MAGIC JOURNEY

MY FANTASTICAL *Walt Disney* Imagineering **CAREER**

KEVIN P. RAFFERTY

EDITIONS

Los Angeles · New York

Jacket photos by Jess Allen
Jacket designed by Winnie Ho

Hard cover illustrated by Nick Balian

Interior designed by Winnie Ho
Composition and layout by Arlene Schleifer Goldberg
Interior pattern created and illustrated by Nick Balian

For information address Disney Editions, 1200 Grand Central Avenue, Glendale, California 91201.

Library of Congress Cataloging-in-Publication Data
Names: Rafferty, Kevin P., author.
Title: Magic journey : my fantastical Walt Disney imagineering career / by Kevin P. Rafferty.
Description: First edition. | Glendale, California : Disney Editions, 2019.
Identifiers: LCCN 2017058405 | ISBN 9781368020480
Subjects: LCSH: Rafferty, Kevin P. | Amusement rides—Design and
   construction. | Walt Disney World (Fla.)—History. | Disneyland
   (Calif.)—History. | Walt Disney Company—Employees—Biography. |
   Engineers—United States—Biography.
Classification: LCC GV1859 .R34 2019 | DDC 791.06/8—dc23

ISBN 978-1-368-02048-0
FAC-038091-19151
Printed in the United States of America
First Hardcover Edition, September 2019
10 9 8 7 6 5 4 3 2 1

SUSTAINABLE FORESTRY INITIATIVE

Certified Sourcing
www.sfiprogram.org
SFI-00993

Logo Applies to Text Stock Only

For the love of my life, Patty Ann,
because the only thing
more challenging than being an Imagineer
is being married to one

And to KJ and Brad,
because the only thing
better than being an Imagineer
is being their dad

And to Marty Sklar,
the best boss, advocate, friend, and "dad"
an Imagineer could have had

Know

Imagi

encircles

ledge

is limited.

nation

t h e   w o r l d .

—Albert Einstein

ACKNOWLEDGMENTS

While this book was still buzzing around in my brain and not yet put into these words that dared to come in for a landing on the most frightening thing in the world—blank paper—I asked my literary agent, Richard Curtis (it's so cool to have a literary agent, especially one who is so renowned and from New York City, which makes him that much more legit), how I should approach and deliver this work. With pencil at the ready to take copious notes, I fully expected him to answer with a long list of strict book-writing rules—a protocol and/or formula for publishing that would ensure the successful delivery on my part of a properly written and formatted book.

But instead, Richard simply answered, "Write the book you want to write. Finish it and be happy with it." That was it. And here it is. Thank you, Richard, for your wit and wisdom, and for accompanying me on this journey.

As free and easy as "write the book you want to write" may sound, it eventually had to be handed over with i's dotted and T's crossed (make that *fingers crossed*), to an editor. But not just any editor: the best editor not only in NYC but the entire world. Make that the universe. Lucky for me, I know her. In fact, there was no one I would rather hand this labor of love over to than my longtime friend and editor extraordinaire, the wonderful Wendy Lefkon.

Wendy and I go way back, back to when she expertly and lovingly edited my writing for the book *Walt Disney Imagineering: A Behind the Dreams Look at Making the Magic Real* (1996). The other day Wendy gave me a gift in the form of one of the greatest compliments I have ever received in my professional life: she called me a *real* writer. Once you've read this book, you'll understand why that comment means so much to me.

Thank you, Wendy, for your treasured friendship and for allowing me to do something I didn't know I could do until I started doing it; and now here it is. That's so Imagineering! Thanks, most of all, for believing in me as a *real* writer—especially since I have never quite believed that myself. My deepest gratitude to Wendy's talented team, especially Winnie Ho and Nick Balian, for so wonderfully and whimsically designing and illustrating my story.

Ironically, the most difficult thing about writing my Imagineering story was having to talk about myself and my accomplishments. But it was the only way I could give heart and meaning to this "Hero's Journey." I cringe when I think someone may misinterpret this book as an "I did this" and "I did that" collection of boasts, because, truly, boasting is not in my nature and those who know me know I am not that way. When I talk about projects I've worked on, I certainly did not do any of them alone.

The only thing that's impossible for an Imagineer is accomplishing an Imagineering project on his or her own. The truth is, no Imagineer is an island. We are all in this together and we need each other to get there. But writing this book from a first-person perspective, talking about myself and the stuff I've done, was the only way I could communicate how an entry-level foot-in-the-door "nobody" somehow beat the odds to effectively contribute to the creative cause at the most creative company in the world. And although this book is a joyful and playful series of withdrawals from my memory bank, my journey was often not that easy. But that's what made the sweet moments and accomplishments even sweeter.

So, gosh, I hope you don't perceive the following pages as being boastful. My intent was to use the examples of those goals achieved as proof dreams really do come true. I could not have done the things I was able to do without the help, encouragement, and support from many fellow Imagineers over the years—and I would like to acknowledge and thank them all, past and present. I may have ignited a few creative sparks for ideas that actually made it into the Disney parks, but making those dreams come true took many hearts, minds, and hands. At Imagineering, dreams come true because teams come through!

When I was being swept away by the theatrical production *Wicked*, the song "For Good" brought me to tears because the lyrics brought to mind and heart some of my very favorite colleagues—my family, really—whom I've worked most closely with and most admire. Their goodness, talent, help, encouragement, and love have not only made me a better Imagineer and human being, but each, in his or her own special way, has changed my life for good, especially the following Imagineers and ex-Imagineers, who most inspired me and continue to inspire me more than even they could possibly imagine: Marty Sklar, Randy Bright, Rob't Coltrin, Tom Fitzgerald, Kathy Mangum, Joe Herrington, Nick Ross, Jeffrey Shaver-Moskowitz, Ryan Adams, Chris Turner, Mark Rhodes, Tracy Smith, Mark Panelli, Mary Ane, Charita Carter, Tom LaDuke, Mason Lev, Bryan Jolley, Nancy Hickman, Jeff Webb, Mindy Wilson, Ken Horii, Chris Runco, Bob Weis, John Schmidt, Dave Fisher, Jim Clark, Bruce Gordon, David Mumford, Ray Cadd, Nancy Seruto, Tony Baxter, Adam Hill, Dave Scott, Steve Litten, Josef Lemoine, Thomas Niederhiser, Lori Coltrin, Dex Tanksley, Sally Judd, Jodi McLaughlin, Dave Durham, Blake Ostrowski, Frank Reifsnyder, Mouse Silverstein, Sue Bryan, Dustin Schofield, Sandi Sullivan, Doug Griffith, Cliff Welch, Tom Leach, Kyle Barnes, Tom Morris,

Tim Delaney, Michael Sprout, Alfredo Ayala, Shelby Jiggetts-Tivony, Laura Alletag, Chuck Miller, Chris Mais, Jason Grandt, Steve Kirk, Janny Mulholland, Heidi Rosendahl, Barry Braverman, Raellen Lescault, Chris Beatty, Oscar Cobos, Greg Wilzbach, Stephen "Toaster" Gregory, George Scribner, Louis Lemoine, Bobby Brooks, Ray Spencer, Tim Kirk, Ed Nemeth, Bruce Vaughn, Bran Ferren, Ray J. Warner, Michael Browne, Chrissie Allen, Brian Nefsky, Chris Merritt, Amy Greive, Kathryn Klatt, Rick Adam, Aristeve Trotter, Jody Gerstner, Glenn Barker, Brandon Kleyla, Chris Crump, Mike Jusko, Daniel Jue, Vicky Todd, Diane Scoglio, Neil Jones, Ted Robledo, Diego Parras, Peggy Van Pelt, Judy Liss, April Warren, Dave Minichiello, Eric Jacobson, Marnie Burress, Scot Drake, Kirk Winterroth, Meghann Morris, Joe Lanzisero, Mary Carver, Brian Houle, Daniel Joseph, Denise Brown, Mark Schirmer, Nina Rae Vaughn, Robert Zuber, Peggie Farris, Trish Cerrone, Vanessa Hunt, Steve Spiegel, Mike Iwerks, Dustin Eshenroder, Zsolt Hormay, Jon Georges, Avi Tuchman, Justin Newton, Scott Trowbridge, Paul Baker, Andrea Lawler, Chuck Myers, Becky Train, Scott Hennesy, Doris Woodward, Scott Mallwitz, Barb Dietzel, Billy Almon, Taryn Stickrath, Rhine Meyering, John Mauvezin, Kathy Rogers, Michael Herman, Chris Carradine, Cathy Ritenour, Larry Nikolai, Maggie Elliott, Greg Randle, Becky Bishop, Anne Osterhout, Paul Osterhout, Skip Lange, Brian Crosby, Bob Stephens, Jennifer Schwartz, Joe Rohde, Ann Myers, Norita Cullen, John Dennis, Michelle Landouw, Mark Diwas, Rick Rothschild, Nick Roedl, Mike Fracassi, Michael Wallden, Pam Fisher, Dan Beaumont, Stacie Covington, Art Verity, Andrew Fisher, John Hench, Debbie Gonzales, Frank Villalpando, Tori (Atencio) McCullough, Mike McCullough, Craig Russell, Kim Irvine, Steve Roach, John Gritz, Josh Gorin, Debra Kohls, Lori Gonzales, Ann Pynchon, Michael Valentino, Dave Crawford, Alec Scribner, Marianne McClean, David Stofcik, Mark Mine, Todd Homme, Paul Rudish, Chris Willis, Cory Sewelson, Ryan Donoghue, Aurelio Garcia, Luc Mayrand, John Bradbury, Jeff Kurtti, Mark LaVine, Amber Samdahl, Coulter Winn, Dan Granberg, Patrick Brennan, Hannah Brennan, David Odom, Antony Capstick, Joe Garlington, John Horny, Jillian Rothman, Derek Howard, Rhoi Carpena, Jess Allen, Scott Goddard, Todd Neubrand, Steve Cotroneo, Owen Yoshino, Suzanne Holzer, Virginia Foote, Kiran Jeffrey, Don Goodman, Kevin Lively, and last but not least, my Pixar project pals, Roger Gould, Liz Gazzano, Tony Apodaca, Jay Ward, Bob Pauley, Bill Cone, Jerome Ranft, Andrew Stanton, Darla Anderson, Pete Docter, Jonas Rivera, and John Lasseter.

My most sincere and heartfelt thanks to each and every one of you. You're the ones who have made this journey so magical.

CONTENTS

ACKNOWLEDGMENTS   *vi*

FOREWORD   *x*

INTRODUCTION   *xii*

WHEN YOU *DISH* UPON A STAR   *1*

FROM RAGS TO . . . RAGS   *13*

WED BEHIND THE EARS   *25*

SCOPING OUT A NEW ROLE   *41*

A STEP IN THE *WRITE* DIRECTION   *59*

I'VE GOT NO STRINGS   *71*

FROM WASHING DISHES TO SPINNING PLATES   *79*

SINK OR SWIM   *89*

PAN GALACTIC PIZZA PORT   *107*

THE DISNEY-MGM STUDIOS EXPANSION   *125*

YOU CAN'T ALWAYS GET WHAT YOU WANT   *143*

NONSTOP '90s   *159*

THE BIRDS AND THE BEES   *177*

TEST TRACK   *199*

MICKEY'S PHILHARMAGIC   *211*

OCEANS OF FUN   *219*

TOY STORY MIDWAY MANIA!   *233*

THE ROAD TO CARS LAND   *251*

TO THE NEXT-GENERATION IMAGINEERS   *287*

WHAT A RIDE!   *297*

FOREWORD

You'd think that if my dad wrote a book about his forty-year career as a Disney Imagineer, I'd ask him if I could read a draft before it came out. Or he would offer to let me read it.

I didn't ask—and he didn't offer!

I suspect we share the same reasons for keeping it a surprise.

The first is anticipation. I'm probably more excited than anyone to read his book. Having a hard copy will be more fun than reading a draft. The same goes for my dad: he probably would rather let me find it, or give it to me as a gift.

The second reason is my experience handling communications at Disney. I might've suggested wording something differently. Don't get me wrong—I'm not expecting anything negative. He's told me several times along the way that this book is not about airing dirty laundry. This book is about the real stories that help illustrate what Walt Disney Imagineering is all about. You may wonder how I know that, since I haven't read it yet. Truth is I don't need to read it to know that. I already know what my dad has contributed to Disney parks, and I can't wait for you to learn about it in this book.

I have many memories with my dad at 1401 Flower Street (Imagineering's headquarters in Glendale, California). I remember as a child meeting Jimmy Macdonald, John Hench, and other Disney Legends there. Macdonald, a sound effects pioneer, was the voice of Mickey Mouse, succeeding Walt Disney. He also did the yodeling, whistling, and sneezing for the dwarfs in *Snow White and the Seven Dwarfs*. Macdonald had a house in Glendale, and I remember after he died helping my dad run errands and doing chores for his wife, Bobbie. Another time, my dad brought me into Hench's office, and I got to spend time with the great artist and designer. I didn't think twice about these opportunities at the time, but what special moments they were looking back.

My dad has spent a lifetime creating special moments for me, our family, and Disney parks guests as a "second generation" Imagineer. In my admittedly biased opinion, he is the *ultimate* dad and Imagineer. I can also tell you without having read this book that it is about more than dreaming up ideas for Disney parks. It is about the *American* dream—after all, he started as a Disneyland dishwasher and became a seasoned creative executive. I'm certain you'll notice themes of hard work and a can-do attitude. That's the spirit of Walt Disney Imagineering.

I had the opportunity to work at Walt Disney Imagineering for a short period. I worked on the communications team during an eight-month assignment away from my regular role as a writer for the *Disney Parks Blog* and a media spokesperson at the Disneyland Resort. My time at Walt Disney Imagineering was a real window into my dad's career. One of my favorite memories there was when I supported a series of presentations given by former Imagineering president Marty Sklar at a creativity conference for California arts teachers. One presentation was with a panel of Imagineers that Marty facilitated. He asked my dad to call him on his cell phone in the middle of the presentation so he could tell my dad, in front of a very confused audience, what a good job I was doing behind the tech booth. I was honored and embarrassed.

That was about a month before Marty passed away. Marty's family called to ask my dad to speak at his funeral shortly afterward. I was so proud of my dad at Marty's service. He honored Marty beautifully, describing him as a difference maker and life changer—qualities I would use to describe my dad as well.

I was equally proud of my dad when he spoke at the 2017 D23 Expo weeks earlier to describe the Mickey & Minnie's Runaway Railway attraction to an audience of nearly seven thousand Disney fans. Marty was in the audience and we watched as the chairman of Disney Parks introduced my dad as the Imagineer working on this special attraction—Disney's first ride-through attraction built entirely around Mickey Mouse. Of course it takes an entire team, as my dad was very quick to point out. I think my dad closing out his career with Mickey Mouse, and the company trusting him to lead the project creatively, speaks volumes to my dad's truly being, as a colleague once described him, the heart of Imagineering.

After decades of waking up before the sun rose to drive from Orange County to Los Angeles for work, my dad has earned such an accolade. If you are a local to the area, you know that's no picnic—whether it's done in daylight or not! So what made the drive worth it? You'll find out in the pages ahead.

As Marty always said, there's only one name on the door: Walt Disney. That's probably why you're not familiar with my dad. But I'd be willing to bet you're familiar with his work—having read, heard, or experienced something (or many things!) he has created in a Disney park. I can tell you my dad has always gone to work for the right reason—creating happiness and magic—and that it's always been an honor describing him as a Disney Imagineer. It still is!

Kevin Rafferty, Jr.
Anaheim, California
February 2018

INTRODUCTION

WED Enterprises was an exhilarating beehive of activity when I began my career there in 1978. The spark of an idea for both Epcot Center and Tokyo Disneyland had ignited, and the place was on fire. John Zovich, then vice president of engineering, had a sign on his office door in the executive "Gold Coast" just inside the front lobby that read: LEAD, FOLLOW, OR GET THE HELL OUT OF THE WAY. And boy, did he mean it. At the opposite end of the Gold Coast resided Marty Sklar, who, with John Hench, his fellow senior vice president of the creative division, was manning the helm.

Marty and John were larger-than-life to me, not only because they knew and had worked with Walt Disney, but also because they were now the top dogs of the design and development of two major new Disney theme parks—one of which would be the first in a foreign country. I, on the other hand, was, well, in the grand scheme of things, nobody. I didn't know a single person at WED when I started and my noncreative position was so entry-level that I took a cut in pay from my previous hourly job in the foods division at Disneyland. No kidding, I went from $5.75 an hour down to an even five bucks. And now I had to drive an extra fifty miles to work in a car that behaved like it didn't have ten miles of life left in it. Friends told me I was crazy. But I didn't think I was crazy, because I was crazy about this place from the first day I got my entry-level foot in the door.

At that time Randy Bright, who would later become my mentor, worked under Marty as the vice present of creative development and show writing. Every Wednesday morning from 8:00 a.m. to 9:00 a.m. Randy hosted something he called "The Wednesday Morning Breakfast Meeting" (breakfast not included). Every week he invited experts from across a broad spectrum of the entertainment industry to come in and help stimulate the creative juices at WED. The event took place in the center of our headquarters building at 1401 Flower Street in Glendale, California.

As busy as everyone at WED was, this weekly Wednesday morning meeting was an eye in the middle of the work storm, so it was always well attended. I was happy to get permission to attend my first one, which happened to feature a too-high-energy-for-the-time-slot improv troupe. The four improvers rushed onto the tiny temporary stage and immediately shouted out for volunteers from among the approximately two hundred sleepy, coffee-sipping Imagineers. (I was soon to discover that most Imagineers are not morning people because they stay up most of the night working on "work stuff" or filling their heads and hearts with just about everything and anything they can learn more about.) There weren't any takers. "Here's a volunteer!" proclaimed a boisterous member of the troupe as she ran to the second row and grabbed and dragged onto the stage a reluctant participant named Peggie. "Need one more," suggested another improver, who ran all the way to the back of the room to grab another young lady seated in the last row. At that the audience gasped. And I mean a serious collective gasp, as if the building were about to collapse. "What's going on?" I whispered to the drop-jawed person sitting next to me.

"They could not have picked a worse person for this," he whispered.

"Why?" I inquired.

"That's Lindsay," he continued. "She is the shyest person here. She never speaks. She doesn't even look at you. This is going to be a disaster."

I scanned the now wide-awake crowd and the expressions on everyone's faces; and the murmuring clearly verified what my neighbor had just shared with me. Meanwhile, Lindsay wasn't budging. It finally took the combined force of the entire troupe to carry her up to the front, where they sat her and Peggie side by side in folding chairs facing the audience. I could see Randy Bright in the front row bury his face in his hands. "Okay, ladies!" the improv leader bellowed after asking their names (though he had to ask Lindsay several times because he couldn't hear her response). "Here's your situation. You, Peggie, are Calamity Jane. And you, Lindsay, are Annie Oakley. Ready? And . . . GO!"

But nobody went. Neither of the two women said or did anything. The thirty painful silent seconds that crawled by felt like an hour. Peggie bit her upper lip with her lower teeth and looked prayerfully towards the ceiling as Lindsey sat motionless, staring down at her hands folded tightly in her lap. This was going on way too long. Why, oh, why, I thought, didn't the improv people do something?

Then it happened. Lindsay launched out of her chair with such thrust it snapped over backwards and folded flat on the floor with a bang. "Calamity," she cried in her best Broadway stage–projected Western-style Annie Oakley voice. "We've been stuck on this here mountain fer over a month . . . AND I NEED ME A MAN!"

The place exploded. I guarantee that in the history of the world there has never been an audience reaction like the one I experienced in my first Randy

Bright Wednesday Morning Breakfast Meeting. The whoops, whistles, and thunderous standing ovation lasted for a good five minutes. As a brand-new Imagineer, I remember asking myself at that moment, *What just happened? What does this have to do with designing theme parks? What is this place?*

Well, after all these years I think I have it figured out: this place was not at all what I expected. And everything I did there was not what I expected to do. What's more, everything that happened there, no matter how strange or unexpected, had everything to do with designing Disney theme parks. When you get to be my age after having had such a rare job in such a rare place for such a long time, you can't help but experience things, moments, and events that are so unbelievable or weird that they fall under the category of "You Can't Even Make This Stuff Up." What does *that* have to do with Imagineering? Why would an Imagineer ever do something like *that*? Who could have possibly guessed that my childhood interests, my hobbies, and even my favorite TV shows and TV and movie stars would someday be a part of my career? Strange that so much of that stuff would later intertwine. Or is it?

Here's why. Walt Disney Imagineering has a mind, heart, and spirit of its own. It brings things together and draws people together as well. It does what it needs to do when it needs to do it. It survives and it thrives. It falls but leaps way back up. It calls talented people with varied interests to itself and gives them a chance to discover who they are so they can make a difference. It presents impossible challenges and helps its Imagineers, like Lindsay, rise to the occasion when they need to the most.

In a recent meeting, I was asked by a colleague to share a particular story they'd previously heard me tell (several times) with the younger Imagineers in the room. Whenever I'm asked to tell one of these stories—and I do love to tell them—inevitably, one of my colleagues asks when I'm going to write my book. In addition to that, I've been asked hundreds of times by new friends I've met along the way or by young people interested in becoming Imagineers themselves to tell "my story," the personal story of how I became an Imagineer. Still others are interested in a detailed description of my typical day.

Well, after four decades of leading, following, and getting the hell out of the way, I've never had a typical day.

This book is for all of you. In it I'll explain how I became an Imagineer and all of the crazy stuff that happened because I did, all of which will help explain why I have never had a typical day. Forty years of helping conceive and deliver shows and attractions for Disney parks around the world has been my extreme honor, profound privilege, and joyous pleasure. I have never taken it for granted, not a nontypical day of it. Ever. Putting these personal experiences on paper is going to be difficult because I've always said I was going write about it all "someday" at the end of my career, a career that has meant so much to me and has been so much a part of who I am that writing my memoirs means it's all wrapping up. Wrapping indeed this beautiful gift I've been given!

There are hundreds of thousands of different jobs in the world, and there are hundreds of thousands of people who do the same job. But how many Imagineers are there? Well, only a few, really. And I was called to be one of them during the busiest heyday of Walt Disney Imagineering.

On that first Monday in 1978 when this new bee buzzed into the beehive I had no idea what I was doing, where I was going, or how long I was going to last. Fresh out of college, inexperienced, and dreadfully insecure, I found myself surrounded by the wizards, masters, dreamers, and doers of legend. These men and women were the best in the business. Many of them invented the business—or various aspects of it. Could I ever really be one of them? Would I ever be good enough? Did I really have what it took to be a real, honest-to-goodness contributing Imagineer? Most importantly, could I pull my weight in sharing the daunting responsibility of continuing Walt Disney's theme park legacy?

For a shy young artist, it was a mountain of pressure. By Wednesday, though, the place had provided me with some insight for success. Sometimes you just gotta be Annie Oakley.

WHEN YOU *DISH* UPON A STAR

IN 1974, I was studying to become a Roman Catholic priest. Throughout my studies, however, my anxious creative mind would oftentimes wander to all things pop culture, music, movies, art, and animation, especially during Latin class. As my mind would start to *Rome*, I'd turn all of the margins in the pages of my thick Latin textbooks into animated scenes à la a flip-book. While my studious classmates were focused on translating Cicero and Virgil, I was focused on animating toga-clad maidens dancing on ancient urns and Romans in chariots racing across my pages. I even animated an "aqua duck"—which consisted of a duck sliding across a stone aqueduct. (Decades later I remembered that when I was asked to come up with a name and story for a waterslide on a Disney Cruise ship.)

Latin was not my favorite subject. That's why I added this poem, and made it appear as if it had been done with an ancient hammer and chisel in a stone-style font (as best I could with a ballpoint pen, anyway), to the inside cover of my textbook:

LATIN'S A DEAD LANGUAGE

THAT'S PLAIN ENOUGH TO SEE

IT KILLED OFF ALL THE ROMANS

AND NOW IT'S KILLING ME!

There it was, a foreshadowing of my future: art, animation, and poetry all in one Latin book. I was drawing and creatively writing when I was supposed to be mastering an ancient language. Then one day, after miserably failing a Latin test, I felt God saying he had other plans for me. (Though I don't think it was the Latin thing as much as it was the celibacy thing. There were more dancing maidens in my margins than anything else.) Good call, God.

Yet I did deeply treasure my seminary experience, and it did help to calibrate my moral compass and establish a strong work ethic that would serve me well in my career. During my five formative years in the seminary, my professors were brilliant priests and nuns with high moral, disciplinary, and educational standards; and they expected nothing less from me (which is why, for the record, I did ace my Latin final. *Deo gratias!*). These dedicated men and women taught me well and set me up for success in the future, both in learning and in life. At the end of the school year I bid them all a fond farewell and departed St. John's Seminary in Camarillo, California, for California State University, Fullerton, where there were girls and an art department with a new animation

You would never know it, but I was wearing Mickey Mouse shorts under there. It's okay, they were *holey*.

instructor who came from Disney. With a dream to become a Disney animator myself, I switched majors from philosophy to art. Cicero would have been cool with that. After all, it was he who wrote *In virtute sunt multi ascensus*: "There are many degrees in excellence."

"You're too smart for art!" exclaimed my uncle Bob, who worked for the district attorney in Los Angeles. "What you need to do," he advised, "is get your butt into Loyola Law School [in Los Angeles]." My parents, however, were fully supportive of my artistic aspirations. "If it doesn't work out, honey," assured my mom, "you could always work with me in the grocery store."

My Italian grandmother, who dropped to her knees and sobbed uncontrollably when I told her I was leaving the seminary, pulled herself together long enough to insist I go to business school so I could run my uncle Lou's pasta factory, which for an Italian grandmother is the next best job after being a priest.

And so it began. Friends and relatives warned me, begged me, and even bribed me not to be an artist, all claiming that an art degree was worthless and it would never help me land a *real* job. One of my best friends even claimed that artists are weirdos. "You don't want to be a weirdo, do you?" To prove them all wrong, I naively made it my mission to get a job in the field of art even before I earned my art degree. With that goal in mind, in May 1974, I filled out a summer job application at Disneyland.

How could it not work out perfectly? I loved Disneyland, it's just down the street from where I live and go to college, I can draw, and a job there would be a foot in the door with Disney as a young artist (so when I did get my art degree they would simply transfer me up to the Walt Disney Studios in Burbank). Piece of cake!

"Making *cakes*?" I questioned my cheerful job interviewer at Disneyland, who informed me, as though she were presenting me with a rare and priceless gem, there was a position available in the bakery backstage. "But you don't understand," I reasoned. "The application asked what I was applying for and I stated I wanted to be an artist. I know you have artists here. You're Disney!" My interviewer, whose name was Marsha (and I remember that because she looked exactly like Marcia Brady from *The Brady Bunch*), agreed. "Yes, we do have artists, but currently we have no openings in the art department," she responded. "Well then," I compromised, "if I can't be an artist *yet*, can I operate rides?" Marsha shook her head and said once again, "I have an opening in the bakery. That's it. In. The. Bakery." Her frozen, twisted facial expression looked exactly like Marcia Brady's when she and her brother Greg fought over who got to convert the attic into his or her private bedroom.

"But I've never baked anything," I assured Marsha, hoping she might listen to reason and be swayed by my honesty and puppy dog eyes to dig a little deeper and find something more suited to me. Like maybe in the art department. She fired at me point-blank. "Do you want the job?" I hemmed and hawed while teetering on the fence of this most difficult decision that I didn't know at the time would change my entire life, both personally and professionally. I let Marsha have the attic. "Great!" she exclaimed with a victorious smile. "It starts at three a.m. tomorrow." "*What?*"

I was at Disneyland at 2:00 a.m. so I would not be late on my first day. Wearing my crisp white costume ("costume" is Disneyland speak for "uniform" because Disneyland employees are not considered "employees" but rather "cast members" in that they all have a role in the show. But in my case, I was going to be performing backstage, because my role had to do with baking rolls). I nervously waited near the locked bakery door located on the loading dock behind the Plaza Inn Restaurant on Main Street. The baker to whom I was supposed to report arrived at 3:00 a.m. sharp.

"Who are you?" he asked with great surprise. I introduced myself and reminded him I was the new guy reporting for work, and on time, too. Surely, he must know about me. "I didn't know about you," he said, unlocking the door and flipping on the lights. "Let's go in and check the schedule." His eyes scanned the schedule up and down and all around as he whispered, "Lafferty, Lafferty, Lafferty. . . ." I looked down at the bakery floor whispering, "Marsha! Marsha! Marsha!"

"Aha! There you are on page three!" the baker happily reported. I breathed a sigh of relief, as I was worried there might have been a mistake. "But there's a mistake," he added. "You're not supposed to be working in the bakery at all. You're supposed to be a DMO." "Oh, a DMO!" I said with great relief, as if I understood what a DMO was. "But you're not starting your shift until ten a.m.," he continued. "Come back then and report to the area supervisor three doors down." I had seven hours to wait, which was plenty of time to try to figure out what "DMO" stood for.

Hmmm, maybe it's "Disneyland's Mickey Organizer." That would be great. I could be the guy who helps keep Mickey in line and on time. Or maybe it's "Disneyland Major Officer." Perhaps I was going to be a security guard. How hard could that job be in the happiest place on earth? Yes sir, things were looking up! I was certain that after thinking more about it Marsha had a change of heart and reconsidered my application, finding something much more to my liking, perhaps as a nice surprise. The sun began to rise over the nearby trash dumpster as I continued to ponder all of the marvelous things a DMO could possibly be. Maybe it's "Disneyland Magical Operator." Whoa, maybe I'm going to be a ride operator after all! I will have to send Marsha a nice note once I get settled in to my plush new office.

Ten o'clock finally arrived, as did the area supervisor. "Who are you?" he asked. I introduced myself and reminded him I was the new DMO reporting for work, and on time, too. "Ah," he said, "let's check the schedule." I was certain that once he found me on the schedule, I would be asked to go change my clothes and he would then escort me over to my new office, somewhere in the park, where I would be a DMO, whatever that was. "Yep," he said. "There you are. New DMO."

I couldn't stand it anymore. I had to ask. "What exactly is a DMO?" He looked surprised that I didn't know. "Dish machine operator," he answered. He escorted me through the backstage corridors of the Plaza Inn to the deep dark dank dish room. It was like a steam bath but without health benefits. Or windows. Or girls. My shift was scheduled to last until 6:30 p.m. Dirty dishes, glasses, and pots and pans were piled everywhere. God was clearly punishing me for leaving the seminary.

The dish room was supposed to be manned with four DMOs, but there were only two or three DMOs working at any given time because new hires would show up, take a look at hell, and run for their lives. Two new DMOs arrived on my first day and quit on the spot. That meant I had to cover their now vacant positions and shifts. I worked overtime on my first day, departing at 11:00 p.m. When I finally walked out of the dish room in my once-crisp white costume, I looked like I had been slaughtered in a paintball tournament. The dish room serviced both the Plaza Inn and the Inn Between (the cast member cafeteria), and the action was nonstop. Busy busboys carried bins called "bus tubs" on their shoulders that were heaping with dirty dishes, food scraps, and even from time to time dirty diapers back to the dish room with such regularity that it was impossible to ever catch up. The line outside the Plaza Inn door stretched back to Main Street all day long. Once I jumped into the never slowing, ever growing mess, it felt like I was tasked to dig out the Panama Canal with a plastic spoon. It was relentless. Being a DMO was exhausting work. And the perky pretty girls in the cute green-and-white-striped dresses that served food out front wouldn't give a DMO the time of day. We were the dregs of the earth, the slimy, pasty bottom-feeders. Latin class was like paradise compared to this.

The next morning, as I was about to leave for Dish Room Day Two while wondering why I was going back, my dad asked how I liked my new job. I told him it was awful, horrible, and grueling, and I didn't know hell had stainless steel walls. I explained I had to see the nurse two different times for cuts caused by broken dishes and glasses, that two new guys showed up, saw what I was doing, and quit, and that I had to cover for them, and that when I finally clocked out after thirteen hours of nonstop work—on top the seven extra hours of waiting in the dark because of the bakery snafu—I smelled like a dumpster and looked like a walking Jackson Pollock painting. "Other than that," I told Dad, "it was great."

He smiled and said something that got me through the entire summer (and beyond): "Son, the only time you're going to find success before work is in the dictionary."

Before I stepped out the door, my aunt Darlene, who was visiting from Iowa, walked in and said, "Have fun 'working' at Disneyland. You're so lucky!" By midsummer I had become the old man of the sea of dishes. Dozens of one-day-only DMOs came and went, but I was still there working a minimum of sixty hours a week raking in, after taxes, $60.00. Doing the math revealed I was washing about two thousand dishes for one dollar. Meanwhile, my best friend, Mark, called to excitedly tell me he got a job at Disneyland. "You did?" I asked. "Where?" You can't make this stuff up. "The bakery!"

With my fellow DMOs, and obviously taken before our shift, because we are clean. There should have been four of us in the photo, but the fourth guy did not have the stamina and quit. But I covered for him. I outlasted these other two, too.

A lot happened that first summer even though I spent most of my life in the dish room being avoided like the plague by the Plaza Inn girls. I thought when I left the seminary girls would dance and swoon around me all day long like in an Elvis movie. It didn't matter. I had no time for them anyway. Mark, on the other hand, loved working in the bakery. He was in his element, having baked cakes, pies, and cupcakes just for fun since fourth grade. Part of his job was delivering baked goods to the restaurants around the park, which gave him an opportunity to flirt with all the girls. And unlike toxic me, he smelled like whipped cream.

He was particularly sweet on a girl named Patty, who worked at the Coca-Cola Refreshment Corner on Main Street. When he delivered trays of brownies to Coke Corner in the morning, he wrote notes to her in the frosting. Smooth move. But when Patty introduced baker Mark to her best friend, Evelyn, he fell like an underbaked cake.

This is where the cosmic forces of Disneyland began to kick into high gear for me. Mark and Evelyn began dating and on Mark's birthday, Evelyn came to his house and brought Patty along with her. This is when and where I met Patty. "Small world," she said when she found out I worked at Disneyland, too. "What do you do there?" I crossed my fingers and hoped for the best. "I'm a . . . DMO." "Oh," she said as if she understood what a DMO was. But it was obvious she didn't because she kept talking with me. We had a nice chat that evening but nothing came of it. The next day I ran into her in the cast member parking lot at Disneyland. I also began to see her frequently backstage, and when school started in September, I saw her at Cal State Fullerton.

We both continued to work part-time at the park—and Disneyland, in its wisdom, made sure we kept bumping into each other often, and at the most unexpected times. Patty already had a boyfriend, of course: a conservative Ken Doll dental student that her parents adored because he was one year away from having a real job, not to mention a "Dr." in front of his name. But I liked Patty a lot. She was sweet, beautiful, and wholesome, a true poster girl for Disney. Her sister, Linda, was a dancer at the Golden Horseshoe Revue, my all-time favorite show and her brother, Steve, operated rides at Knott's Berry Farm.

Remembering what my dad said about achieving success before work, I went to work on Patty and ultimately landed a date. When I met her parents her stone-faced, deadly serious intimidating dad asked what I did for work. "I, um, . . . am a DMO, sir." "What the hell is that?" "I, uh, wash . . . dishes." He grimaced and growled. And I swear this to be true: his giant terrifying German shepherd growled at the very same time.

"Are you in school?" he asked. "Yes," I responded. "What are you majoring in?" Gulp. "Art." He didn't have to speak. The look in his eyes said it all: *You are a loser with no future, and you are also a weirdo—and my daughter happens to be dating a dental student who is about to make bank, so get the hell out.* The German shepherd showed teeth. I thought I would never see Patty again. But strangely enough we continued to run into each other in the cast member parking lot. Disneyland clearly wanted us together. It was Patty, after all, who encouraged me to apply at WED Enterprises (later renamed Walt Disney Imagineering)— but more on that later. Let's go back to the dish room to close this chapter, because it sets the stage for what happens next.

Procedure dictated a plumber be called when the garbage disposal went kaput or the floor drains clogged and backed up. Problem was that "a plumber" was actually four plumbers who would take forever to arrive. One would assess the situation while the other three scratched their heads. They'd leave for a while and return with a new part while more than two thousand dirty dishes stacked up. For my own survival, I learned to take these matters into my own hands. I figured out that I could fix the garbage disposal in less than two minutes. When it came to clearing the clogged drains, I turned to the soda fountain. There, behind the fountain, was an array of pressurized carbon dioxide tanks. I would disconnect and "borrow" a CO_2 tank and wrap a towel around the end of its connector hose to create a makeshift gasket. Then voilà! The clog would get blown away with an audible *whoosh.*

One day when the drains backed up, I went to fetch a tank and a towel as usual. After checking to make sure there was no supervisor in sight, I shoved the towel-wrapped end of the hose into the drain, turned the valve, and waited. And waited. I opened the valve all the way. Nothing. Then suddenly I heard the release, but this time it sounded like an underground sonic boom followed by bloodcurdling screams coming from the other side of the door—the door that opened into the onstage restaurant serving area. A Plaza Inn girl popped her head through the door, saw me kneeling over the drain hole with hose in hand, and yelled, "RUN! Run away and never come back!" I hesitated. Is she talking to me? Why would she—"NOW!" I ran like Snow White through a dense forest of mops, shelves, and food racks out the back door, jumped off the loading dock, and crouched behind a dumpster, where I hid frozen in fear for at least ten minutes.

Finally, my fellow DMO came out to find me. "You are not going to believe what you just did," he said as if he were addressing a hero. Well, here's what happened: the floor drains are all connected to one pipeline. When I opened the CO_2 valve, the drains that decided to clear were the ones onstage in the restaurant directly behind the service area where guests stood in line and were served their food by the girls who never talked to me. It so happened, at that very moment, that standing in the fallout zone of what was to become known as "Old Faceful Geyser" were Dick Nunis, then president of Disneyland, and two of his executive entourage (Ron Dominguez and Jim Cora).

Dick was a man who instilled fear in every cast member. The trio was in line with their trays when the drain covers blew off and flipped through the air like pancakes, followed by gushing geysers of thick black muck that blasted out of the ground like a crude oil strike. The muck spattered their faces, coats, and ties. I could and probably should have been justifiably fired right then and there—and that would have been it for me at Disney. But Disneyland protected me. I was destined to be an Imagineer. For the rest of the summer of 1974, I was a Plaza Inn legend. The girls still didn't talk *to* me, but they talked *about* me. I mucked Dick Nunis and lived to tell the tale. (Dick, if you're reading this, IT WAS ME! Can't fire me now! HA HA!)

As summer drew to a close—and I worked more overtime than ever—Disneyland was also working overtime to get my attention. During my breaks, I would head across Main Street, slip backstage behind the Jungle Cruise, and escape through the rubber plants into the tropical paradise of the Tahitian Terrace Restaurant in Adventureland. In a park filled to the brim with summer guests, I happened upon this tranquil eye in the storm that, between live shows, was strangely but serenely vacant. For ten glorious minutes, I had this lovely paradise all to myself, a world away from the deluge of dishes. It was there I hatched a scheme to explore more of the park after dark. At park closing, even after working a twelve-hour shift, I would clock out and then explore every inch behind the scenes, trying to figure out how everything worked and marveling at the showmanship. Sometimes the third-shift maintenance folks were kind enough to give me a personal tour explaining the Audio-Animatronics and ride systems. It was a magical time for me. But it wasn't as magical as that one special night that brought my first summer season to an unexpected grand finale.

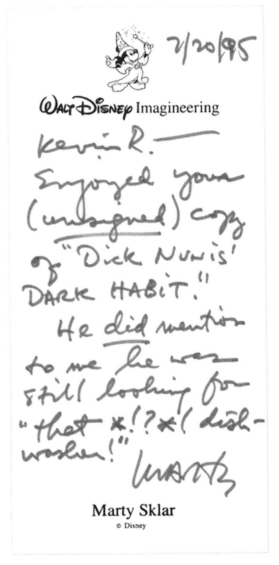

2/20/95

(Walt Disney) Imagineering

Kevin R. —
Enjoyed your (unsigned) copy
of "Dick Nunis'
DARK HABiT."
He did mention
to me he was
still looking for
"that *!?*(dish-
washer!"   Marty

Marty Sklar
© Disney

Overtime carried me to closing shift almost every night. The DMO closer's job included going outside to the Plaza Inn's patio and turning the chairs upside down on top of the tables. While performing that task late one night, for some reason I took notice of the sparkling lights in the trees on Main Street, as if seeing them for the first time. My attention turned to the tired but happy guests talking among themselves about their favorite memories of their day as they strolled past me on their way out. "That was the best day of my life," said a petite

Here I am in the Disneyland cast cafeteria, the Inn Between, happy to be on the other side of the wall from the dish room!

elderly woman whose wheelchair was being pushed by a young girl who smiled and added, "Mine too, Grandma." She was holding the string of a Mickey Mouse balloon in one hand and a giant lollipop in the other—no, not the young girl, but Grandma.

I didn't just see their love, I *felt* it. That moment could not have been staged, timed, lit, or art directed more perfectly or beautifully. Those two, separated in age by sixty or seventy years, brought it all home for me. This is why I was here. This is what Disneyland is all about. It's a reassuring eye in the storm in a turbulent world where friends and family can spend time together and enjoy each other, where dirty dishes remain hidden and a Mickey balloon can lift the spirit of an infirm woman of eighty and make her feel like she's eight again. That night it all became crystal clear: Disneyland was much more than a happy place or a park or even a job. It had the special power to give someone the gift of the best day of her life. I didn't want to be an animator anymore. I wanted to be an Imagineer.

FROM
RAGS
TO . . .
RAGS

I WAS PROMOTED in 1976 to busboy—which may have been perceived only as one small step up from dishwasher. But the transfer brought me to the exclusive members-only private Club 33 at Disneyland. The establishment, located on the second floor of a structure in New Orleans Square, was so elegant that even the busboys wore tuxedoes and appeared as though they themselves could order a martini, shaken not stirred, without blowing their cover.

While I was a waiter at Club 33, my future wife, Patty, transferred from Coke Corner to work in the parking lot and at Great Moments with Mr. Lincoln.

The moment I stepped through the concealed front door into the fancy foyer I felt like Jed Clampett must have felt the day he arrived in Beverly Hills. Prior to opening for business that day, the more experienced and refined busboys, shocked to discover my *blackwater* roots, went immediately to work on me à la Professor Henry Higgins on Eliza Doolittle. They said *"Je ne sais quoi"* and "decorum" a lot. When my etiquette-infused training session ended and the main dining room filled with guests, I was assigned to a table of eight businessmen, all wearing dark suits.

My first duty was to serve an individual pat of butter to each guest. This was accomplished by first lifting said pat from a silver seashell-shaped dish—ensuring it rested comfortably on the curve of the cocktail fork, not stabbed onto the prongs for goodness' sake—and then, while standing behind the guest's right shoulder, to raise the butter-patted fork over said shoulder and place it gently down upon the bread plate, positioned at precisely two o'clock, all without interruption or disturbance.

Then I was to repeat this in a clockwise rotation, from guest to guest, around the entire table. It was like playing two games at the same time: Operation and Twister. The moment I raised my trembling fork over the first guest, the butter pat fell off and landed on the backside of his suit jacket, about three inches below the top of his shoulder. The gleaming butter pat sat there but was not visible to any of the men engaged in lively conversation. I had not yet disturbed. I had not yet interrupted.

Thankfully, my fellow busboy and trainer, David Hunsaker, witnessed the whole dreadful event and sashayed into the scene with the grace of a Baryshnikov. Having commanded everyone's attention, he stopped directly across the table from where I remained frozen and raised his arms in a grand welcoming gesture. "Gentlemen!" he proclaimed while silently screaming to me with his eyes to remove the butter while he was distracting these guys. "Is this your first visit to Club 33?" I caught David's drift and sprang into action, flicking the butter pat off the shoulder and high into the air away from the table. One of the gentlemen responded that yes, it was indeed their first visit to the club. David said, "OH!" But it was not to acknowledge the gentleman's response. It was because his eyes followed the flying butter pat as it splatted onto the lens of an expensive camera two tables away.

"Welcomeandenjoyyourlunch," David then said as he sidestepped over to the table with the buttered Nikon. He scooped up the camera and asked the table, "Would you like me to take a picture of your group?" They'd be delighted, thank goodness. As David raised the viewfinder to his eye, he swiftly wiped the butter off the camera with the side of his thumb, dropping it out of sight into the cuff of his shirtsleeve. Then he exclaimed, "Say butter! I mean cheese! Oh, just pick your favorite dairy product!"

After the butter incident, I quickly got the busboy biz down pat. Before long, Jim Lowman, then manager of Club 33 (who at the time of this writing was retiring after fifty years of service at Disneyland), promoted me to maître d', then sous-chef, followed by waiter, bartender, and finally lead, which was like assistant manager, all in less than two years. From our perspective, Jim managed the club with an intimidating presence disguised behind an ever-present smile. He would position himself where he could watch us work the main dining room via several strategically located decorative mirrors on the walls. He thought he was invisible to us, but I often looked over my shoulder into a mirror, any mirror, and caught Jim's bespectacled eyes and arched eyebrows reflected in the corner of the frame.

Moms have eyes in the back of their heads. Jim had eyes everywhere. The guests loved him. My coworkers were terrified of him. I liked him. But he was tough on me. For some reason, I was the one he always picked to do the hardest or weirdest jobs. For example, one particular night, after already tossing tons of extra work my way, he handed me the keys to a company pickup truck and asked me to run to the store to buy lettuce. On the way back, while driving backstage with the truck cab filled with romaine, I noticed a human-sized rubber mermaid lying on a wooden pallet behind one of the maintenance shops. Naturally I pulled over and tossed the mermaid into the back of the pickup. I parked behind New Orleans Square, threw that heavy mermaid over my shoulder, and carried her upstairs, where I snuck into the club through the balcony back door, which was also the back door to Jim's private office. I sat the mermaid up in Jim's desk chair, stuck his pipe in her rubber mouth, and placed his fancy gold desk pen in her hand to suggest she'd written the following note on his JAMES LOWMAN printed notepad: "Want to go for a swim, big boy?" (Jim, if you're reading this, IT WAS ME! Can't fire me now!) I then delivered the lettuce to the kitchen and got back to work in the main dining room, waiting anxiously for the post-discovery fallout. But neither Jim nor anyone else ever mentioned the mermaid, and her whereabouts remain a mystery to this very day. She simply disappeared.

When I think about it, borrowing a mermaid was really a dumb thing to do. Can you imagine what would have happened if Jim had walked into his office and caught me with my hands on her bare chest as I lifted her into his chair, especially since she was not wearing a pair of strategically located shells? Or worse yet, if Disneyland president Dick Nunis had seen me schlepping a full-sized, half-naked mermaid up the stairs, her tail flapping wildly against my shins? Disneyland was protecting me again. I was meant to be an Imagineer!

After completing my third year at Club 33, I earned my BA in art. I had two 16mm animated short films under my belt along with what I thought was a pretty darned good art portfolio, and although I had my sights set on becoming an Imagineer, I landed an interview with the Walt Disney Studios animation division. To me it was a surefire way to get to WED, since I had heard the first Imagineers all came from Disney Animation. The producer scheduled to review my portfolio was really and truly named Donald Duckwall. I mean, come on, what were the odds of that? That's like a producer at Hanna-Barbera being named Yogi Bearwall, or a producer at Warner Bros. being named Bugs Bunny-wall. It was a sign!

But then something happened. Disneyland, in all its wisdom, stepped in for me again. On my way to the cast member costume window to pick up my tux for work, I saw something on a bulletin board near the administration building. It was a small poster featuring Mickey Mouse holding three Mickey ear hats

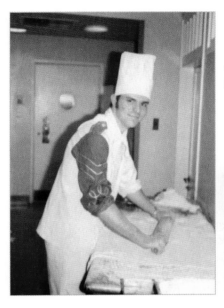

From Club 33 busboy to chef, where I continued to cook up big plans for the future!

This photo may be deceiving. I didn't really stir the pot until I arrived at Imagineering.

Living the good life as lead (assistant manager) at Club 33 before deciding to trade in my snappy tux for a broom, dustpan, and heaping helping of humility.

with the caption MICKEY WANTS YOU! Pinned next to the poster was an official communication from WED Enterprises, home of the Imagineers, saying they were about to design and develop a new park called EPCOT Center and they were recruiting artists and designers. Holy paintbrush, what timing. They need artists, and according to my brand-new college degree, I am one. Mickey wants *me*! I ran to the nearby backstage pay phone and immediately called the number, and a live WED recruiter named Sally actually answered and listened as I told her my entire life story up to that very second.

This is the poster that was hanging on a bulletin board backstage at Disneyland in 1978. It's what started it all!

As Sally was about to schedule an interview for me, saying it was my lucky day because it was the last interview of the day for the last position they had available, the phone operator interrupted: "Please deposit thirty-five cents for three minutes." *WHAT?!!!* In a panic, I pulled my pockets inside out searching for coins but they were empty, which should have been no surprise because it was Wednesday, payday was Thursday, and I usually spent every penny on Patty by Sunday. "Sally, wait!" I pleaded in a panic. "Don't hang up!" "Please deposit thirty-five cents."

At that moment, I would have given a hundred paper dollars for thirty-five cents. Then a voice behind me sternly asked, "Who's Sally?" It was Patty! She wasn't supposed to come to work until later that evening, but they'd called her in early (thank you again, Disneyland!). "QUICK!" I begged her, "I need coins! COINS COINS COINS!" Patty protected her purse, shoving it under her coat. "Not until you tell me who Sally is." In one fell breath, I told her who Sally was and she quickly came up with two shiny, wonderful, beautiful quarters, which I jammed into the slot. "Hello, HELLO! Are you there?" Sally thankfully stayed on the line and we set up the interview, which was oddly on the same day and at the same time I was scheduled to meet with Don Duckwall. I grabbed the appointment, hung up the phone, and asked Patty for more coins so I could call and reschedule Don to another day, you know, just in case. "Naw," she said. "Go for it. Just go to WED." I countered her confidence with a tinge of worry and fear. "But I don't know anybody at WED." She said, "So? Go!"

Lucky for me, my first credit card came in the mail a few days before my interview, because I didn't own a suit, nice shoes, or a presentable portfolio case to hold my artwork. When the big day came for my long trip from Disneyland's Orange County to Imagineering's Glendale locale, I put on my new suit and shiny new wing tips, wedged my large new portfolio case in the faux back seat of my ticking time bomb Fiat 124 roadster named "Old Unreliable," and headed north, praying the car would make the hundred-mile round-trip—or at least the first most important fifty miles anyway. The good news is the car made it. The bad news is there was a heavy downpour the entire trip, and the duct tape patches on the torn convertible top did not hold it together.

By the time I pulled up in front of 1401 Flower Street, my new wool suit was soaked. To add insult to injury, I had arrived two hours early. I sat in the car, even as the rain accumulating above me continued to drip through the roof. I dabbed my eyes with my new tie and stuffed pages torn out of my Thomas Bros. Maps book into the holes in the car's convertible top. The night before, Patty had accidentally spilled an entire strawberry milkshake—which cost all the money I had left—on and between the seats of my little car, and although I thought I'd gotten it cleaned up, my wet wool suit and the rain-soaked carpet around the stick shift made my car smell like a musty sheep eating moldy strawberries.

There were four single-wide white trailers set up in the parking lot directly across from WED Enterprises main lobby. (As a sidenote, these were the very same "temporary" trailers in which, ten years later, Ron Clements and John Musker set up shop with their team and produced the Disney animated game-changer The Little Mermaid.) When it came time for the last interview of the day, mine, and with the rain still falling, I pried my portfolio from the clutches of the back seat and made a mad dash to the door of trailer number two as instructed. The moment I turned the doorknob, a great gust of wind caught the door and slammed it against the side of the trailer with a bang. The receptionist seated inside threw her body across her desk to keep her neat stacks of paper from blowing everywhere—but they still did anyway.

I pulled the door closed behind me, and with my hair matted down around my skull and my soaked suit dripping audibly onto her papers now on the floor, I apologized for the disturbance. "I smell strawberries," she said as I helped pick up her papers. "And . . . sheep." Just as she had them neatly restacked on her desk, however, the trailer door blew open again with a bang and a great gust once again blew everything everywhere. I turned and saw the silhouette of a cowboy sharply defined in the doorframe by a flash of lightning, exactly like when the bad guy steps through the saloon doors in a Western movie. With rainwater pouring off the brim of his hat to add extra oomph to the cowboy image cliché, the man stepped into the light, and I immediately noticed that everything about him was square: his jaw, the top of his hat, the pattern on his shirt, his nostrils, his shirt pocket (and the Marlboro box in it), his license plate–sized belt buckle, his watch; even his mustache was trimmed perfectly square on three sides and open on the bottom. He was like a living caricature drawn by a Disney animator.

Any Disney animator would tell you Mickey is round-shaped because round is friendly. I didn't get friendly from this cowboy. And his hat was black to boot. I can't remember what I had for dinner last night, but I remember every detail about meeting this man forty years ago. "You Kevin?" He caught me off guard, so my first instinct was to answer in his native tongue. "Yup." He extended his square hand. "I'm Don," he said. "Don Tomlin." It's a good thing I'm left-handed because his vise-grip handshake squeezed the life right out of my offered hand.

A fellow wearing a dry suit and tie, the HR recruiter from "Professional Staffing," stepped out from the office door behind the receptionist, introduced himself, and invited Don and me to come in and have a seat. I don't remember his name but Mr. HR looked like the professor from *Gilligan's Island*. Don remained standing in a power position, turning a trash can upside down and placing one boot upon it as he crossed his arms, leaned against the fake-wood trailer paneling, and faced me. This is my moment, I thought, confident that my art portfolio would knock Don's socks off right through his square-toed boots. Today I was going to become an artist and an Imagineer! My nervousness melted away when I began to fantasize about how I was soon going to be able to buy a new car and pay the entire total of my first credit card bill because I was on the verge, right here, right now, of making the big bucks.

"So, tell us, Kevin," began Mr. HR. "Why are you here?" This was the question I had been waiting and hoping for, the one I had answered over and over again in my head. "Well, sir," I answered enthusiastically, "I'm here to help design EPCOT Center. Would you like to see my portfolio now?" Don raised an eyebrow. "No need," he said. *Wow!* I thought. They don't even need to see my work! My reputation precedes me, probably because good ol' Jim Lowman must have already called them to provide a glowing performance review and recommendation on my behalf; probably told them I could do anything and he would miss me terribly, which made me feel incredibly guilty about the mermaid. As soon as I get to my plush new office here at WED I will have to send Jim a nice note.

Don continued the vetting: "Where do you see yourself in ten years?" Again, I answered quickly with confidence. "In ten years, I see myself still as an artist in the creative department here at WED." Cowboy Don and Mr. HR looked at one another as if I had just stuffed firecrackers down the fronts of their pants and lit the fuses with a blowtorch. With both eyebrows now raised, Don turned his head slowly towards me like a praying mantis and stared at me as if I were smoking tumbleweed. I did not realize the gravity of what I had just said. You see, at that time, twenty-three years after the opening of Disneyland, the now seasoned and successful creative department at WED was the castle in the sky, home to kings and queens, gods really, a department of artist and designer deities unattainable by mere mortals like me. I say this not facetiously but with great respect and admiration, because it was true.

Many of the artists and designers in the creative department at WED in the 1970s were still those handpicked by Walt himself to design and develop Disneyland, followed by Walt Disney World, which opened in 1971. They were the pioneers of the Disney theme park industry, and most of them were still at WED "drawing" from their talent and proven experience to create the future. Don Tomlin would have taken a bullet for any of them, as would Marty Sklar, too. Don was still glaring at me with that *how dare you even suggest that you could ever be worthy of rising above the clouds and being allowed passage over the golden drawbridge that leads through the castle portal into the creative department* look as the rain pounded on the aluminum trailer roof even more forcefully. Perhaps this was an exclamation point from the gods themselves.

The hard, cold reality of where all of this was heading stabbed me right through my vulnerable artistic heart when Don finally said, "Hold your horses, fella. Did you think I was interviewing you to be an *artist*? Oh, no, no, no. No, no. No. That's not the job I'm offering." It seemed the smiling Mickey with all the hats on the WED recruitment poster was about to hand me his last hat, and it wasn't the one I was expecting—or even wanting.

Don, who turned out to be the manager of the "special services" department, looked at me square in the eye and began to describe what he referred to as an "entry-level job." As he did my eyes glazed over and his words began to sound like sounds, not words, like when Charlie Brown's mom says, "Wah, wah, wah, wah, wah. . . ." This job was so entry-level, so far below the creative clouds, that it was deep in the dark castle dungeon—the WED equivalent of, God help me, the dish room. How could this possibly be happening again? Don continued to explain that the position would include sweeping floors, emptying trash cans, setting up chairs in conference rooms, dusting models, and cutting cardboard mats to frame the concept art created by the *real* artists, the ones in the creative department. So, I would not *be* an artist, I would be working *for* the artists, and for Don himself.

And then came the icky icing on this rotten cake: the job would pay less than what I was earning at Disneyland. Don wrapped it up by saying he wasn't actually offering me the job then and there anyway. He said he would have to talk it over with Mr. HR to determine if I was *qualified* and get back to me. Drenched, deflated, disappointed, and now $200.00 in credit card debt at 17 percent interest, I thanked them both with the best smile I could muster and stepped back into the now dark, windy, rainy night where Old Unreliable, the only car left on Flower Street, was waiting, or should I say wading, up to her hubcaps in water. The lights went out in the trailers as I opened my car door and plunged my posterior into the cold water that had pooled inches high on my torn vinyl seat. It felt like my career at WED Enterprises was over before it even got started. Old Unreliable didn't start up either.

THE DAY AFTER my "wet WED interview" I was back in my elegant element at Club 33 assistant managing the staff—not emptying trash cans, not sweeping, not dusting, and not earning less per hour than the wage being offered in faraway Glendale! At the club, I was working close to home, hobnobbing with celebrities and dignitaries, and enjoying a steady and comfortable position in a classy joint where my fellow cast members and the members of the club themselves had become dear friends.

But when WED called to offer me the junior job I jumped on it. It certainly wasn't the best job in the world, but it was at the best place. Besides, I figured I could sweep the less-than-impressive job description under the carpet with my friends and family and still honestly tell them I was an Imagineer, granted a spin on the truth similar to when my cousin Robert boasted he worked aboard the *Playboy* jet; he did, but in actuality his job was to scrub the interior, change the satin sheets, and empty the plane's waste tank after every flight. My elementary-school chums turned me into a playground hero because I had a direct connection to the *Playboy* jet, which linked me to Hugh Hefner and his no-attire empire. When you're an eighth-grade boy at a parochial school who actually had never laid eyes on a copy of *Playboy* magazine (because that would be a mortal sin—which of course seals the deal on ensuring the forbidden fruit remains unreachable and therefore all the more mysterious and enticing), knowing someone who knows someone who is in the "know" put me in the category of an expert who could answer all of life's most intimate questions. Thank goodness, they never asked, but I can only imagine they imagined there was nothing left to my imagination. But I had plenty to go around: imagination, that is.

Two weeks after giving notice at Disneyland, my magic journey began in an orientation class at the Walt Disney Studios in Burbank, three miles up the road from my new employer, WED Enterprises. An hour early, I was the first one in the "Disney University" orientation room. On the table inside the door was a tall stack of MY NAME IS ___ stickers and a pen. I wrote KEVIN in perfect bock letters on the top sticker, but I felt it didn't look artsy enough for WED, so I tossed it into the trash can and tried again, this time in a whimsical cursive of my own design. It looked fun but too frilly.

I tried a version with shadowed box letters that made my name seem to appear in 3-D. Getting there but not yet worthy. I filled half of the trash can with rejects before landing on a design that had that certain creative gestalt one would expect from an Imagineer, even one that was about to receive that title from a collective company perspective and not an individually earned one. Ten minutes before the session started, about a dozen new Imagineers began to trickle in for their half-day of pixie dusting, and I must say that their name stickers were surprisingly and disappointingly blah, which led me to believe they were probably on the business side of the business.

A man wearing a glowing white belt and matching white loafers, the kind with those frilly little tassels on the tops, sat next to me wearing a name sticker that had such poorly scrawled letters that it looked like a doctor's prescription. I could hardly make it out. The man, about twenty years my senior, seemed out of sorts while fidgeting impatiently and scanning the room. He looked as if he needed a friend. "I'm Kevin," I said, proving the point by pointing proudly to my name sticker featuring the best design in the room. "You're gonna love WED, Earl!" He stopped shaking my hand and said, "Carl. It's Carl." He seemed nice enough but appeared as though he had other things on his mind and not all that excited to be there.

Well, considering where *there* was, that raised a warning flag with me. I decided to ramp up my nerve to pump up his verve. "Carl, did you know the 'WED' part of WED Enterprises stands for Walter Elias Disney? It was his own personal company and it's where Imagineers still design stuff for Disneyland and Walt Disney World. I mean, holy cow, Carl, WED is it, the mother ship! Walt himself handpicked people from his studio to become the first Imagineers, and here we are today about to become Imagineers ourselves! Pretty special, huh?"

Carl nodded in agreement. I was getting through to him. By that time our instructor, Barbara, had arrived to start the orientation, which was perfect timing because I had just set the stage for Carl. "Huh," Barbara began. "I thought I had a lot more stickers than that. Well, it looks like everyone has one." I thrust the sticker side of my chest forward so mine would stick out and be noticed; and Barbara took the bait: "Ooooh," she said. "Nicely done, Kevin!" I was off to a good start!

The orientation was fun and informative. I felt bad for Carl, though, because every time our enthusiastic instructor asked questions about Walt Disney Productions or WED Enterprises to test our knowledge—or rouse our curiosity—he was the only one in the room that did not have an interest in participating; it was almost as if there was somewhere else he'd rather be. Oddly, he didn't seem to know anything about Disney, and I hoped he wasn't thinking he was about to start a normal, run-of-the-mill-type job that anyone could get anywhere. We are about to become Imagineers here, Carl!

I never asked what position he was going to start that day, but I wanted him to know how privileged he was to work at WED. At the end of orientation, we had earned our official oval name tags featuring a WED logo—a badge of honor. "When you get your CARL, Carl," I said, pointing to my newly minted name tag, "think about how many people in the world get to wear these, okay?" As I began to depart, I pivoted around to call out to him one last time to drive the message home. "Hey, Carl!" I exclaimed while walking backwards. "Remember what we saw on the film today. Walt said Disneyland would never be completed as long as there is imagination left in the world. That's what Imagineers are for! It's not just a job, Carl. We are about to head over to 'THE Mecca of Magic'!"

I arrived in the WED lobby at 1401 Flower Street, adjusted the alignment of my new WED name tag to perfection—a process that poked about twenty new pinholes in my best shirt—and glanced up the stairs, where I noticed a large black-and-white photograph, circa 1955, of Walt Disney stepping through his newly built Sleeping Beauty Castle. "Well, Walt," I whispered after taking a deep breath to calm my nerves, "here goes nothin'." With my new blue WED identification card, my golden ticket into the chocolate factory, I was now among the rare few authorized to step through the lobby door into the secret inner sanctum.

On my first day at WED, the first thing I saw was this photo of Walt taken in 1955 prior to the opening of Disneyland. It has not moved from this spot the entire time I've been here. It has become my favorite image in the whole place.

On my walk through the seemingly endless maze of corridors to find the special services department, where I was to report to my new boss, "Sheriff" Don Tomlin, I passed dozens of Imagineers on the move. Some were carrying rolled-up plans, others were huddled together (and speaking over each other with arms flailing to emphasize their points), and two were carrying a four-by-eight-foot storyboard (one on either end, with one puffing on a cigarette so rhythmically that he was perfectly synchronized with his hurried and purposeful gait, which made him look like the Disneyland steam train when it's barreling down the track).

Clearly these were all men and women on a mission. Arranged in perfect order along the length of the corridor walls were framed screen-printed attraction posters, the very same ones found in the Disney parks. And to think this— THIS—was the very place in which these very attractions were dreamed up and designed. Right here! (Later that same day I would find out these posters were screen-printed right here, too, in a room across the hall from special services.) At last I was in the belly of the magical mother ship; and despite the fact it looked like an old mid-century concrete industrial building like a million others on the outside, on the inside its exuberant Santa's workshop vibe was everything I had imagined.

Some male Imagineers scurrying through the ant farm–like corridors had long hair and long beards, and some were dressed in loud double knit leisure suits with long collars and even longer sideburns. A woman (who I later found out was a designer from the model shop) walked by wearing a Girl Scouts uniform she'd handmade entirely out of paper; and here it was still two months shy of Halloween! What the heck was that all about? Despite spending my wonder years smack-dab in the middle of the Haight-Ashbury hippie heyday, I was always a clean-cut conservative kid. But this place was a frenzy of far-out fashion and fuzzy faces. Growing up attending Catholic schools, I had to follow strict dress codes and abide by the rules set for length of hair (atop the head) and, God forbid, facial hair, which was was not allowed—at any measurable amount.

At Disneyland, strict dress codes and rules about length of hair and, Dick Nunis forbid, facial hair, were also strictly enforced. As a result, I never had long hair or facial hair, which was a bummer, man, because this was the 1970s and I looked like I was living with Ozzie and Harriet. We could not even let our sideburns grow past mid-ear at Disneyland. I decided to wait a week and then start not shaving or getting haircuts simply because I could.

I felt so liberated and rebellious, like I was free to sin with no consequences. And I hoped Dick Nunis would make it up to WED on occasion so I could walk right up to him with my long hair and bearded mug and say, "Hey, man!" HA

HA! I happened upon another mustachioed, long-sideburned Imagineer who, wearing rose-colored granny glasses and green-and-orange-checked pants, could have passed for Sonny Bono. He stopped to show some sort of an architectural plan to a well-dressed conservative-looking woman in high heels who was with a Drew Carey-like guy with a crew cut, a tie, and a pocket protector containing at least six pens.

Wow, this place was like *Mod Squad* meets *The Lawrence Welk Show*. It was Monday but it felt like *Freaky Friday*. I was not used to this upside-down dynamic in a work environment, or any environment for that matter, so the first thing I felt in my first few minutes at WED was a culture shock of sorts.

Right off the bat Imagineers proved themselves to be an interesting bunch. They were both straightlaced and loosey-goosey—and everyone seemed to be fine with that. I was totally fine with that. The best part was it appeared as though there were no rules!

"Rule number one," said Sheriff Don, who looked at his watch when I stepped through the door into special services for the very first time, "is to be on time." And I was, as always. "Starting tomorrow," he continued, "your shift will begin at precisely 8 a.m. Not 8:01. At 10 a.m. you will take a break until 10:15 a.m. Lunch is from 12:00 until 1:00, and that doesn't mean until 1:01. Your last break is 3 p.m. to 3:15 p.m., not a minute more, and your shift ends no earlier than 5 p.m., unless I need you to stay longer. Any questions?" I looked around the room, which was approximately four hundred square feet. In the dead center was a giant well-worn worktable with razor cutters and overhead retractable heating irons for use in spot tacking mounting paper to the back of photos and artwork. Along the walls were rows of wooden bins jammed with mat and illustration boards, and in the far corner was a large heat press for dry mounting art onto board stock.

There were also several trash cans around the room, all of which needed emptying. "Yes, I, uh, do have a question. Do I have an office?" I replied. Don repeated my question back to me twice: "Do you have an office? Do you have an . . . *office*?" After his long laugh (that started off low and breathy like the sound a '52 Plymouth makes when you try to start it after a long hard winter in Fargo, North Dakota, and progressed into the helium-induced high-pitched sound a fairy would make while humming into a kazoo), he snapped into a dead serious demeanor, pointed to the centrally located worktable, and said, "That is your office!" Just for the record, there was no chair. Or phone.

Don, suddenly distracted like Dug the dog in the movie *Up* whenever he'd see a squirrel, looked past me to the double doors through which I had entered and called out to someone in the same sweet voice that the smarmy Eddie

Haskell of *Leave It to Beaver* would switch to when Mrs. Cleaver walked into the room. "*Helloooo!* Nice shoes!" I turned to find out who had distracted Don and couldn't believe my eyes. It was the white-shoes, white-belted-wearing Carl—the same Carl from my orientation class!

What the . . . ? I'd left the studio lot before he did, so how could Don possibly know Carl already? "How do you know Carl?" I had to ask. "How do I know Carl?" Don repeated twice. "How do I know . . . *Carl?* That's Carl Bongiorno, our president." "President?" I repeated in disbelief. "As in *president*, president? Of WED?" Don laughed. "Yup!" He continued, "Didn't they teach you guys anything in orientation?" (I later discovered Carl had attended orientation with us that morning out of curiosity to check the content of the program and to see how it was handled. You would think that of all people, the president of WED would have written his name on his sticker with a little more artsy-fartsy flair. At least I thought so until I found out that before Carl became president of WED he was an accountant at Walt Disney World. Then it all added up.)

My job in special services provided no opportunity whatsoever for me to use my bottled-up-and-ready-to-erupt-like-Mentos-in-a-Coke-bottle imagination and contribute anything creatively to the Epcot cause. It was mindless busywork smack-dab in the middle of a land flowing with creative milk and honey; and for that reason I could not understand what was so "special" about these "services." I felt like a sports car parked backwards in a garage watching all of the other cars happily zooming by all day.

But that was then. Now that I look back on the experience four Disney decades later I realize my time in special services was a blessing in disguise and meant to be because it established a solid foundation upon which I built an informed and much-appreciated career. You wouldn't think performing simple and repetitive tasks to support the real artists and designers would have any growth potential whatsoever. But it truly did have value—and here's why: special services was located in the corridor crossroads of the 1401 headquarters building between the main model shop, the heart of the place, and the executive "Gold Coast," the brains of the place. It was WED's impromptu gathering place, a bustling Grand Central Station through which all the key artists and designers flowed as they stopped in for a chat, to tell a quick story or pick each other's brains while gathering up materials or having their original art and designs mounted and matted by me.

And I was all ears. (To this day, some of the best ideation and cross-pollination at Imagineering happens at random times in random places when folks are on their way to someplace else, like the bathroom.) They were always excited about their work, and when they weren't having a meeting of the minds or exchanging ideas among other designers who wandered in, they were happy to tell me all about it and/or about themselves. And I was more than happy to learn about their exciting concepts in progress and about them personally. That's how I got to meet and know them and their projects, and through them I became aware of and eventually part of the close-knit culture and family of WED.

Although I knew their work, I did not know any of the legendary Disney designers who actually created that work until I met them at WED and started to connect the dots. I began to learn who they were and what they had done through Don Tomlin, as they'd come in and out of our area. "Ya see that gal over there with the pearl necklace?" Don would say to me. "That's Harriet Burns. She started with Disney in 1955 working on the props and sets for the *Mickey Mouse Club*." The *Mickey Mouse Club* was the very first show I remember watching on TV. Among the many memorable sets Harriet designed and constructed was the show's famous clubhouse. She would always wear high heels and a nice skirt as she out-sawed and out-hammered the construction guys who worked alongside her.

She also made the first scale model of Sleeping Beauty Castle. Truly a class act, Harriet worked on the other side of the wall from me in her own little corner of the main model shop. Even though foam dust flew (one of the reasons I dusted models, by the way) and table saws buzzed around her all day—and even though she always seemed to have wet glue and/or paintbrushes in her hand—Harriet always dressed impeccably, looking at any moment as if she were about to step out onto the White House lawn for a photo shoot as first lady. She was actually the first lady of WED.

Almost every working day I experienced one-on-one encounters with the founding fathers and mothers of WED, including Harriet, Herb Ryman, Claude Coats, John Hench, Blaine Gibson, Maggie Elliot (then head of the model shop, whose father, an art director, had worked on thirty-one films and later became executive vice president and chief operations officer at WED), Harper Goff, X Atencio, Ward Kimball, and even Marc Davis on occasion. Although I was nobody, they treated me like I was part of the family. Prior to coming to WED they were all successful art directors, animators, production designers, layout artists, and more in the film industry.

After becoming Imagineers, they quickly learned how to adapt their two-dimensional filmmaking savvy to create the three-dimensional worlds and stories of Disneyland and beyond.

That's why they were all so good at what they did at WED, creating the classic and timeless attractions everyone knows and loves. They were showmen and women, first and foremost. Considering their remarkable histories, accomplishments, and positions in the company at the time I arrived, it pleasantly

Almost all of these first-generation Imagineers were still on campus when I arrived at WED Enterprises in 1978. These were my earliest mentors and heroes.

surprised me none of them walked around with their noses in the air. And that's not just because they kept them to the grindstone. They were genuinely good, kind, and extremely likable people, all of them great storytellers who loved what they had done and what they were doing so much that they enjoyed taking the time to share with me—the bright-eyed and bushy-tailed new kid—their histories and whatever was currently on their minds or sketch pads.

Through their example, I began to recognize and learn that the greatest creative talents at WED were humble and dedicated servants to the Disney design cause because they understood with great respect that there was only one name on the front door: Walt Disney. It wasn't about them. It was still about him. Through them and their stories I got to know the Walt Disney they knew and loved, the one never written about so matter-of-factly in books. I heard firsthand from Herb Ryman his story about that legendary weekend he and Walt spent together to create the first-ever hand-drawn bird's-eye view map of Disneyland and about how his sister Lucille kept them fed. I always thought Herbie was so fortunate because he was the first person ever to see what Disneyland looked like, because it appeared out of the tip of his pencil. (When I did eventually get into a creative leadership role, I always made sure the artists on my teams knew how fortunate they were because they were the first ones to get to see what the big idea would look like!)

I began to look forward to Herbie's frequent "pop ins" to special services because he was a bundle of energy, happiness, and unbridled enthusiasm. He was a pure joy to be around, like a kid on Christmas morning every single day, and as exuberantly colorful as his art, which helped us begin to see what Epcot and Tokyo Disneyland were going to look like. His many sketches and oil paintings filled me with awe, but they also made me realize that the quality of my art was not even close to that of the resident masters like him who were helping design the Disney parks of the future.

The world-class quality of the original art being produced at WED made me realize I had put my own artistic ability into a category much higher than it deserved. When I went in for my interview, I thought I was ready to jump right in and design away that very day. But I was clearly not ready, and therefore grateful my portfolio case was never opened. My work compared to theirs was as if I were plinking a tiny toy piano at Carnegie Hall, thinking it worthy of such a venue, before suddenly discovering the terrible truth when the real virtuosos take the stage, sit at their concert grand Steinways, and fill the hall with so much perfection and emotion that they make the audience weep.

Getting to spend time with Herbie, the most talented in my opinion and yet most humble of them all, and all the others I came to respect and admire so much made me realize how far away I was from their echelon. As I became brutally aware of how many dues I would have to pay to even begin to contribute in some small way, if even at all, to the creative process at WED, I began every new day by leaving my unjustified frustrations and even more unjustified ego outside the front door.

Still I could not help but wonder: Did I even belong here? Did I really have the chops to continue to entertain my aspiration to be an artist here? Despite the misgivings I had about whether I possessed a creative soul I stuck it out, month after month, keeping my eyes and ears open while climbing the steep mountain to learn everything I could, directly and indirectly, from the gurus who resided at the summit of the art of WED Enterprises. And by that I don't mean visual art only; I mean *the art of the process* of creating enjoyable, memorable, and operational three-dimensional immersive entertainment experiences for our park guests.

With the premiere of *Star Wars* still fresh in my mind, I began to fancy myself as farm boy Luke Skywalker trying to learn from the WEDi Knights how to discover my true creative force and use it to help the "WED Alliance." But

Luke had it much easier than I did. Turns out he had the Force already built in because he got it from his father. My father worked for the gas company, and I was a still a schmuck from the dish room. At least my father was a good guy.

No college offers a major in Imagineering. But working in special services was like taking Imagineering 101. It's where my real education began. Although it wasn't a proper classroom, I felt as though my encounters with the original Imagineers, whether it be up close and personal or within earshot of a group of them engaged in lively and informative conversation, were the finest education I could have received while aspiring to be one of them someday. Sure, I took a cut in pay to take a job others may not have been willing to take (perhaps that's why it was the last one on the list?), but befriending and learning from the giants of the industry was priceless.

And what I found fascinating and just plain weird is every one of them had somehow already touched my life long before I met them, not just in some fleeting way but in an impactful way; a way that would influence my future, whether it be something they had created for Disneyland, the movies, or TV. Harper Goff—the designer of Main Street, U.S.A.; Jungle Cruise; and more—regaled me with mesmerizing stories from his past. He had come up with many successful ideas, but the most surprising one for me was his concept for a TV Western that featured two secret agents who used clever spy tools fabricated from objects and crude-by-our-standards technologies from the mid-1800s to thwart evil: sort of James Bond meets *Bonanza*. Their home base was a fancy railroad car that was lifted and carried from place to place by a hot-air balloon. The balloon part never made it, but the TV show sure did. And it was one of my all-time favorites as a kid: *The Wild Wild West*.

Harper also told me the story about the time he met Walt Disney in a model shop in Europe. They wanted the same model train, engaged in a conversation, and discovered shared interests, and Walt invited him to come work at his studio. Harper became art director on the movie *20,000 Leagues Under the Sea* and designed the iconic exterior of the *Nautilus* and all of its richly appointed interior sets. Of course, his stories included working with Walt to design Disneyland, their meetings, their research trips, and many tales never written about. But I got to hear in person from the person who was there. Harper often talked about the trip he and Walt took to Dearborn, Michigan, to visit the Henry Ford museum, which, along with his hometown of Fort Collins, Colorado, influenced his designs for Main Street, USA.

Although I held Harper and his inspiring colleagues in the highest regard, I also discovered they too had humble beginnings and experienced problems like the rest of us. Many shared those types of never-written-in-any-book stories with me as well, such as this little gem from Harper: while attending Chouinard Art Institute in Los Angeles, Harper lived in a tenement building, which had only one tiny bathroom per floor. While he was walking to class one morning, about halfway there, he felt a sharp pain in his stomach, which meant he had to find a bathroom pronto. With all of the residents on his floor already gone for the day, he ran like the wind six blocks back to his building, flew up the fire escape, dove into the bathroom window, and perched himself on the pot with his face buried in his hands. "When the fireworks were over," he admitted, "I finally looked up and lo and behold there was a woman in the bathtub right in front of me."

After getting to know the wonderful and kind Sam McKim, another talented WED artist with a film industry background—though only in Sam's case as a child actor—I discovered he was the one who'd created the souvenir map of Disneyland I'd had hanging on my bedroom wall since 1963. What surprised me the most, however, was finding out decades later that he had served in the army during World War II with a dear friend of my family's, Walt Ehlers, who because of his heroic actions on the beach at Normandy on D-Day was awarded the Medal of Honor. He was often present at the flag-raising ceremony at Disneyland. When I arranged a celebration for Walt's eightieth birthday at Club 33, I about fell over backwards when Sam McKim entered the room. I had no idea he knew Walt Ehlers. Sam had never talked about his army days with me, so that's how and when I found out. To this day, when I visit The American Adventure at Epcot (and I do every time I'm in Walt Disney World, which is quite often), I enjoy seeing Sam's paintings framed in the lobby and featured in the show itself (because I saw him working on those very pieces in the days before computers, when you could walk upstairs at WED and smell the wet oil paint).

These connections between the masters and me—and there were many— were uncanny. John Hench told me the story about how Walt Disney asked him to design a restaurant for Disneyland. After John told him he didn't know anything about the restaurant business, Walt suggested he learn. The restaurant John designed was the Red Wagon Inn, later renamed the Plaza Inn, home of the dish room where I got my start! John also designed Flight to the Moon, a life-changing attraction for me, because as a kid I believed every part of the experience. I really believed I was being launched from our planet and heading in a rocket to the moon. I watched the actual liftoff through the lower window of the rocket and felt the pressure of it under my seat!

Finding out from a friend you really don't fly to the moon was like finding out there is no Santa Claus. Devastating. But that personal and memorable experience of perceived reality would serve me well in my later years as an

Imagineer in the sense that if you can create an attraction that keeps guests in its spell, that's the art and magic of Imagineering.

Just for the record, I still believe in Santa. So, kids, if anyone tells you otherwise, tell that person to take a flying rocket to the moon.

Some people have sports heroes. Others have military heroes. My heroes were from the musical, visual, and theatrical arts. Among them, especially while I studied animation, was Claude Coats. His exquisite and truly inspiring backgrounds for the movie *Pinocchio*, especially the nighttime Italian village in the opening sequence, so filled me with awe, appreciation, and emotion that his work was one of the reasons I wanted a career in animation in the first place. Regarding Claude's film work, I often asked myself, *How can something that extraordinary come from a mere mortal?* Especially since the watercolor medium is so unforgiving when it comes to making changes such as can be easily accomplished by computer these days. Claude worked his visual magic on many Disney films, and his hand-painted animation backgrounds were my absolute favorites. To discover that he was full time at WED and to have the opportunity to meet him and get to see him every working day was a thrill. His office was right around the corner from special services.

One of the key designers and creators of Pirates of the Caribbean, Claude was a shy and gentle soul and always took the time to explain whatever he was working on. As fate would be so kind, later in my career I would have the opportunity to work with Claude as my creative partner on a theatrical show that would celebrate the sixtieth birthday of Mickey Mouse. We designed the show for installation in the Carousel of Progress theater at Disneyland. The traveling carousel venue was originally designed to deliver a sequential passage-of-time-style show, so our multimedia Audio-Animatronics show was the story of Mickey's life as told in four acts. I titled the show *Mickey Mouse Through the 'ears*.

One night the two of us went on a field trip to Disneyland to do an after-hours research walk-through of the Carousel building while it was still home to America Sings. It was a lifesaving trip; and I mean that literally. While standing stage left, I noticed Claude near center stage stepping slowly backward towards one of the open character lift pits located directly behind him—and he was one step away from an eight-foot drop right through the stage floor! I lunged at him with just enough time to grab his belt and pull him towards me and out of danger. The poor man probably thought that I had gone berserk until I caught my breath and pointed to the dark open pit just behind his heels. In typical Claude fashion, being a man of few words, he simply smiled and said, "Oh, gee. Thanks."

Once Claude and I had the story beats and show sequence for our Mickey show fleshed out and ready for presentation, Randy Bright, vice president of creative development, fell in love with it and asked us to go to Disneyland and present it, which really meant "go sell it" to the executives there.

When we arrived at the conference room in the administration building at Disneyland, it was clear the execs had something else on their agenda and were not expecting us. I interrupted their animated conversation when I opened the door. At that moment, all I could think of was that I used to work for these executives and it was the first time I'd ever seen them all together in one place. Claude looked over my shoulder into the now deathly quiet room. One of them asked why the two of us were there and I explained we had developed a new attraction concept for the Carousel building and wanted to present it to them. They were obviously surprised and began to murmur among themselves in jury-like fashion.

The quick and unanimous verdict was they didn't need or want a new attraction for that venue. They crossed their arms and stared us down, and although they didn't say a word, their eyes were communicating, "Scram!" My gut told me not to budge but my brain warned me I didn't have a plan B. This time, and quite surprisingly, Claude grabbed me by the belt and pulled me backwards into the corridor. "Listen," the tall man whispered loudly, bending down to put his nose almost against mine, "we have a great little show here and they need to see it. Now you go back in there and tell them that!"

Wow! That was so un-Claude-like! His spark really lit my fuse. Now all charged up, I walked back in and got them to agree to give us ten minutes of their time. After our forty-five-minute pitch the surprised and delighted execs, now genuinely excited about our proposed Mickey concept, began to murmur again among themselves. The unanimous verdict now was that they wanted to do it!

Like countless other good ideas, however, it never did happen for a variety of reasons. But after telling us point-blank that they didn't want it, and then to have them completely turn around and become believers as a result of my pitch? Well, I became a believer in the persuasive power of pitching a good "gut feel" idea. That realization alone, in addition to working closely with Claude, of course, made the entire design and development effort on the Mickey show worth it as both a growth experience and an example of trusting myself for all concept pitches in the years to come. Claude, who was not at all a squeaky wheel—which made his corridor coaching to me even more meaningful—taught me to jump in and fall on my sword for that which is worthy. He was so right, because later in my career I jumped in and pitched many ideas I totally believed in with mind, heart, and gut; and ultimately, many of those ideas made it into the parks.

For Kevin — very best wishes and thanks MARC DAVIS 1980

In the late 1950's, Walt Disney introduced the concept of a pirate adventure to his staff at WED. Like so many other Disney dreams that eventually became a prodigious reality in the Magic Kingdom, the idea for a pirate show was far ahead of the technology required to achieve the desired effects. It was not until the middle 1960's that the *Pirates of the Caribbean* show could move forward toward actual realization.

In simplest terms, Audio-Animatronics combines and synchronizes sound and animation by means of electronic systems. Every movement of each member of the cast is "programmed" into a sequence of action that can be repeated over and over again throughout the day.

The success of the first Audio-Animatronic show (the Enchanted Tiki Room at Disneyland) and the overwhelming public response to the four Disney shows at the New York World's Fair 1964-1965, indicated that Audio-Animatronics was ideal for the pirate concept.

From the Disney World's Fair experience came one more conception basic to the pirate show: the idea of guiding the guests through the adventure aboard flat-bottomed boats propelled by silent (and unseen) jets of water. This idea was first proven in the *It's A Small World* attraction at the New York World's Fair.

The WED artists began to create pirates in myriad phases of their notorious lives. Sketches, such as those above, eventually evolved into a unified tale in pictures—called a "story board." The pirate at the right, for example, portrays the pictorial development of one performer in the show.

In 1967, when Pirates of the Caribbean made its debut, I took home a souvenir picture book about the making of the attraction. Thirteen years later, I dug up that buried treasure (see above), brought it to work, and asked Claude, Marc Davis, X Atencio, and everyone else who had worked on the attraction and was still at WED to sign it for me. Had I not taken the entry-level job at WED, my souvenir book would be nothing more than just that today. Having the rare and remarkable opportunity to get to know those whose TV shows, movies, and beloved attractions I enjoyed my entire life was about to change the rest of my entire life.

SCOPING OUT A NEW ROLE

PELICAN ALLEY was one of my favorite places at WED from 1978 to 1981. It was located inside the massive MAPO building (short for *MAry POppins*, because it was funded by the proceeds of the successful 1964 Academy Award–winning film that featured a scene with Mary singing with another talented actor, an Audio-Animatronics bird perched upon her finger) in the backyard of the 1401 Flower Street headquarters in Glendale. Pelican Alley was affectionately named after the first family of fine feathered friends brought to life using Audio-Animatronics technology—and was home to dozens of lab-coated technicians, machinists, and tinkerers who were busy building all of the animated show props and life-sized Audio-Animatronics actors for our two groundbreaking (literally and figuratively) new parks: EPCOT Center (now known as Epcot) and Tokyo Disneyland.

Unlike the precise assembly plans created today with computer-aided design software, the folks at MAPO didn't have much in the way of detailed drawings to guide the manufacturing of their figures. They did a lot of shoot-from-the-hip inventing and fabricating right at their workbenches. The place, which was always bustling, smelled like plastic, steel, and hydraulic oil. It was never quiet because of the cacophony of mechanical and percussive sounds emanating from drills, hammers, ratchets, part-making machinery, and the distinct "clickity-clicks" made by animated eyelids, mouths, and beaks opening and closing. These *fasten-atin'* rhythms could have perfectly played along with the song "Heigh-Ho" from *Snow White*. Oftentimes I imagined the "Mechanical Musicians of MAPO" breaking into song like in a movie musical (imagine along . . .):

We tap tap tap tap drill punch drill making figures all day through
To saw saw saw saw tap drill grind is what we like to do
It feels so great to animate
Then pack it up and put it in a crate
For a ride! For a ride! For a show! For a show!
Where a billion guests will go!
Heigh-ho, Heigh-ho
We're working in MAPO
(Whistle)
Heigh-ho, heigh-ho, heigh-ho, heigh-ho . . .

If ever there was a place that personified the vibrant vibe of Santa's workshop, this was it. MAPO was established in the mid-1960s as a state-of-the-art facility in which all future Audio-Animatronics design and development could be housed in one place with plenty of space close to the WED headquarters building. By the time I happened upon the scene, MAPO already had a most interesting and successful history, because it was here that the famous actors from Disneyland and the Magic Kingdom in Walt Disney World, including many of the ghosts in Haunted Mansion, the pirates in Pirates of the Caribbean, the cast of America Sings, and several others, were produced.

Talk about cool! Standing in the heart of the MAPO building, I often thought about those late nights I spent sneaking through the shadows behind the scenes at Disneyland, before I even knew there was a MAPO, to study the costumes, staging, and inner workings of the Audio-Animatronics actors that began their life right here. (At the time of this writing, the MAPO building, which no longer houses animated prop and figure production, is a mysterious, top secret facility accessible only to the team of Imagineers who are working to bring the worlds of *Star Wars* to life in our parks. MAPO the Force be with them.)

Several months after being hired, as I started to settle in and become more comfortable with my surroundings and responsibilities, I looked forward to spending my two daily fifteen-minute breaks combing the campus in an effort to stay up to speed on what everyone from almost every discipline was dreaming and doing. Stops along my regular route were the massive main model shop, where development of the giant walk-on-able room-sized model of Epcot was well underway; the sculpture shop, where many maquettes and character busts were taking shape; the special effects department, where among many other mind-blowing things, there was "hot" glowing lava oozing out of a volcano mock-up for the Universe of Energy pavilion (thanks to the unorthodox use of an industrial dog-food pump); and of course MAPO, where there was always so much activity taking place. Amid the shelved robotic bits of history and "spares" were many birds, feathered and unfeathered, bodied and bodiless.

There were also dinosaur heads, skinned and skinless, and other recognizable and not-so-recognizable animals, figures, and related parts. The MAPO team was literally putting together the entire cast for two brand-new theme parks before my very eyes.

Inevitably, whenever I'd happen upon one of the A.A. figure technicians who was ready to try out a new function or movement, my break time would be over—and darn, I'd have to miss it. "Hey," a technician would call out to me as I strolled by with a curious look. "Wanna see how Will Rogers is gonna twirl his rope?" "YES!!!" But then I'd glance at my watch. "NO! Gotta go, or Sheriff Don is gonna twirl his rope around my neck!" All of this dashing around to satisfy my curiosity while the break-time clock was ticking down reminded me of *Supermarket Sweep*, a 1960s TV game show in which contestants were given the opportunity to run through the aisles of a supermarket with a shopping cart and stuff all the groceries they could into it in sixty seconds. I only had a few minutes to run around to one or more of my favorite places to stuff all I could into my "snooping cart" before booking it back to special services not a second too late—or face the steely-eyed wrath of Sheriff Don! I never had to face his wrath, by the way. It turns out Don's bark was worse than his bite and he had a heart as big as Texas.

Blaine Gibson, the head sculptor at WED (he was the head sculptor because he sculpted heads), was the busiest artist on earth when he started working on the busts for the actors slated to perform at Tokyo Disneyland and Epcot, including the hosts of The American Adventure (Mark Twain and Benjamin Franklin); a cast of dozens of others for World of Motion, Horizons, and Spaceship Earth; and Dreamfinder for Journey into Imagination, to name a few. (Many of his originals can still be seen today in the sculpture shop at 1401 Flower, which looks and smells exactly the same today as it did back then.) As Blaine was trying to stay ahead with the heads in our headquarters building, MAPO was building their aluminum and steel human frames, skull structures, clear plastic body panels, mechanical eyes, teeth, skin, and the crazy quagmire of quirky hydraulic actuators and related technology stuffed inside of them that would ultimately bring them to life. Truly it was glorious watching them all come together knowing full well the secret of where they would be going and what they would all be doing.

One day in 1980, while on break and making tracks over at MAPO, I ran into a highly animated figure I didn't at all expect to see—and it was quite a wonderful surprise. Mark Rhodes, who had worked with me at Club 33, had transferred to WED as I did and was on his way to find and surprise me. I had no idea Mark was at WED, and his abrupt arrival was quite a surprise to him, too. As fate would have it, his becoming an Imagineer was meant to be and would eventually benefit both of us "creative types" even though neither one of us started in the creative division.

But hold that thought. Just as MAPO was built from the proceeds of a movie, Mark, an actor, musician, sculptor, snake oil salesman, and published novelist, used the proceeds of his two best-selling novels, written while he was in college no less, to build something tied to what he most dearly loved: movies. Unheard of at the time, especially in his hometown of Woodland Park, Colorado, Mark boldly built something called a Cineplex. But it turns out his small town was not big enough to support a Cineplex, so he lost his shirt. Flat broke, he packed a borrowed car with what little he had left, including his brother, and drove out to California to apply for a job at Disneyland because, and I'm not kidding (and he himself will validate this), he was after *Walt's old job*. In fact,

My old pal ex-Imagineer Mark Rhodes recently stopped by Imagineering for a visit, and we enjoyed a happy reunion. In the background is the MAPO building where he surprised me forty years prior in our early days as young and feisty Imagineers.

when he arrived at the Disneyland casting office, that's the very three-word job description he penciled in on his application. Disneyland didn't hire him, go figure; but they did hire his brother on the spot, who stated on his application he "would do anything."

Mark applied a second time hoping that perhaps his charismatic charm, good looks, and acting experience would land him a job as a Jungle Cruise skipper. They did not. Taking advice from his newly hired brother, Mark's third application declared he "would do anything." He was hired on the spot and assigned as a busboy ("Utility Man") at Club 33, where we met in 1976. Kindred spirits, Mark and I quickly became friends and spent a lot of time together in and outside of work. Like me he was a dreamer, creative to the core, with big plans for a future at Disney.

Since he'd written a screenplay for Paramount, albeit for a film project that got canceled, I always thought movie-buff Mark would end up at the Disney Studio writing and directing, especially after he rented an apartment in Anaheim and filled it not with furniture but with movie posters that completely covered every square inch of the walls. During my last few months at Club 33, Mark became maître d' and then bartender, because he was over twenty-one and had tended bar in Colorado, which was a surprise to me, but it was typical of Mark to be so Walter Mitty. The man was ahead of his time and wise beyond his years and on top of all that fancied himself as the swashbuckling Errol Flynn.

And darned if he wasn't the spitting image of Errol Flynn, sans the mustache, because he had to shave it off to work at Disneyland. No one at his tender age of twenty-three could possibly have experienced as much in life as Mark had by the time I met him, including marrying Jeannie the popcorn girl from his failed Cineplex.

A natural-born storyteller, Mark claimed everything he ever told me about himself was true, which was hard to believe. And although he doled out some doozies, even his tallest of tales always turned out to be true. An expert about all things related to cinema, he once boasted his uncle worked on the movie *The Wizard of Oz*, claiming if you look in just the right place at just the right time you could see him pop out of the background forest by mistake while Dorothy, the Cowardly Lion, and the Tin Man were skipping along on the Yellow Brick Road.

Of course, I didn't believe that. Who would? And there were no VCRs at that time to freeze-frame and prove it. So, one night, when *The Wizard of Oz* was scheduled to be on TV, Mark invited me over to his apartment so he could prove his point by pointing out his uncle. (By the way, the first piece of furniture Mark bought for his apartment was a TV so he could watch movies.) "Ready?" he said as the moment drew near. "Okay, watch closely and don't blink," he said excitedly as he pressed his finger on the TV screen at the spot where his uncle was supposedly about to appear. "And . . . THERE! See?" But I didn't see anything, just as I expected.

A few years later, when VCRs did come along, I did the step-through-the-frames thing on the tape of the movie looking for that blip of a moment in that scene, and by golly there was the vague shape of a man partially popping out of the trees beside the Yellow Brick Road noticing it was a hot set and popping back in!

For this and for more reasons than there is room to write in this book, Mark Rhodes was The Most Interesting Man in the World long before that bearded beer guy on TV had garnered that title. (The weird thing is, if you see Mark today, he looks exactly like that bearded beer guy.)

Having had all those unbelievable but true experiences—and the creative talent to do anything in the entertainment industry—Mark was a true Imagineer in the making; yet he didn't even know it. But WED knew it and began to put all of its Donald Ducks in a row to make it so. When I transferred out of Club 33, I left many friends behind, including—and mostly—Mark. As noted earlier, I didn't know anyone when I arrived at WED. I was a wayward orphan of sorts, trying to survive the best I could on its crazy streets of dreams.

During that very same week when I came to WED, and "suffered" a demotion to do it, Mark got a promotion to lead position at the Mile Long Bar in

Bear Country at Disneyland. Shortly after that he became lead at the Blue Bayou Restaurant in New Orleans Square. We kept in touch, of course, but I didn't know he would be coming up to WED because he didn't know it either. All Imagineers have their own unique and interesting stories about how they became Imagineers, but surprisingly, when compared to the collective numbers through the decades, there have been relatively few of us Disneylanders that made the transfer from Anaheim up to glorious Glendale (the most noted and celebrated, of course, being Marty Sklar and Tony Baxter).

But here's how Mark did it without even realizing he was doing it: while he was lead at the Blue Bayou, Tokyo Disneyland was being planned at WED. One of the requirements of the Oriental Land Company, Disney's business partner in the bold new venture to build the first Disney theme park outside of the United States, was that every shop, restaurant, and attraction at Disneyland and at Walt Disney World provide them with a Standard Operating Procedure (SOP) from which they could study and learn how Disney operated their American parks. Since SOPs did not exist for many locations, or were so old they were no longer relevant, a major task began park-wide to begin writing new ones or updating old ones to send to our Japanese partners. This task was put upon the leads of all park locations. Since Mark was the lead at the Blue Bayou, he was asked to write the SOP for that location; and since he had professional writing experience they tossed in the Mile Long Bar and Cafe Orleans as well.

After completing the three SOPs in his entertaining yet informative style, Mark was summoned to meet with Disneyland vice president Jim Cora, who had embarked on a new role to work in close liaison with the top executives of the Oriental Land Company. As Mark was climbing the stairs behind the Fire House on Main Street to Jim's office, he naturally thought he was going to be fired (as he often thought—and sometimes rightfully so). But Jim liked Mark's SOPs so much he asked if he would be interested in writing all of the SOPs for Disneyland! After working on them for several months and consistently delivering the quality goods, Mark was surprised when asked if he would consider transferring to WED to head up a new department called "Scope Writing," which was established to create descriptive documents that would capture every detail about every element of the Tokyo Disneyland, EPCOT Center, and future Disneyland projects. (When I arrived, they put a duster in my hand, and when Mark arrived they put an entire department in his! Sheesh. And he got a raise! *Double*-sheesh!)

And here's the clincher: Mark didn't even know what Epcot or WED Enterprises was, but when told he'd make more money there than as lead at the Blue Bayou, he jumped at the chance to become an Imagineer, whatever that was. (As a sidenote, writing SOPs for the new attractions, shows, and shops at Tokyo Disneyland is how my dear longtime friend and colleague, ex-Disneyland sweeper and current Imagineering show writer Dave Fisher, got his broom in the door at WED.)

The week-old Scope Writing department, which was composed entirely of Mark, one electric typewriter, and a stack of blank paper, was part of the Project Estimating department under the project management division. Not the creative division, mind you. "Project Scopes" as they became known were matter-of-factly written descriptions of every element of every new theme park project in the hopper. They also included all of the pertinent facts and figures, such as facility square footages, animated figure details (including number of functions), lineal feet of ride track, ride vehicle specs, audio and lighting equipment, etc.; the list goes on and on.

These handy all-encompassing encyclopedias, which became the "go to" source for all project information, were attached to the cost estimates for everything being designed and developed, including shops, restaurants, back-of-house facilities, shows, attractions, entire lands, and entire parks. In a nutshell, the scopes, which evolved concurrent to the evolution of the projects themselves, helped explain and therefore justify the numbers in the estimates. Since there were so many projects going on in different phases of development, keeping up with the sheer number of scopes ended up being a big daunting deal for Mark, especially since changes were being made every day; and each and every one had to be captured to ensure the scopes were relevant and useful. Within the project management division, there were plenty of estimators, project managers, and coordinators to cover all of the bases. But there was only one scope writer. Mark needed help.

Don Tomlin gave me my foot-in-the-door first break, but I will forever be indebted to Mark Rhodes for giving me my second break, which led to my big third break, which ultimately led to my even bigger fourth break. That's the one that helped launch and establish my professional career at WED. Mark approached me with his plan to expand "Scope Productions," as he renamed the department because the word *productions* sounded more movie-like, as in Walt Disney Productions, by bringing me in as a "graphics specialist" (not an "artist" because, after all, it was on the project management side of the fence). My job would be to embellish the scopes with the latest facility plans, elevations and ride layouts, related concept art, and progress photos. "Basically, Kev," as Mark put it, "to make them pretty!"

At the same time, to complement our two right brains, he would bring in left-brained Bob Stephens, another pal from the park, who would gather all of the numbers, facts, and figures from the project teams. My handling of the plans and graphics, and Bob's handling of the data, would free Mark up for the markups! He completed his department expansion plan by bringing in an eccentric, hyperactive hooligan named E. J.—who looked exactly like Elton John but behaved like Kramer from *Seinfeld*—to support the department with general administrative assistant duties, comedy, and the never-ending binding and distribution of the latest scopes.

There was no fancy-schmancy publication software then because there were no desktop computers. The ongoing production of scopes was accomplished with a typewriter, copy machine, and tons of three-ring binders. I did the graphics old school—by hand on the master documents. Granted, transferring into the scope department wasn't the best use of my artistic talent, but at least it was a step up because it came with a fifty-cent-per-hour raise, plus my own phone and drawing table! (I have had that same phone number for almost forty years.)

Our little department had a big task at hand and we needed a lot of room to roll out plans and assemble all of the scopes. We set up shop in a temporary trailer parked adjacent to the cafeteria patio (known today as the Big D), not far from the trailer where I had my WED interview. As you can imagine, trying to keep up with scope production during the busiest and most expansive time at WED took a lot more time than forty hours a week. It was stressful because we all had obsessive-compulsive tendencies and would let nothing slip through the cracks.

To let off some of that pressure, we often played practical jokes on each other, especially on E. J. because, well, he deserved it. Here's one of my all-time faves: since we didn't have voice mail, pagers, or cell phones, the company issued little PLEASE CALL notepads. If you were away from your desk, and someone answered your phone for you, they'd write the name and number of the person who called on your pad. One day, I left a note on E. J.'s pad that read PLEASE CALL MR. LYON, with a phone number. E. J.'s pad had never been used because no one had ever called him. When he burst into our trailer Kramer-style and spotted the note he struck a pose of excited shock. E. J. then exclaimed, as if we didn't know it, "Hey! Somebody called me!"

He looked closely at the note. "Mr. Lyon? I don't know any Mr. Lyon," he said. "What did he want, this Mr. Lyon?" I was straining so hard not to explode with an atomic bomb–force guffaw that tears spurted out of my eyes the way streams of water do in leapfrog fountains.

I noticed E. J. watching me mopping away the flood of tears, and I played

it for all it was worth. "I don't know, E. J. But it sounded urgent, really urgent."
To that Mark added, "Gee, *Eej*, hope everything's all right. Maybe you should
call right now."

E. J. scooped up the phone. "I . . . I'd better call right now!" Here's how the
call went down:

> VOICE ON PHONE: "Los Angeles Zoo. May I help you?
> E. J.: "Yes! I'd like to speak to Mr. Lyon. It's urgent!"
> VOICE ON PHONE: "Well, *Mr. Lion* is napping.
> Would you like to speak to *Mr. Giraffe*?"

While on the subject of phones, WED had an in-house intercom paging
system. You could hear every page from any place you were in the building.
There were so many Imagineers on the loose away from their offices or work-
stations you'd hear someone's name being paged every couple of minutes. It
sounded something like this: "John Hench, please dial station six. John Hench,
station six." In every hallway, there was a wall phone for answering such a page.
You would push whatever number was announced after your name and then be
directly connected to whoever was trying to reach you. The telephone operator,
Sandy, would announce company-wide any name you would ask her to page
without question. And I mean any name! We heard them all, from "Seymour
Butts" to "Ebb Cott" to "Cindy Rella" to countless others.

A big hit song in 1979 was "My Sharona" by the Knack. One of our Epcot
project coordinators was named Les Skalota. Every time we heard Sandy's
gravelly Roz-like voice announce, "Les Skalota, please dial station five," every
Imagineer everywhere would break into this rousing vocal rendition to the tune
of "My Sharona": "*Bum bada bum ba* Les Skalota." Really, whenever that happened we were all like Pavlov's dogs, instantly singing the Les Skalota song at
the sound of his page. It happened so frequently for such a long time that we
just did it without giving it a thought. Here's proof: I was standing at the urinal
in the men's room one day next to author Ray Bradbury when there was a page
for Les. I have no idea who it was, but the guy in the nearby stall sang the Les
Skalota song with me. At the end of our impeccable performance, "stall man"
brought it home with a perfectly timed toot. Afterward I heard the renowned
author whisper to himself, "Remarkable."

While on the subject of phones, we all had plain-Jane desk phones like the
kind you had in your house in the 1960s. If you wanted to put someone on hold,
you'd simply tap one of the two plastic spring-loaded thingies on top of the cra-
dle where the handset rests; to return to the call, you'd tap it once again. One

day it dawned on me that you might be able to turn this "tap 'n' hold" into a fun feature. I tried out my theory, and to my great delight discovered you could call someone, quickly tap to put them on hold as they were answering, then quickly call someone else, tap again, and the two parties would be connected with neither one of them knowing that a third party, me, had connected them! As far as the two connected parties were concerned, they each thought the other one had called because they were both receiving calls simultaneously. And boy, was it fun listening in on their confused conversations!

PHONE 1: Hi, it's Raellen.
PHONE 2: Oh, hi, Raellen. What can I do for you?
PHONE 1: What do you mean?
PHONE 2: What do you mean what do I mean?
PHONE 1: I mean you called me. What do you want?
PHONE 2: I don't want anything. I didn't call you!
PHONE 1: Then why am I on the phone speaking with you if you didn't call me?

(LONG PAUSE)
PHONE 2: You called ME!
PHONE 1: I did not call YOU! WHO IS THIS?
PHONE 2: I have to go. Les Skalota just walked in.
PHONE 1 AND PHONE 2: *Bum bada bum ba* Les Skalota!

No one knows this, but I used this tele-technique to randomly connect project team members who ended up making good use of the call to work out solutions to design challenges, like, "Hey, I don't know why you called, but while you're on the phone, how do you think we can solve that issue with the such and such. . . ." It was surprising how many great ideas and healthy project-advancing discussions and solutions came out of those no-one-really-called phone calls. I guess you could say my high jinks helped move the design of Epcot along!

The reality, though, was there was little time for such entertaining breaks. It was our job in Scope Productions to constantly scout out the latest designs and plans and attend as many project team meetings as we could around campus. Like news reporters, we would also frequently meet with and interview the team leaders and designers responsible for the ideation and development of all concepts to get all the latest scoops for the scopes.

While at special services, I had the opportunity to chat with and learn from the artists. But in Scope Productions it was also my job to be in constant contact with everyone contributing to every project. That being the case, my fount of learning about the company and its projects went from a trickle to a flood! It was a wonderful time to be at WED because the first generation of Imagineers was starting to merge with the second generation. There was a remarkable cross-pollination going on between the seasoned masters and the enthusiastic new writers, designers, and thinkers who had a rare world of opportunity at their feet.

Generation 2 learned the ropes at the best school in town. The Gen 2 designers were brilliant, and it was fun to watch them in action. In covering the design process and progress of the Imagination! pavilion, for example, I kept in constant contact with the young designers Steve Kirk, Tony Baxter, and Tom Morris, who were working together on the Journey into Imagination attraction. Tony was leading the overall design and development, Steve was the show designer, who also designed and sculpted the little purple dragon-like Figment character, and Tom was my age, just a kid, hand-drawing the show-set packages. We in Scope Productions relied upon their regular input to keep our scope current for the overall pavilion. All three became key creative powerhouses at Walt Disney Imagineering and each later led the design and development for a future park: Tony for Disneyland Paris, Steve for Tokyo DisneySea, and Tom for Hong Kong Disneyland.

Randy Bright, already a key creative leader in the pre-Epcot days, was second in creative command to Marty Sklar and was also writing and directing The American Adventure, including the lyrics to the song "Golden Dreams," which still gets me every time. Randy, and his producing partner, Rick Rothschild, a theatrical genius, were our scope go-to guys for that pavilion.

Now multiply those teams by the number of other pavilions and attractions for two new parks and that's a lot of Imagineers to meet! I didn't know any of them when I arrived at WED, but it didn't take long before I came to know most of them. It was an incredible time of wonder, awe, appreciation, inspiration, perspiration, and growth.

Once our department really got into the groove, Mark, Bob, and I could accurately tell you anything about everything that was going on, and who was working on what. Although not even built yet, we knew the layout and content of every element of Epcot, regardless of whether it was an entire pavilion or an area restroom, right down to the number of sinks and stalls. While the park was under construction, I supported the work on the home front, so I never had the opportunity to travel to the actual site, nor was I present at the grand opening. But years later, when I finally made it to Epcot, it felt so surreal to know a place so well that I had never actually visited in person.

The first time I stepped through the main gate it felt as though I had shrunk down to scale and was placed on the Epcot model I had studied every day as it was being built from beginning to end. You could have put a blindfold on me that first visit to Epcot and I could have taken you on a grand tour of the entire park, pointing everything out in great detail. All of the Audio-Animatronics actors I had watched coming together limb by limb and eyeball by eyeball at MAPO were performing for guests exactly as I had imagined they would. "Ben Franklin," I whispered the first time I experienced The American Adventure. "I knew you before you learned how to walk."

Today it's hard to believe how the Imagineering team could have pulled off such a fresh and epic-scaled park as Epcot without cell phones, laptops, computer-aided design software, e-mail, or teleconferencing. Throughout its design and development, our two most senior creative leaders, Marty Sklar and John Hench, did not have the luxury of staying connected to Imagineers using texts or e-mails. But I'm glad they didn't, because I believe direct contact between individual Imagineers and core project teams was far more impactful, valuable, and appreciated.

Marty and John were constantly on the move so they could check in with everyone and give direction, redirection, approval, a slap on the hand, a pat on the back, and, most importantly, their support and encouragement. You just never knew when Marty was going to pop over to see how you were doing and discuss what you were up to, business-wise and family-wise. He was passionate about his projects and his people, and as a result his people burned the midnight oil to deliver excellence—because they loved him, not because they feared him. For decades Marty was our advocate and champion, and the buck always stopped at his desk. He wrote everything by hand, red Pentel pen to paper.

All company communication was done via hand-carried interoffice mail, but the most effective and appreciated method of communication was the personal visits and handwritten notes and sketches from Marty and John. No one knew better than Marty how to light a fire under someone's butt that would result in their turning out more brilliant work than they had expected to put out themselves. Whenever someone went the extra mile, Marty would always send a personal note of appreciation with his famous red pen on note cards printed with his name. You'd see these red badges of courage proudly and prominently pinned to cubicle and office walls in every corner of the building; and when you'd spot one, you knew that person must have done something special. Folks would boast, "I got a Marty note today!" as if it were a winning million-dollar lottery ticket. Today I have hundreds of "Marty notes" that I consider to be among my greatest treasures. But it took many years of learning before earning my first one.

As I was a noncreative contributor during the design phases of Epcot and Tokyo Disneyland, Marty didn't get to know me that well. But I knew him. He was a force, *the* force at WED, and if he wasn't on the move in our hallowed hallways or on the road for research or at a project construction site, he was out wheeling and dealing and schmoozing with potential or existing corporate alliance partners like General Electric, General Motors, General Dynamics,

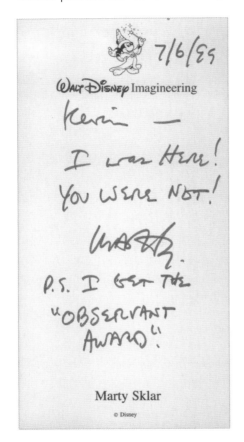

Oftentimes I'd return to my office and find a note from Marty on my chair. He was always so good about stopping by to check in on his "kids."

Marty was always good about sending a note to me after I pitched an idea to Michael Eisner and/or Bob Iger.

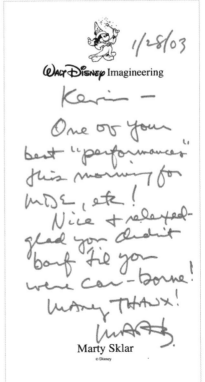

I wasn't there because I was somewhere else in the building actually working. Unlike some people.

MON 1/07/11

RA FARTY

YOU WERE
NOT HERE —
SO I did
not SAY hello.
uz.

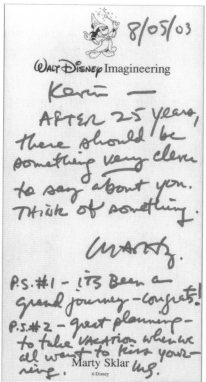

8/05/03

Walt Disney Imagineering

Kevin —
AFTER 25 years,
there should be
something very clever
to say about you.
THink of something.

Marty.

P.S. #1 – ITS Been a
grand journey – congrats!
P.S. #2 – great planning –
to take VACATION when we
all want to kiss your
ring.

Marty Sklar uz.
©Disney

Received on the occasion of my twenty-fifth anniversary with Imagineering. Oh, that Marty!

and in general, many other major American companies. Whenever *our* general was away from WED, his support people would ask me to deliver giant piles of interoffice mail and paperwork, sometimes heaping boxes full, to his house in Anaheim, just down the street from Disneyland.

I lived in California's Orange County as well, so I often dropped the stuff off at his house on my way home. I had great respect and admiration for Marty and I worried about what I would say to him if he ever appeared at his front door when I rang his doorbell. Would he even know me? I used to rehearse greetings and pleasantries should that ever occur. But it never did. I did, however, spot him sometimes in the morning barreling northbound on the Golden State freeway in his battleship gray, battleship-sized company car. That big-boat Buick would swerve, and I'd see his stacks of papers swaying back and forth on the back seat as he talked into a Dictaphone.

When I worked in special services, I'd catch a fleeting glimpse of the man on occasion, a star sighting if you will, but never spoke to him other than to offer a shy hello in passing. After all, I was the guy that emptied trash cans and set up chairs and easels in conference rooms for his meetings, not the guy that was *invited* to his meetings. My first actual one-on-one encounter with Marty, the first time he spoke to me directly, was when I was a new kid on the block. There I was, busy cleaning and setting up a conference room, when he unexpectedly stepped in. And he didn't look happy. Uh-oh. I swallowed hard, hoping he wasn't angry with me. But how could he be? I hadn't done anything wrong. And then he pointed at my shoes and said, "You see that original art you are standing on?" I looked down and, yipes! I was standing on the edge of a painting that was poking out from under the conference room table. He continued, getting more upset with each word, "That is a Bob McCall original we are using . . . for . . . Space . . . ship . . . EARTH!" I jumped off and he stepped out. How could Marty ever let me be an artist now that he thought I had no appreciation or respect for art? I was certain he was on his way over to tell Sheriff Don to boot me out the door. Les Skalota got paged and I didn't sing.

Thank God Marty didn't fire me. Working in Scope Productions was the best learning and growing experience any young and inexperienced Imagineer could have had. Plus, it was great fun to be traveling along with everyone on the rocky road to reality for Epcot and Tokyo Disneyland. Our little department grew quickly, not in the number of staff but in the volume and output of work, and before long our little trailer was bustin' at the seams. Happily, we moved across the street to the historic Grand Central Airport Terminal building where we set up shop on the entire second level. It was fun to learn that the air terminal was built the same year Mickey Mouse was born and that it boasted the first paved runway west of the Rockies, which served such notable aviators as Charles Lindbergh, Wiley Post, and Amelia Earhart.

The beautiful California Spanish colonial meets art deco–style terminal was also featured in several motion pictures. Now it was ours, and the view of the Verdugo Mountains from our spacious new digs was breathtaking. Mark and I joked about how great it was that two busboys ended up in the penthouse suite at the most unique, most secretive, most respected theme park design and development company in the world.

Life was busy but good for a couple of years. Then, before we knew it— and a zillion scopes later—Epcot and Tokyo Disneyland had been completed, opening six months apart. To celebrate, all the Imagineers gathered and jammed together in the Retlaw Enterprises parking lot behind Marty's office and we arranged ourselves to spell out WE DID IT for a photographer on top of a ladder.

But there were so many of us jammed together that we looked more like what's packed in a can of sardines rather than legible words.

WED Enterprises had grown from only a few hundred Imagineers in the late 1970s to almost three thousand in 1983. But now our work was done. The good news was that two brand-new and beautiful Disney parks had been introduced to the world. The bad news, however, was WED Enterprises had no choice but to embark on a massive staff reduction. I was able to hang on for a few months, but the downsizing finally caught up with me. Six years after I was hired in a trailer on a cold rainy day I was laid off in the same trailer on a cold rainy day. The worst part was not being laid off. The worst part was never getting the chance to prove to Marty, the other company leaders, and to myself that I had the creative chops to transfer out of project management into the creative division. It was even more painful, thanks to my scope experience, that I had gained great and useful knowledge about the company, its people, and processes, and that I had to let it all go.

In the final act of every good story, when all is lost and the goal seems impossible, the protagonist is faced with the decision to either toss his or her sword to the ground and run away in fear or raise it up defiantly to face the fire-breathing dragon. Sure, getting laid off was devastating, especially for a young newlywed with a car payment and a new mortgage. But ceasing to be an Imagineer made me a better Imagineer. And I didn't even have to raise a sword. It turns out the pen was mightier. It took me in the *write* direction.

IT'S NOT SURPRISING how many professionals in business and industry today admit their careers ended up being different from what they originally set out to do. This is especially true at Imagineering. Many Imagineers are enjoying careers they never imagined they would have, and some never imagined they'd be at Imagineering at all. Executive Vice President Kathy Mangum, for example, went to my alma mater, California State University, Fullerton, and majored in English. Kathy also started out at Disneyland, where she wore a snazzy tropical muumuu while working at an outdoor merchandise cart in Adventureland. She now leads the Atlantic Region and is responsible for all new development for Walt Disney World, and the Disney Cruise Line ships.

That's quite a leap for someone who stood at the exit of the Jungle Cruise and sold rubber snakes and shrunken heads. Although her role today is not what you'd expect a muumuu-wearing, shrunken-head-hawking English major to be doing, I will say that her spelling, punctuation, and writing are always spot-on. (I had to ask her how to spell *muumuu*).

I use Kathy as an example not only because of her phenomenal success story but because we've worked together on so many major Imagineering projects through the decades that we've become family. Her first park project as producer was also my first attraction-based project as a newly minted show writer (more on that later). "Now, wait just a minute," you say. "How did you go from getting tossed out in the cold after having your umbilical cord cut from WED to coming back to the warm embrace of the mother ship to become a show writer?" It wasn't easy. I think Mama pushed me out of the nest so I would either start flying or hit the ground trying.

Sometimes when you reach the age that you begin to worry about your future, you so concern yourself with trying to figure out what you are going to do for a living it suppresses that skill, talent, or passion hiding deep inside of you that can tell you not what you could be doing but what you should be doing. Kathy certainly could have been an accomplished English professor or a successful anything else related to English for that matter. But I'm glad she ended up doing what she's doing because she is a powerhouse producer with a brilliant talent for leading brilliant talent. She was meant to be an Imagineer—more specifically, an Imagineering leader.

Today English is to Kathy as art is to me (in the sense that we both still apply what we learned in college—though you could never guess what our majors were based on our job titles or professional passions). As an art major, I intended to make a living in the visual arts. I thought you had to be able to put pencil to paper and draw to be an animator. From the practical visual perspective of animation that is true. But from the emotional perspective, which is the very heart of animation, it is not.

It's better to draw crude stick figures that help communicate a compelling and logical story than draw amazing art that does not. (I intercepted Marty Sklar in the hallway one morning and pulled him into my office to pitch the story sequence for Finding Nemo Submarine Voyage with "fish stick" figures I crudely drew on three-by-five-inch index cards.) Animation was my career goal because I wanted to touch people, to make them laugh, to make them cry, to make them feel. This does include drawings, of course, both character and background. But the emotional part of animation comes more from the heart than the art, and the heart of that art is story.

What I didn't know then is that I should have been aspiring to be an animation story guy, not an animation artist guy. It wasn't until after my layoff from WED that my natural knack and love for storytelling awakened, perhaps at the proper time, to tell me what I should be doing. Yep, I was always the distracted kid that drew on the walls of the house and in the margins of textbooks. But looking back on those years, it dawned on me that those were not simply drawings of things. Everything I drew served to tell a quick little story. The dancing lady on the Grecian urn in my high school Latin book turned flip-book ended her brief act by whipping around to reveal this advertisement on the back of her toga: EAT AT ZORBA'S.

In college my animation professor, Carm Goode, told me he really liked my story ideas, but I needed to work on developing my drawing skills. He recommended I take all of the life-drawing classes I could even if it meant sitting in on extra classes I wasn't enrolled in. I dismissed what he said about my story ideas because all I heard was my art was not good enough.

When you're aspiring to be a visual artist, that kind of comment, especially from a onetime Disney animator, raises a big ol' red-flapping warning flag that commands immediate attention. In a panic, I reacted by zeroing in on that which wasn't working rather than regrouping and refocusing on that which was. I went to so many life-drawing classes that I'll bet I saw more naked people than earth would have ended up with had Adam and Eve just left that apple and those fig leaves on the tree (though the muumuu then would probably never have been invented). My life became all about working hard to support the art when the reality is, in animation and at Imagineering, it's the art that supports the story.

The following sequence of events led to the "I could-a had a V8" realization that my real art, though untrained and untried, was writing. After the layoff, with some graphic art and layout experience at Disney on my résumé (it always helps to have Disney on your résumé), I hit the streets with my now expanded visual art portfolio and landed a job at a correspondence school headquartered in sunny Newport Beach, California. Similar to the work I did in Scope Productions, my job was to design layouts for printed materials, in this case lessons written by a staff of instructors.

The good news was I didn't have to commute to Glendale, California. But the bad news was it wasn't Disney. It felt different and because of that my attitude was indifferent. My heart just wasn't in it while I was preparing all of the master material to hit the presses in the in-house printshop, including proofing all of the work. Sure, there was value to the work, as it was contributing to the education of learn-at-home students, but I used to contribute to the enjoyment of Disney park guests, which to me was more of an honor and privilege and a heck of a lot more fun. Things started looking up, however, when in addition to the print design and production I was given the opportunity to work under an art director to create nifty new advertising brochures and magazine ads for the school.

The small company had a small budget, so instead of hiring models for their ads and brochures they dressed me up, along with some of the women from the office, to portray happy correspondence school graduates that, thanks to the training received, now had exciting, high-paying jobs as business professionals and electricians. (I still have a pile of *Popular Mechanics* magazines from that time in which I'm dressed as a plaid-shirted, hard-hatted, conduit-carrying, widely smiling and big-moneymaking electrician. Shocking, I know.) In addition to modeling for the photos and designing the layouts, I also started writing some of the copy for the correspondence school ads that included such attention-grabbing all-cap gems as LEARN AT HOME AND EARN BIG MONEY!

I became obsessed with the ad biz, which shed a lot of light on my lifelong love for TV commercials and clever print and media product slogans; and I wanted to learn everything about the industry. When I started diving into all of the advertising trade magazines, I found in one of them a help wanted ad for a junior-level layout artist at a small agency in Orange County. The agency handled local accounts, including food markets, mom-and-pop restaurants, and a time-share resort company. Landing the job, I was able to parlay my graphic design and advertising experience, as minimal and unseasoned as it was, into designing resort brochures and creating and mechanically preparing print ads for magazines and newspapers, including final proofing and editing.

As I was designing and laying out ads, I began to get frustrated because I thought the copywriting and ideas for the ads themselves were, well, kinda lame. I'd wince when listening to local radio ads from our little agency because the ultrashort dialogue between characters was not clever or compelling and the jingles were a jumble. I often said to myself, *Boy, if they just said* this *instead of* that, or *Man, why did they rhyme* that *with* that? This was coming from a kid who grew up in the late 1950s and through the 1960s, when brilliant advertising became an influential force in our culture and people would use slogans in their everyday speech like "I can't believe I ate the whole thing" and "Nothin' says lovin' like something from the oven." The lack of quality and cleverness being delivered by the little ad agency I was working for made me ask the following question: "Where's the beef?"

One day I couldn't stand it anymore and cornered the creative director, asking if I could take a stab at copywriting for print and radio. Naturally he asked, "Do you have any writing experience?" Considering I had a little but not enough, I honestly responded, "Yes and . . . no." He continued, "Maybe you should just stick to layout." To pry open that slammed door and better advertise myself, I continued by listing my favorite TV commercials and what I loved about them.

And then to try to seal the deal, I sang a medley of my favorite catchy jingles, bringing it all home with "New Ajax laundry detergent is stronger than dirt," because its hard-hitting *BA BA BA BUM* downbeat ending served as the perfect finale. As I stood there in my ta-da pose—and he stood there in his "go away, kid, you bother me" crossed-arms shaking-head pose—I knew I had to keep selling myself to get him to budge.

"As you know, good ads can touch your heart or funny bone, or both," I continued. "A Hallmark card commercial can make you laugh and cry in thirty seconds." Maybe it was just to shut me up, but he caved and said, "Okay, okay, you can give it a try." To that I happily sang, "Plop-plop, fizz-fizz, oh, what a relief it is!" He told me not to push my luck.

Copywriting for advertising was great fun, and I really had a knack for making each and every word count, as driven by the brevity of the ads that had to appear in a little box of space in a newspaper or magazine or were heard in a ten-second radio spot. Advertising, after all, is really the shortest form of entertaining storytelling there is. Before long I worked my way up to writing and directing local daytime TV spots that were shot at the KDOC Channel 56 studio a few blocks away from Disneyland. This experience was most useful in my outside-of-Disney development because attraction stories are also short stories that need to be written and directed. Some attraction stories are so short that they last a whopping ninety seconds!

Copywriting forced me to distill the story and/or message down to its purest essence. The other growth experience that came out of working in the ad biz was learning to pitch an idea for a single ad or an entire campaign. You can imagine how this was useful in my continued career as an Imagineer in boosting confidence when it came to quickly and clearly communicating ideas for shows and attractions to busy executives. As far as I'm concerned, every good pitch should begin with a solid attention-grabbing, hit-'em-over-the head and slap-'em-into-submission statement—aka the one-liner. Here's the starting line I used that took an attraction idea all the way to the finish line: "YOU GET TO HOP IN A CAR AND RACE ACROSS ORNAMENT VALLEY LIKE LIGHTNING McQUEEN." I mean, c'mon, who wouldn't want to do that?

Today, when young writers and designers ask for my advice about pitching, I always tell them the trick is to reduce the enormity of their big idea into one little descriptive but powerfully compelling intro line that will grab, even shock their audience and make them want to know more. If you start a pitch way down in the weeds by saying something like, "This idea uses a twenty-wheel coaster bogey system on a track hidden under a surface that looks like a road," it'll get choked out before it has a chance to grow. Start by telling them what the heck it is and what you get to do, then unleash more information once you have 'em hooked on the line like a fish. For example, you pass by a newspaper stand and the headline reads UFO LANDS ON CITY HALL. "What?" you gasp in shock. "I have to know more!" So, you read the secondary line: "At 8:30 Monday morning an unidentified flying object landed on top of city hall and seven purple, two-headed beings jumped out and danced the cha-cha."

You double-gasp, "What? What?! Then what?" Now the only way to satisfy your curiosity is to buy the paper to get the whole story. That is the art of the pitch, of which I would argue the root is in advertising. Grab 'em and hook 'em, and then you can sell 'em. And once you've got 'em, go ahead and do the cha-cha!

As I continued to study and learn everything I could about the ad biz, another help wanted ad in an industry magazine caught my eye. Southern California Edison was looking for a proofreader/copy editor. Although it wasn't directly related to the advertising industry, the ad was attractive for two reasons: it was a night shift position, which meant I could try to take on two jobs for a while, and it came with health insurance and other big-company benefits the small ad agency could not offer. This was an important consideration because Patty and I were expecting our first son, Kevin Jr. Edison hired me for their corporate communications department where, for a change, it was all about words, words, nothing but words.

One evening as I was arriving at work I was surprised to see an ex-Imagineer,

George Anderson, heading to his car in the employee parking lot. I had no idea George worked at Edison and I ducked behind a van to hide because I had a score to settle with him. During the Epcot project, George was a planner/scheduler and had an office next door to us in Scope Productions. He carpooled with my compadres Mark and Bob, and for months, every time their car would stop in traffic, George would whip out a spray paint can, open the car door, and mark the freeway with a spot of Day-Glo orange. Why? I can only speculate that because they commuted all the way from Rancho Cucamonga (yes, that's a real place in California—and they really did commute all the way from there), their long drive drove George over the gorge. It was really something traveling on that freeway during non-traffic hours and seeing miles and miles of George's Day-Glo dots.

Now, though, I'd be able to get my sweet revenge for something he had done to me in our days of practical joking back at WED. George never knew I knew he did this, but he had sent me a letter typed on official Walt Disney Productions stationery signed by a name he'd completely made up: Vic Shapiro, Vice President of Corporate Considerations. The opening line read something like "I have been considering your performance and as a result you are being strongly considered with serious consideration, but only if you improve your . . ."

A long list of unrealistic improvement stipulations followed, which threw me for a loop because I worked my tail off to be a model Disney employee. But it looked like the real deal because it was on real corporate letterhead and was signed with a real signature in real ink. The letter never did say what I was being considered for, but its tone freaked me out. It was as if Big Brother were watching my every move. After a few weeks of losing sleep over it, I found out crazy George was the sender because I overheard him bragging to someone about it and how dumb I was to believe it. We both got laid off before I could one-up him. But here was my chance!

Working at Edison's corporate communications office, I had total access to official company letterhead. When George received his official typed letter I'm sure he was taken aback, especially since it was signed in real ink by a major company honcho: NICK SHAPIRO, VICE PRESIDENT OF EMPLOYEE HISTORIES. It seems Mr. Shapiro had received troublesome information about a certain orange spray paint incident and for this reason would be keeping a watchful eye on George for the duration of his employment, which would be reinstated subsequent to his full payment for damages caused to the California Highway Department in the amount of $134,025.03.

I wasn't at Edison long before I received an unexpected message on our home answering machine from Steve Sock, manager of the estimating department at WED. When I returned Steve's call he surprised me with the news that Mark Rhodes was transferring out of project management into show writing in the creative division. Mark, God bless him, recommended I take his place as head scope writer, so Steve called to ask if I'd consider coming in to interview for the position. I remember at that exact moment thinking had I not been laid off and remained on staff at WED doing graphics, such that they were, in the estimating department, I would not have been qualified to be considered for a writing position. But now that I had had several months of practical writing experience under my belt, I thanked Steve for considering me and told him I would be happy to come in for the interview.

That's how I returned to the wonderful world of WED. But this time as a more experienced, more valuable, and more-appreciative-of-being-an-Imagineer Imagineer. Without that outside writing experience and Mark's inside recommendation, I may not have ever returned to WED, which means I would have missed out on that rare opportunity to come up with ideas for shows and attractions for Disney parks all over the world. Had I declined Steve's invitation because I was mad at Disney for laying me off—or had I opted to stay to find my way in the ad biz—there would be no Twilight Zone Tower of Terror, it's tough to be a bug!, Toy Story Midway Mania!, Radiator Springs Racers, Luigi's Rollickin' Roadsters, or others.

But that almost didn't happen anyway. When I returned to WED in 1984, it was in trouble.

During my absence, the once gushing fire hose flow of approved project work had slowed to a trickle. That was bad news for Scope Productions. The good news was it gave Mark Rhodes time to moonlight from writing scopes to writing shows, even if they were in the form of blue-sky speculative ideas. He was more than happy to lend his time and talent to new concepts being tossed around in the interim. Post Epcot and Tokyo Disneyland, there were a few new ideas being kicked around, including an interactive attraction called The Black Hole Shootout, inspired by the movie *The Black Hole*. (Imagineering industrial and vehicle designer George McGinnis also designed the robots for that movie.) There were a few other ideas in production at that time, including The Country Bear Vacation Hoedown, *Captain EO*, Star Tours, and Splash Mountain (which started out being called simply Splash, per Michael Eisner's request to name it after the Tom Hanks and Daryl Hannah movie of the same name. But there's more to that story: it almost became our first mermaid-themed attraction long before Ariel made a splash! Good thing we had the entire cast from America Sings waiting in the wings).

Another of the blue-sky ideas starting to grow legs was a new attraction for the Norway pavilion at Epcot called Maelstrom. Mark Rhodes was cast as the show writer for Maelstrom, working alongside an energetic young art director named Joe Rohde. This was Mark's golden ticket out of estimating and my golden ticket back into the chocolate factory, though still not in the creative division. But I figured Mark had been able to make the chocolatey-smooth move into creative, so maybe there was hope for me someday.

I was delighted to have this opportunity to come back to WED, especially since I was in charge of an entire department, comprised of, well, me. The great news that made my return even sweeter was the company bridged the time I was away, which meant I was able to reinstate my original hire date. The not so great news about my return was that it happened at a not so great time. WED was in a state of flux both project-wise and direction-wise, and although a few of the concepts being explored were picking up steam, the company was in limbo, especially from a corporate perspective. Marty Sklar, WED's biggest advocate, champion, and savior, really was proactively scrambling behind the scenes, dreaming, scheming, and charting the course for its future.

Meanwhile, WED was under serious scrutiny as certain new corporate board members, with a bent for big business, questioned the fact that it spent money but did not make money. Imagineers knew our work helped spin the turnstiles at the parks, but the corporate books did not reflect that because it was something that could not be quantified. We did not manufacture and sell widgets to the masses; so, to a WED outsider we appeared to be a financial burden. Feature Animation was in a slump at that time too, but the rumor on the street was that WED was going to be shut down. But thanks to Marty Sklar and Roy E. Disney, it didn't happen. They wouldn't let it happen. Marty did not return calls or accept meetings from corporate to buy us more time while Roy was working on bringing in the dynamic duo of Michael Eisner and Frank Wells, who came as close as anyone could in replicating the hit- and history-making chemistry of Walt and Roy O.

Already giants in the movie industry, Michael was the creative half and Frank was the business half—and they could have not come to Disney at a better time. When Michael became our CEO, Marty immediately latched onto him to show him the tremendous value of WED Enterprises as a capable creative contributor to the future of the company and to the future in general. Michael, who had a fascination for how things work and how things are made, was quick to appreciate and recognize the potential for WED to contribute to all things entertainment and industry. He could not come over often enough to "the toy box at WED" and admitted it was his favorite place to hang out in

On the set with the boss , Michael Eisner. I loved pitching new ideas to this man!

the entire company. Michael honestly believed we could do anything (as do all Imagineers) and he launched us out of limbo into the limelight.

One of Michael's first requests of WED was to look at ways to design and improve many things people use in their everyday lives, including the automobile. (Alas, the Disney car was short-lived.) In 1985, Michael and Frank officially changed the name of WED Enterprises to Walt Disney Imagineering and, *whoaaaa*—hold on to your hats and muumuus—from that moment on it was one heck of a wild ride! With a new name, a new spirit, and a new corporate boss who ignited and challenged us to change the world, Walt Disney Imagineering soared with great purpose and passion into the future.

I feel so blessed and am so thankful to have been a creative contributor at Imagineering during that remarkable, almost unbelievable period of tremendous theme park, resort, nighttime entertainment, and cruise ship growth. For ten years, until his tragic death in 1994, Frank Wells continuously placed big bets on us as Michael relied solely on his gut to green-light one risky project after another. And guess what? That's how you grow a company. During Michael's twenty-one-year tenure, Imagineering launched one bold and gutsy moon shot after another.

And that's when I got my chance to step up to the launchpad.

THE FIRST THING I did upon my return to WED was march upstairs to get a whiff of that wonderful fragrance of oil paint wafting from the artist's offices as a welcome home. It was like comfort food for the nose. The second thing I did was learn the new Wang word processing system (the next step up from an electric typewriter before there was such a thing as a desktop computer) upon which I would be writing and printing the project scopes.

Waiting for me in my new office, located on the ground level in the main building, was a new word processor and a request for three new project scopes: one was for Maelstrom; another for a "freak storm–themed water park" being considered for Walt Disney World that was so early in development it didn't even have a name; and a third for a dark-ride concept inspired by the Disney movie *The Black Cauldron* (an idea that soon went to pot).

On my first Monday back at the company, I was already behind in my work because one of the scopes was due on that upcoming Friday. To catch up, I worked long hours Monday through Thursday researching and writing, and then late into the night on Thursday-into-Friday to keep that little printer wheel on the Wang whizzing as sheets of paper emerged out the other side like a spooling roll of paper towels having convulsions. Each page had to then be torn from the long and serrated printout.

As luck would have it, I had just enough paper left to print the scope, which I had finally completed by 2:30 a.m. Good thing, too, because it was due in six hours. I laid the long printout, not yet torn into individual pages, across my office floor until it stretched out the door like a thin carpet runner and dropped to my knees to start tearing and sorting. That's when I heard a strange jingling sound approaching my office. When I looked through my door, what should appear but the furry face of a perky puppy! Feature Animation was making *Oliver & Company* across the street and in my dead-tired delirium I thought one of their model mutts had escaped. But on the other end of the jingling leash appeared Chuck the chipper security guard. "Chopper's making the rounds with me," Chuck reassured me.

I was down on the floor because I was about to tear the printout into pages, but Chopper interpreted that as a friendly human getting down to his level to play. He reacted to that assumed invitation with great gusto and ran towards me directly over the entire length of my printout, all the while doing what excited puppies do on paper. There wasn't a dry sheet in the house. Chopper turned my entire night's work into a doggie Slip 'N Slide. While the puppy did his darnedest to clear my puddled pages with his high-speed, windshield-wiper tail, Chuck apologized and offered to help clean it up. But I sent them both on their merry way with a plan to let the pages dry and send them through the copy machine for a clean fresh copy. Good thing we didn't have color copiers then.

Later that morning, when I reviewed the water park concept scope with show designer Richard Vaughn, I found out to my great surprise he had a link to my past. Richard, whom I worked with on the concept development of many fun projects over the years, was the son of bandleader Billy Vaughn, of whom my dad was a huge fan. While growing up I heard Billy Vaughn's records a lot because Dad had them spinning on his phonograph every weekend throughout my wonder years. Dad's favorite song of Billy's was "Sail on Silvery Moon," which was the tune Richard's doorbell played when he was growing up (I'll bet I still heard that tune more often than he did). One weekend when Billy Vaughn and His Orchestra were playing at Carnation Gardens at Disneyland, Richard invited me to go see them as his special guest. Hearing the music I grew up with being performed live sitting next to my colleague (who grew up with the actual guy who was performing the actual music) really added to the uniqueness of my already unique past-life-connects-with-my-Imagineering-life life!

Richard and I worked together on some of the experiences and visual gags for Typhoon Lagoon and Blizzard Beach, which makes me think of Randy Bright, the man, the mentor, who helped me take the creative division by storm.

Randy was the vice president of creative and the head of show writing at that time. He and I attended many of the same meetings while I was gathering information for the project scope documents. Randy liked the way I had written the descriptions of the projects in the scopes and noticed the way I squirmed restlessly in concept meetings because, as a scope gatherer/hunter (and not a creative contributor), it wasn't my place to toss out ideas or add anything to the lively and most exciting early-concept discussions being enjoyed by "the creatives."

Although I had enough pent-up energy and gumption to change the world, I'd sit there silently biting my tongue, just like the days in advertising when I had to lay out stuff I wanted to change but couldn't. Randy would oftentimes read my body language, wink at me, and interrupt a brainstorm to ask for my thoughts about the subject, at which time everyone would cross their arms and stare at me. It was fantastic! Upon these most-welcome valve-releasing invitations I'd unleash a steady stream of ideas and opinions related to the topic, or toss out a different topic altogether (does it have to be a light bulb?) and sometimes they would stick! Then I'd read the room and shut up so as not to push my luck.

But to keep that creative torch lit, I started sending follow-up memos to Randy with more thoughts and ideas about the many goings-on going on—and

I became Marty's left-hand man!

as a result he started calling me into his office to join him in bouncing stuff around. "So, Kev," he'd say, "I've been playing with this idea about some kind of a live show starring Mickey Mouse where he's staged high up on Sleeping Beauty Castle fighting the forces of evil. What if we had some sort of an inflatable thing that would make Maleficent rise up out of the castle moat, where she turns into the giant dragon and blows real fire around?" Sometimes Randy's crazy concepts became the real deal, and in this case, his "playing with an idea" ultimately became *Fantasmic!*

Randy, who also started his Disney career at Disneyland, on the Rivers of America as a sailor aboard the sailing ship *Columbia*, was a real showman. He had a lot of ideas a lot of the time and I loved those occasions when he'd call me in to help answer the question "What if . . . ?" Sometimes he had specific requests for me such as naming a restaurant or shop in one of the parks; and other times he would ask me to help him "knock around" the story for something.

The first big story I ever helped Randy knock around in great detail was for the freak-storm-water-park concept, which started as a request from Walt Disney World for a separately gated water park because River Country at Fort Wilderness campground was extremely popular and not big enough to accommodate our guest demand. Where do you start when you start to ideate something new? You start with a story. "What if a typhoon swept in and turned a resort town upside-down?" pondered Randy. "Everything is topsy-turvy after the storm leaves and it's all fun and funny. You know, what if the storm had a sense of humor? What are those things, those quick-read, visual-gag things the storm left behind?"

Kathy Mangum had transferred from the Disney Studio to Imagineering to become Randy's associate producer by that time and she ended up being the real deal producer for Typhoon Lagoon. I was not in the creative division yet, but I got to work with Randy, Kathy, show designers Chris Runco and Richard Vaughn, and a few others who were developing the concepts for the water park. And boy, oh boy, was that fun! (Marty was right when he said, "You can't make fun unless you're having fun yourself!") I even got to name everything in Typhoon Lagoon and became its official show writer, even though I wasn't officially a show writer because there were strings attached.

In grand Disney tradition, if you sit in enough meetings with Disney artists, you're bound to see yourself as they see you. This caricature is by Chris Runco.

I was still assigned full-time to produce project scopes under the project-management banner. Essentially, I was moonlighting for Disney creative. Working on many special projects for Randy and a few others on my own time as a show writer wannabe, I'd burn the midnight oil after work and on the weekends, paying my dues and coming up with a lot of stuff that was up to snuff, because it started to find its way into actual park projects. I was starting to contribute creatively, legitimately. I was starting to find my way.

After more than a year and a half of working on many show-writing and story-development efforts with and for Randy Bright to prove to him (and especially to myself) I could really do this, I got the nerve to point-blank ask him, in the same apprehensive, say-a-lot-very-quickly-without-taking-a-breath style Ralphie used when asking his old man for a Red Ryder BB gun in the movie

A Christmas Story, if he thought I was good enough to, dare I suggest, transfer out of project management into the creative division as an official show writer. (I actually got to work with Jean Shepherd, one of my favorite storytellers, who wrote and narrated that movie, on the refresh of the Carousel of Progress at the Magic Kingdom in 1993.)

"I do and you are," he responded with his warm and contagious smile. He then added, "As a matter of fact, I've been thinking a lot about that myself. Let's make it happen." At that very moment, I felt what Ralphie felt when he was surprised with a Red Ryder BB gun after being told by everyone, including

TRANSFER APPLICATION

NAME: Kevin P.   DATE: July 15, 1987

DEPARTMENT: Estimating/Scope Writing   JOB TITLE: Senior Scope Writer

PHONE NUMBER: _____ / _____
                        Home   Work Extension

Position applied for: Show Design Writer

*Please use reverse side for any applicable experience or training.

DEPT. HEAD EVALUATION OF TRANSFER APPLICANT

	5	4	3	2	1
Shows interest in work	✓				
Follows directions	✓				
Initiative	✓				
Working relationship with peers	✓				
Working relationship with Management	✓				
Dependability	✓				
Attendance	✓				
Leadership ability	✓				
	Excellent				Unsatisfactory

Is this transfer applicant recommended for a transfer at this time? YES ✓ NO _____

Is the department able to release the applicant at this time? YES _____ NO ✓

If "NO" date able to release Sept 15ᵀᴴ

Why should/shouldn't this employee receive a transfer. If employee should not be transferred, how can he/she improve to become eligible for a transfer?

_____   _____
Dept. Head Signature   Employee

Hallelujah! My ticket to creative!

his old man, he could never have one. After thanking Randy, I left his office in a shock-induced dizzy haze of "this really can't be happening" and leaned against the wall in the hall to take a deep breath and let it all sink in.

My impossible dream to be in the creative division was coming true. Like Pinocchio, having proven myself to be brave, truthful, and unselfish, Randy pulled a few strings and I became a real show writer.

This was a big deal. Despite the odds and obstacles, I finally made it into creative, the very division in which I was told I'd never be.

FROM WASHING DISHES TO SPINNING PLATES

WHILE BRAINSTORMING ideas for the 1988 "Blast to the Past" event at Disneyland, Randy Bright and Kathy Mangum challenged me—now an official show writer about to work on my first official attraction (albeit an overlay to an existing attraction)—to team up with Mark Rhodes to create and write a special show for the Submarine Voyage that would play only through the duration of the summerlong 1950s-themed event.

We came up with the crazy idea that a 1950s-radio disk jockey, named "The Ghost of Nemo" (as in "Captain," not "Finding"), would mysteriously take over the sub. During the voyage both he and the sub captain would communicate with the first mate, named Mr. Rhonda, in the form of edited snippets from popular fifties and early sixties songs. Here are a few excerpts from the show, which only one summer's worth of guests got to hear (probably a good thing).

After the sub is taken over by the ghostly DJ who says he's going to take us on an "Undersea Blast to the Past," the first mate discovers the captain is missing:

MR. RHONDA
Captain! Captain! Where are you?

CAPTAIN (sung by the Drifters)
Up on the roof.

MR. RHONDA
Oh, no! What should I do?

CAPTAIN (sung by the Beach Boys)
Help me, Rhonda, help, help me, Rhonda.

While passing mermaids, the DJ impresses the first mate with his knowledge:

MR. RHONDA
How do you know so much about mermaids?

GHOST OF NEMO (sung by the Beach Boys)
I get around.

At the volcano:

MR. RHONDA
Oh, no! A volcano!

GHOST OF NEMO (sung by Jerry Lee Lewis)
Goodness gracious, great balls of fire.

After passing the sea serpent:

MR. RHONDA
What was that?

GHOST OF NEMO (sung by Sheb Wooley)
It was a one-eyed, one-horned flying purple people eater.

MR. RHONDA
That thing sure had a weird face. What did it look like to you?

GHOST OF NEMO (sung by Ernie K-Doe)
Mother-in-law, mother-in-law.

Okay, I won't put you through any more of that. But dig this, daddy-o—the exit song was the same song you hear in the subs today, which is Bobby Darin's "Beyond the Sea." At the end of the summer, Kathy came into my office and slapped a guest letter on my desk. "Congratulations, you knucklehead," she exclaimed. "This guest claims your Blast to the Past Submarine Voyage is the work of the devil." Yikes! Well, I sure didn't love that, but I did love the fact that twenty years later, Kathy and I would team up once again at the same sub lagoon, this time with Tony Baxter and my best pals from Pixar, to create the Finding Nemo Submarine Voyage.

Since the moment I became a show writer to this moment there has never been a dull moment. In all these years, I have never experienced any slack time, and there was never a time when I worked on only one project at a time. Over the years I've been blessed with keeping a variety of project plates spinning, each in various phases of development, at all times, and I've been double-blessed to have had the energy and drive to keep them all going.

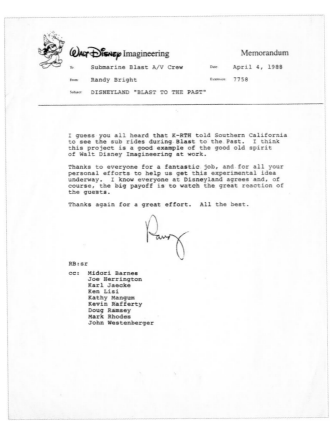

Walt Disney Imagineering   Memorandum

To: Submarine Blast A/V Crew   Date: April 4, 1988

From: Randy Bright   Extension: 7758

Subject: DISNEYLAND "BLAST TO THE PAST"

I guess you all heard that K-RTH told Southern California
to see the sub rides during Blast to the Past. I think
this project is a good example of the good old spirit
of Walt Disney Imagineering at work.

Thanks to everyone for a fantastic job, and for all your
personal efforts to help us get this experimental idea
underway. I know everyone at Disneyland agrees and, of
course, the big payoff is to watch the great reaction of
the guests.

Thanks again for a great effort. All the best.

RB:sr

cc: Midori Barnes
     Joe Herrington
     Karl Jaecke
     Ken Lisi
     Kathy Mangum
     Kevin Rafferty
     Doug Ramsey
     Mark Rhodes
     John Westenberger

I love Randy's line "The big payoff is to watch the reaction of the guests," because one of them thought the Blast to the Past Submarine Voyage was the work of the devil!

Executive vice president Tom Fitzgerald used to pass tons of work my way because, as he often said, "If you want something done, give it to a busy Kev."

There was a crazy busy period, for example, when I was working on two full-time jobs at once—Toy Story Midway Mania! and the entirety of Cars Land. Fortunately, the Mania! focus was winding down as Cars was gearing up, not to mention we were delivering two Manias in two different parks on two different sides of the country at the same time. And they weren't exactly the same. Even though some may think we create exact replicas, also referred to as "cookie-cutter" attractions, the reality is none of them is the same as the other. Even the first two simultaneous Midway Manias were different in that one was designed to fit thematically at the Boardwalk in Disney California Adventure and the other was designed to fit thematically in Pixar Place at Disney's Hollywood Studios.

The charming exterior façade and exterior queue for the California version were themed as an attraction you might discover on a turn-of-the-century boardwalk, while the interior queue for the Florida version was designed as *Toy Story* Andy's bedroom in which you were the same scale as his toys. Its exterior façade was designed as if it were part of Pixar Animation Studios. The Twilight Zone Tower of Terror is another example of each subsequent rendering not being the same as the last. Although today there are four versions of the attraction simultaneously entertaining guests in locations around the world (and one has even been thematically changed to host a new *Guardians of the Galaxy*-themed story), the first one completed in 1994 for Disney's Hollywood Studios in Florida is the only one in which the elevator car suddenly and mysteriously "breaks out" of the shaft and travels horizontally into the Twilight Zone.

When the second version opened in Disney California Adventure in 2004, it was delivered without that exclusive-to-Florida feature. And when the third was built in Tokyo DisneySea in 2006, the physical ride experience was the same as in California, though the story was altogether different because the *Twilight Zone*, an iconic TV franchise in the United States, was not relevant to the Japanese audience. That explains the creation of the story of Harrison Hightower, a member of the Society of Explorers and Adventurers and a collector of rare antiquities. The fourth version, known as La Tour de la Terreur—Un Saut dans la Quatriéme Dimension, which opened at the Walt Disney Studios Park in Paris in 2007, is closest in overall experience to the California version. But it is still not a cookie-cutter replica, as the building height, some of the interior spaces, and the language is different.

The Many Adventures of Winnie the Pooh in the Magic Kingdom at Walt Disney World was the first of many projects I helped create with my longtime creative partner in crime, Rob't Coltrin. (His real name is Robert but he uses the apostrophe because he is an impatient fellow. Just think of all of the time he has saved over the years by not having to add that unnecessary *e* and *r*.) Although the two attractions share the same name, our Magic Kingdom version of Pooh was not the same as the one at Disneyland, because a different team of Imagineers had a different vision for their version. (For the record, I did not work on the Disneyland attraction, although the Anaheim team borrowed from the music soundtrack we created for the Magic Kingdom.)

Having the once-in-a-lifetime, unforgettable, and remarkable opportunity to work with Rob't—one of the most passionate and brilliant theme park designers and storytellers I've ever had the honor to share the same rarified air of endless blue-sky possibilities with—was one of the greatest joys of my career. Working at Imagineering means working with geniuses every day. I don't mean that to sound commonplace, especially since Imagineering is not a common place. But Rob't is a design genius times a gazillion, the guru on the summit of the art and purpose of Imagineering. He is as good with story as he is with show—and attraction design and ride layout—and he understands all of the complicated and sophisticated "Swiss watch" mechanisms, math, and real-world physics and dynamics that must orchestrate seamlessly together to deliver excellence in a ride-through attraction.

It's one thing to come up with an idea for an attraction but still another to completely figure out every part of it and then prove it's going to work all day, every day, for years to come. Rob't and I call that hardest part of our art "Day Two," the time when you roll up your sleeves and battle it out with both sides of your brain.

Allow me to give you an example of a "Day One" idea that didn't have enough meat on the bones to make it to Day Two. Not too long ago a young illustrator (not a designer; there's a difference) came into my office to pitch an idea for an attraction. "Are you ready?" he asked excitedly. "Give it to me!" I said with great anticipation. "It's an avalanche!" he proudly proclaimed with a *Well, sir, how do you like that?* smile. "Okay, what happens?" I asked, anticipating the story beats. He looked bewildered. "What do you mean what happens? Don't you get it? It's an avalanche! Don't you know what avalanches do?" I responded, "Yes, of course, but what do the *guests* get to do? Tell me about their experience." His face got all scrunchy and then he blurted out, "Their experience is they experience an avalanche. An AVALANCHE!" "Okay!" I said. "Let's go to the entrance of your attraction. Take me through the scenes all the way through to the finale." He had nothing and was getting upset.

I felt bad for him as this idea was stuck in the snow with nowhere to go, so I started asking questions that might help him dig his way out, such as What is the story? Where is the place? Is there a preshow? What are the beats that lead to the avalanche? Are there any characters in the show? What is the avalanche made of? How does it drop and then reset for the next group? What is the ride system and what is the ride vehicle—some sort of snowmobile? How many guests does the vehicle carry? How many guests per hour can the attraction accommodate? Do you have a particular park location in mind for this? I had hoped that these tough but necessary questions would help him understand there wasn't enough *there* there for him to communicate and elaborate on the idea and to help him realize how hard it is to do what we do. It's really hard.

Puzzle-solver Rob't is a master at making an idea makeable. No one outside

When it comes to creating rides, Rob't and I have a pretty good "track" record together!

Imagineering really knows of him, because Imagineers don't get their names on the credits—there are no credits. Plus, Rob't's focus is purely on the up-front stuff, the ideation, and the figuring-it-all-out part. He rarely sticks around on a project once it moves into the actual production phase because he prefers designing things, not building them. When you see Imagineers in the limelight at attraction-opening media events, you won't see Rob't there in all the hoopla— even though he helped design or even led the design of the attraction that was just unveiled—because he is in Glendale, California, working on the next great thing. His mind, heart, and hand are in many of Imagineering's most beloved attractions. All together, I believe he has worked on more than seventy projects— and I was right there along with him on many of them (although once I help get them started I like to stay with them all the way through to opening day).

I will cover our project-prolific years together later on, but when I was getting my creative career cooking, Rob't was still a kid in school at Cal Poly, San Luis Obispo. He studied architecture, art, and design, and while still in school produced, directed, and choreographed student plays and musical revues on his own time and dime. After graduating he landed a job in Burbank as a TV art director and fine-tuned his natural showbiz chops by designing sets for the Bob Hope specials, *The Oprah Winfrey Show*, and award shows honoring recipients of the Golden Globes and the Grammys year after year.

I believe Rob't was born to be an Imagineer. His entire life, including being obsessed with the souvenir Disneyland map that hung on his bedroom wall for years (as I was with mine) in his hometown of San Jose, California, was indeed the very map that grabbed him and guided him to the road to Imagineering. He arrived in 1990 with a lot of creative ammunition in his camp, because by that time he was a seasoned show designer in the entertainment industry. He brought all of that experience along with him to our table, which was lucky for Imagineering and even luckier for me. Shortly after his arrival we teamed up, fused our brains together, and effected a lot of change. In fact, some colleagues have referred to the two of us as the "Clements and Musker of Imagineering." But no one outside of Imagineering would know that. (Ron Clements and John Musker, directors at Disney Feature Animation, teamed up to produce a long list of animated classics, starting with *The Little Mermaid*.)

For those of you out there that don't know Rob't, I wanted to introduce him to you at this point in the book because he is such an integral part of the rest of my story; and I will continue to mention him and some of the results of our fabulously fun Rob't & Kev collaboration as we go along. But before we go there, let's go back once again to the pre-Rob't period in 1987 when I started spinning all those project plates from the very moment I transferred into the show design department in the creative division and became a show writer. Those plates, by the way, have never stopped spinning to this day. That is a statement, not at all a complaint. When you're on the creative development side of things, also known around Imagineering as "Blue Sky," you're always busy because you're constantly dreaming up and working on many different new ideas long before they are presented and approved—*if* they are presented and approved.

Sometimes you don't even have to be proactively dreaming up new ideas, because they have a way of dropping in on you, when you least expect it, when it is time for them to happen. Like potential project paratroopers, they drop out of the blue sky. And just before coming in for a landing, they yank the chain of the light bulb that illuminates that *aha!* moment in your brain, causing you to smile and whisper to yourself, *Oooh, yeah.* Hanging on my office wall is a sign that speaks to the power of an idea. It reads: YOUR SPARK CAN BECOME A FLAME AND CHANGE EVERYTHING.

In the 1980s, after a bit of a post-park-opening dry period, a sudden out-of-the-blue (sky) Roman candle-like spray of sparks descended upon Imagineering, set all that dried brush aflame, and changed everything. Let me tell you, it's quite a challenge to keep flames under control when you're drinking out of the fire hose!

IT WAS THE BEST of times . . . and the worst of times: best because there was suddenly too much to do and the work kept coming. But worst because there was suddenly too much to do and the work kept coming. The Blast to the Past Submarine Voyage was just a drop of water in the ocean of new projects I found myself jumping into. There was no easing into my new role as a show writer; and now that I was one, I suddenly didn't feel talented enough, experienced enough, or worthy enough to finally start doing what I had dreamed of doing. I felt like a Little Leaguer in my very first game stepping up to the plate to swing against Hall of Fame pitcher Nolan Ryan—armed with a toothpick. It used to be "Holy smokes, when am I gonna be a show writer?" Now it was "Holy crap! I'm a show writer!" It even said so on my new business card. It was time to sink or swim.

I continued to storm in on Typhoon Lagoon as it went into its production phase. This entailed polishing and finalizing the backstories and park-wide nomenclature, show graphics, and signage. At the same time, the Disney-MGM Studios (now Disney's Hollywood Studios) was under construction and Bob Weis, overall park creative lead, and Tom Fitzgerald, creative executive for the new project, asked me to lend a hand with several of the shows already in development. One of them, the Monster Sound Show, had a postshow that featured some of the handmade sound effects instruments created by Jimmy Macdonald, longtime sound effects master at the Walt Disney Studios. Jimmy was also known as the voice of Mickey Mouse, personally chosen by the man who first gave Mickey his voice, Walt Disney, and he performed that iconic falsetto for thirty-eight years. Joe Herrington, Imagineering's own longtime sound effects master, worked with Jimmy, Mark Rhodes, and me on the hands-on, voice-on, and ears-on postshow experiences. In addition to the audio effects exhibits and experiences, guests could create their own sound effects and dub in the voice of an animated character in an exhibit called Movie Mimics.

Shortly after Disney-MGM Studios celebrated its grand opening on May 1, 1989, I spent a day there with the voice of Roger Rabbit, Charles Fleischer, at the request of Bob Weis, who was hoping we might be able to polish up and add material to the live shows. But first Charlie wanted to see Movie Mimics. Arriving there, we found a mom and her young daughter about to dub their voices to a scene from *Who Framed Roger Rabbit*. The two characters featured on the clip were Jessica and Roger Rabbit. Charlie asked them, "Hey, do you mind if I try this with you?" The mom was surprised at Charlie's request but graciously agreed to let him give it a go. "Okay," she said. "You be Roger and I'll be Jessica." He responded, "I'll give it a try." When it came time for Mom to record her voice, the script scrolled on the screen to prompt her and she

After Joe Herrington and I went over to the Disney Studio lot to collect Jimmy's collection of his handmade sound effects, we staged this fun celebratory moment with Maestro Jimmy!

performed her line into the microphone in her best Jessica Rabbit, which sounded more like Popeye's Olive Oyl.

Then came Roger Rabbit's part. When Charlie leaned into the mic and sounded like the real deal because, well, he was the real deal, the daughter dropped her jaw to the floor. "Wow!" She exclaimed, "You're really good!" Charlie never told them who he was, but he ramped up his Rabbit act and performed as the character all the way out the door, leaving behind an entire post-show's worth of shocked but delighted guests.

After we had a good laugh over that, Charlie and I headed over to the tram tour to take a ride and see if we could add some polish to the live spiel. All morning he had been carrying a pair of silver Chinese Baoding balls, which he nervously clicked and clacked in his hand. We boarded the tram in the first row of the last car. When our tram stopped inside the Catastrophe Canyon portion of the tour and the outdoor set suddenly exploded with fire effects as part of the show, Charlie flinched and dropped his precious Baoding balls onto the tram floor, where they rolled out of sight behind us. In the midst of all the catastrophic mayhem, as the fire spread across the set and cascades of water gushed down towards our tram, now rocking wildly on a shaker floor, Charlie stood up, whipped around to face our fellow tram tourists, and shouted, "My balls! My balls! Somebody grab my balls!" Somehow, I don't think that was quite the material Bob Weis was hoping for.

Recalling that story reminds me of another totally unexpected moment that happened with a character voice actor I was with a few years ago while in Seattle. We were guest speakers at the Pacific Northwest Mouse Meet Disney fan convention—and by *we*, I mean me, Tony Anselmo (the voice of Donald Duck), and Bill Farmer (the voice of Goofy). After picking the three of us up at the airport, our host and the organizer of the event, Don Morin, treated us to lunch at a local burger joint. A minute after we sat down, an elderly couple slid into the booth next to ours, and I noticed the gentleman was wearing a T-shirt with a giant Goofy face printed on the front. And here I was sitting next to the real Goofy! I mean, come on, what are the odds? "Bill," I whispered, "check out our neighbor's shirt." Bill glanced over and smiled. "You've gotta talk to him on our way out," I suggested. Bill wasn't so sure about that. "C'mon," I pleaded, "it'll make his day!" The couple was still there as we rose to leave. I didn't think he was going to do it, but he then stepped over to their table. "*GAWRSH*," he exclaimed in perfect-cuz-he's-Bill-Farmer Goofy-speak. "I sure like your shirt, young feller!" The man, who I would say was in his mid-eighties, didn't miss a beat when he replied to Bill in perfect Goofy-speak himself, which floored us. "*Gawrsh*, thanks, pal!" Bill kept the goofy Goofy conversation going. "Say, you from around these parts?" The man laughed, "AH-*HYUCK*! Sure am." "*Welp*," said Bill, "it's sure been swell talkin' to ya!" To that Goofy 2 replied, "*Welp*, same to you, pal. So long!" Bill never did tell his Seattle soundalike who he was.

Welp, things really got goofy while trying to keep up with my many projects in various phases of development, which besides Typhoon Lagoon also included the Comedy Warehouse live show at Pleasure Island, Pan Galactic Pizza Port and Astrozone for Tokyo Disneyland, Magic Kingdom Railroad, and Mark Twain at Disneyland script enhancements; plus there were a few side jobs for Randy Bright. And on top of all that, I was also working with fellow show writer Mark Rhodes and a bright new Imagineer who came to us from Feature Animation, Joe Lanzisero, on a bunch of new attraction ideas, including a potential new show replacement we came up with for Walt Disney's Enchanted Tiki Room.

Our proposed show included a new cast of bird characters, one of which was a Latin parrot bandleader named Chicky Chickardo. Joe designed Chicky and the MAPO team built a beautifully feathered mock-up (or shall I say a "squawk-up") of the bright blue new show bird. Imagine my surprise when I turned on a network news program and saw Michael Eisner being interviewed standing proudly next to Chicky! But our bandleader bird's brief few minutes of television fame was his first and only public appearance, as our concept never left the nest.

Speaking of Michael making the news, at that same time in 1988 when he and Chicky were appearing together, he had also made the cover of *Time* magazine. Pictured behind him was a happy Mickey Mouse. The headline read: WHY IS THIS MOUSE SMILING? The second line of the caption under Michael's photo, read: "Because Michael Eisner's magic has transformed Disney into a $3 billion kingdom." Michael was smiling right along with Mickey because, according to the cover story, he had cashed in on a $6 million bonus.

The week that magazine hit the newsstands I was walking with two colleagues in the long corridor that runs from east to west all the way through the center of the main Imagineering building, and we were naturally chatting about Michael's big bonus. The corridor has a shiny concrete floor, and when a forklift operating behind us hit the brakes it dropped a wooden pallet onto the floor with a loud, resonating *KA-BANG*! "D'oh!" I blurted out loudly. "EISNER DROPPED HIS WALLET!" I know you are not going believe what happened not three seconds after I opened my big mouth but it's true, so I'm going to tell you anyway. From around the corner, a mere ten feet away from me, appeared Michael Eisner, Frank Wells, Marty Sklar, and I don't even know who else because my eyes were fixed on Michael as he reached around to the back of his britches to check for his wallet. He apparently did have it as indicated by his overacted huge sigh of relief and exaggerated wipe of his brow. Frank Wells tried unsuccessfully to suppress his chuckling. Marty shot me a look exactly like your dad would after you backed his new Buick into a police car. And that was that. No one in the Eisner entourage said a word as they continued on their merry way. Of course the timing of that wallet incident could not have been worse, because the very next day my wife, Patty, and I were invited to attend an executive retreat and brainstorming weekend at the Ritz-Carlton Hotel in Laguna Beach, California, with guess who? Yep. I had just made a fool of myself in front of Michael and all of my key Imagineering leaders—and they were all going to be there. I don't even know why I was invited to join them, because I was not an executive then; the only invitee that wasn't. Heaven help me.

The weekend began under perfect weather conditions with a lovely buffet dinner on a beautiful bluff overlooking a divinely art-directed Orange County beach. After Patty and I loaded our plates with wonderfulness we sat down at one of the fancy-schmancy tables set up on the lawn. We had the table all to ourselves, which was perfectly fine with my shy wife. But then, lo and behold, who should suddenly appear in the distance, walking across the lawn directly towards us? Yep. Patty panicked. "Oh, my gosh," she whispered worriedly. "Is that? Is that? Here comes Michael Eisner! Is he really . . . no . . . is he really coming over here? What if he sits with us?" "*Pah!*" I countered, following up with an absolute guarantee he would never sit with us, especially after I put his wallet in my mouth. "Come on, honey," I assured her. "I'm not even an executive. Why would he bother with me? He doesn't even know my name."

"Kevin!" Michael called out. "Mind if I join you two?" Patty sucked sea air and turned whiter than our tablecloth. "Please, do!" I offered, and he draped his coat over the back of the chair right next to Patty's to reserve his spot. She shoved her pointy shoe into my shin under the table like this was all my fault. "OW!" I cried out. "What was that?" Michael asked. I responded, "OW'd like to introduce you to my wife!" After the introduction Michael went off to the buffet table.

"Oh, this is just great!" Patty exclaimed, sincerely worried she might do or say something that might embarrass us or even jeopardize my career. "What am I supposed to say? What if I say something stupid? What if—" I interrupted her. "Look, no one is saying you have to say anything," I said. "It's just a dinner. At the Ritz-Carlton. With my boss's, boss's, boss's boss—who happens to be the rich and famous CEO of the entire Walt Disney Company who, by the way, just stuffed his mattress with an additional six million bucks, which is more money than you and I and all of our combined friends and relatives past, present, and future will ever see at one time. That's all. What could possibly go wrong?" She didn't respond.

"Besides," I continued, pointing over to the buffet, "our corporate attorney Merritt Farren has joined him. I'm sure the two of them will come back here together and they'll have a lot to talk about among themselves, especially now that Michael's magic has transformed Disney into a three billion dollar kingdom." Patty choked on her mint-infused water.

As predicted, the two men sat with us, just us, now a table of four: the movers and the shakers (shaking attributed to nerves). Merritt wore high-end, impeccably pressed suits and he always looked picture-perfect, not a hair out of place, like a living, breathing *GQ* magazine cover. Patty didn't say much during our dinner except when she excused herself to get dessert. Upon her return, I noticed she was joyously carrying a big chocolate brownie, topped with more whippy chocolate frosting than there was brownie, all on a fine china plate. Brownies are to Patty what catnip is to cats. She was clearly rewarding herself with *Patnip* because she had successfully made it through the meal without doing or saying something stupid, as she was so certain she would.

And it turned out she really enjoyed our two delightful tablemates. Seeing her finally happy and relaxed made me happy and relaxed. The strife was o'er, the battle won. But then, as she approached the table, she tripped on a dip in the grass and fell forward. As she tried to course-correct from her forty-five-degree angle, she thrust the plate upward in a swooping arc, like a bowler releasing a bowling ball, and its top edge caught the underside edge of table, catapulting the brownie high into the air. I swear, the entire thing happened in slow motion as the flip-flopping fluffily frosted brownie flew, end over end, in an arcing trajectory towards Merritt. I watched in helpless horror as Merritt's eyes widened and his lips puckered way out in the exact shape of a corona on a daffodil to cry (say the following in slo-mo), "*NNNNWOOOOOOOOOO!*" Flip . . . flop . . . PLOP! Frosting side down on the crotch of his probably Prada pants.

One minute Patty and I are enjoying the lap of luxury. The next minute her dessert is on the lap of a lawyer. Fortunately, good-natured Merritt laughed it off, graciously refused our insistent offer to have his clothes dry-cleaned (which at the Ritz probably would have cleaned me out), and validated he was the class act I thought he was. Living with Patty is like living with Lucille Ball in my very own situation comedy—as if life is not sitcom-y enough being an Imagineer!

Meanwhile, back at the Imagineering ranch, ex-animator Joe Lanzisero was invited by his friends, animation directors Ron Clements and John Musker, to come over to their trailer to check out their new project in the works. Joe grabbed Mark Rhodes and me and we took the five-minute walk over. Scattered about the trailer were animators who were hard at work hand-drawing as Ron and John took us through the rough storyboards for something called *The Little Mermaid*. After they brought Ariel's incredible journey to life for us, Ron popped an audiocassette into a tiny tape player and we listened to a homemade scratch-track recording of composer Alan Menken playing his piano and singing the songs he and lyricist Howard Ashman had written. And I was smitten. Although still in the stages of storyboarding and scratch-tracking, the movie already looked, sounded, and *felt* like it was going to be a game-changer. After a few years of an animation dry spell—which was so dry that they had moved the animators into the cluster of trailers on our Imagineering parking lot—it was clear this new mermaid movie was going to make a huge splash.

Even though we already had more work than we could handle, Joe, Mark, and I still got caught up in the excitement of what we had just seen and heard; we literally bolted back to our building, sprinted past the guard in our main lobby, and flew up the stairs to get right to work on new attraction ideas inspired by *The Little Mermaid*. Within a few days of our inspiring check-in with Ron and John we had a board filled with a variety of concept sketches for small- and large-scale attractions. One, I remember, was a double-decker musical carousel. The lower part was "under the sea" and the upper part was "above the surface" featuring characters from both worlds. We excitedly carried our concept board into Randy Bright's office for the big pitch. Although he really liked our ideas, he didn't know all of the great stuff we were privy to about this very special movie in development. Being wary of basing a long-term attraction on a possibly short-term animated feature, he suggested, "Let's wait and see how the movie does." I'll always regret missing the opportunity to open a *Little Mermaid*-themed attraction day and date with the theatrical release because, as we all know, that movie had legs.

Even though our *Mermaid* concepts never surfaced, there was still plenty to do. I wore out my word processor but happily traded up for a boxy new Apple Macintosh floppy-disk computer. That little Mac was a giant godsend, considering all of the projects I had in the hopper. But first I had to learn how to use it. Imagine my awe and delight when I discovered the computer had a feature that allowed you to type a sentence and then have the computer actually speak the sentence in a weird electro-robo female voice. It really cracked me up because none of the inflection was correct. I really didn't have time to play, but I spent at least a half hour typing different sentences just to hear how the Mac would say them. My first typed sentence, I DO NOT HAVE TIME FOR THIS, sounded like I DONUT HALFTIME FOWTHUS. MARTY SKLAR IS A DOO DOO HEAD sounded like MAW TEASE CLAW IZZUE DWUDWED.

Amazing! I could not believe this crazy computer was smart enough to talk! It was time to press this thing into action, especially since I had received my Mac before my colleague and cubicle neighbor, show writer Michael Sprout, with whom I was working on some Disney-MGM Studios stuff, received his. This meant he had not yet had a chance to learn of its humanlike capabilities.

The other fortuitous thing is we had recently received a telephone voice-messaging system. My plan was to wait until Michael was gone, call his number, wait for the beep, and let my computer do the talking. Here's the message he received when he got back. Now imagine that cliché, monotone, incorrectly inflected electronic voice saying, "Hello, Michael Sprout. This is Lucille in Michael Eisner's office. Michael wants you to get a tattoo of his face on your butt. Have a nice day."

Originally from Detroit, Michael Sprout aspired to be a Claymation animator but instead came to Imagineering and became an Audio-Animatronics figure animator. Then he, like me, became a show writer. It was so much fun working with Michael over the decades, and he is personally responsible for some of the longest oxygen-depriving almost-fatal bouts of laughter I've ever experienced. One day, while we were in the Bowling Alley building (Imagineering purchased an actual bowling alley located in Glendale on the nearby corner of Flower and Sonora Streets and turned it into a work space, save four lanes, which remained usable) working together on future expansion concepts for the Disney-MGM Studios, Michael was thumbing through an outdoor clothing catalogue and said, "Say, take a look at this." He was referring to an item called UNDERWEAR WITH WIND-PROOF PANEL. It was funny, but not that funny, because it kind of made sense. What made it funny was when soft-spoken, mild-mannered Michael put his finger directly on the picture of the item and asked—quite seriously, because he sincerely wanted to know the answer—"Why do you suppose they put the windproof panel on the *front*?"

After turning to look at each other with doglike cocked heads—and holding that pose for a long while of bewilderment—the ridiculousness of the whole thing hit me and I fell to the floor, laughing uncontrollably. Then Michael started laughing uncontrollably as well. This went on and on until I thought I was going to need one of those windproof panels myself. When we finally ran out of gas, he sputtered out one last gasp of a giggle, which started me laughing again. Our laughing attack lasted until it was time to go home. But when we both returned the next morning, my stomach and ribs still aching, all it took was one look at him to start it all up again. I would have called *The Guinness Book of World Records*, but there was not enough air left in me to speak.

So much work time was lost because of our hysterics that I had to stay late to get my task done because I had something due the next morning, which was no laughing matter. At around 11:00 p.m. I finally finished my work on the computer, glanced at Michael's open catalogue, and started laughing again so hard that I slapped the top of my desk, which caused a little sad face icon to appear on my Mac screen. And then it went black. I had killed my computer! All my work was lost! Now what?

Enter Chris Carradine, always hyper, blowing into my office with the unbridled bluster of an untied balloon because he was over-the-top excited about something he obviously wanted to share with me. Chris, son of actor John Carradine (and the brother of actors Keith, Robert, and David Carradine), did not get into the family business himself because he wanted to become an Imagineering architect. He was still there working late on an early concept for a nighttime dining and entertainment center being planned for Walt Disney World, and he wanted to tell me the backstory of Merriweather Pleasure, the founder of Pleasure Island. It was the longest backstory I had ever heard, but I'll distill it down to one sentence: Merriweather Pleasure was a sailmaker and Pleasure Island is the waterside spot where he set up shop.

The concept for Pleasure Island sounded like fun, and Chris, project creative lead Rick Rothschild, designer Joe Rohde, and their concept team were creating backstories and designs for the proposed clubs, restaurants, and shops that were "once buildings that housed the various manufacturing shops of Pleasure's sail-making business." The story about Pleasure's power station turned warehouse got my attention. It would be the home of the Comedy Warehouse. The very next day Rick Rothschild gave me a call to ask if I would team up with two comedy writers he was bringing in to create, write, and mount the live show for the Comedy Warehouse. I agreed but under one condition—that I get a new computer! The premise for the scripted show was to poke fun at ourselves—Disney. We were to write a satire about a Walt Disney World vacation as experienced by a family of four (mom, dad, sister, and brother); the roles would be performed by a comedy troupe. To research the guest experience, we went to Walt Disney World ourselves to "walk in our guest's shoes." It was my first trip there, but I already knew the place well.

Our first stop was Epcot. Upon entering the park, we followed the other guests as they entered and immediately got into the long line at Spaceship Earth (because it is the first thing you see and the first thing to do). I knew from my scope days that there was a lot more to see and do on the other side of that giant geodesic sphere, but since we there to intermingle with and observe the guests, we waited with them in line for over an hour in the heat of summer. This inspired me to write the first song of the show, entitled "Super Conscientious Friendly Disney World Employees," as sung by the comic actors portraying Walt Disney World cast members. I won't include all of the lyrics, but here's one verse and chorus sung by a "Spaceship Earth Hostess" (sung to the tune of, forgive me, dear friend Richard Sherman, "Supercalifragilisticexpialidocious"):

> I work up at the giant golf ball they call Spaceship Earth
> One day a lady in the line there started to give birth
> The baby came and everyone around her was relieved
> They'd been in line there waiting since the kid was first conceived!
> I'm a . . .
> Super conscientious friendly Disney World Employee
> I'm here to help and wave hello, I hope you all enjoy me
> I never sweat, I always smile wherever they deploy me
> A super conscientious friendly Disney World Employee!

Our completed show script had this preface on page one:

> Michael Eisner gave Walt Disney Imagineering this assignment: "Create a show for the Comedy Warehouse. It should be funny, light, satirical—the first Disney review that pokes fun at the Disney Guest Experience. Be bold. Use this as your measure—create a show that, if someone else did it, we'd sue 'em."

And boy, did we ever! The idea for the Comedy Warehouse was to provide a place in which adults could relax and enjoy a properly chilled adult beverage after a long day at the parks having had many of the experiences we re-created with a tongue-in-cheek twist in the show. Since it was late-night comedy, we didn't write it for a family audience. Still, it wasn't too over the edge. But it was filled with more Disney self-poking joking than you can shake a *schtick* at. Some considered the content controversial, so it ran for less than a year before it was replaced by other comedy acts, including stand-up. In case you missed it, here are snippets from two of my favorite sketches.

SNIPPET ONE:

The curtain opens to reveal two PIRATES OF THE CARIBBEAN and the REDHEAD.

PIRATES
(Sing)
Yo ho, yo ho, a pirate's life for me . . .

They stop and relax after the guest boat passes them by.

PIRATE ONE
Okay, they're gone.

PIRATE TWO
So, listen, you wanna go out tonight?

REDHEAD
No, I'm going out with two little guys from "it's a small world."

PIRATE ONE
We should sing a different song for a change. Hey, how about this one!
(Sings)
Hey there, Georgy Girl, walkin' down the street so fancy-free . . .

Pirate Two looks offstage.

PIRATE TWO
Uh-oh, here come more people.

PIRATE ONE
(Sings)
People, people who need people . . .
A boat approaches.

PIRATE ONE
Stop it!

PIRATES
(Sing)
Yo ho, yo ho, a pirate's life for me!

Blackout. Curtain closes.

SNIPPET TWO:

Mom and Dad step out of the Main Street, U.S.A. Emporium, each carrying bags.

DAD
What's in your bag?

MOM
I got you a little gift. Here.

From the bag, he retrieves JUMPER CABLES. A plush CHIP is attached to one end and a plush DALE is attached to the other.

DAD
Oh, boy! Chip 'n' Dale jumper cables! How did you pay for them?

MOM
I charged 'em.

He hands her a bag.

DAD
I got something for you, too.

She opens the bag and pulls out a little shovel with a Winnie the Pooh attached to it.

MOM
What's this?

DAD

It's a Winnie-the-Poohper Scooper!

On opening night in May 1989, I was upstairs standing against the railing of the wraparound warehouse balcony with my fellow writers watching our one-hour show for the first time with guests. It was fun to see our material come to life for an audience! But I was exhausted, having worked many extra hours helping to deliver the show while also working on other projects at the same time, including one in Tokyo from where I had recently returned. So, I was jet-lagged and punch-drunk. As a matter of fact, I was real drunk, too, because every time the audience laughed at a joke the three of us writers would raise a toast to whoever wrote that particular bit and say, "This one's for you!" All those toasts hit me hard, because I am not a drinker.

But this was opening night after all. As we were in the back corner upstairs out of view and out of the room light, we were making total fools out of ourselves among ourselves while reacting to the audience's reactions. Plus, I felt happy and proud every time my two comedy compadres raised their glasses to me and said, *"Thish wansh fer yewww, Kev,"* especially since they were seasoned pros in comedy screen writing and television. I was playing in the big league now. That first audience loved the show and the cast got a standing ovation. As the guests below us began to leave, I finally let go of the railing, turned around, and was shocked to discover there were two people sitting at a candlelit table against the dark back wall less than four feet away from where I was standing. Considering my uncharacteristic behavior and cockeyed condition, I was beside myself with embarrassment when I came to the realization that someone had been sitting directly behind me and observing my immature worst. And worse than that, you're not going to believe who that someone was. My heart dropped straight into my shoes as my boss Marty Sklar and his wife, Leah, raised their glasses and said, "This one's for you, Kev."

This was a gratifying moment for Marty because he loved to give me a hard time in a fun and playful way. It all began almost a year to the date before his toasting of my being toasted that opening night, when I took three paper toilet seat covers out of the bathroom dispenser to craft one Mickey Mouse–shaped cover. When unfolded, the seat part was the same, but seamlessly spliced and taped to the top were two rounded Mickey ears cut out of the same material. I didn't really know Marty that well then but decided what the heck, I'd have a little fun with him, attributing my courage to deliriousness from working too much overtime. I folded up the Mickey-shaped cover and paper-clipped on the following note that I then stuffed it into an interoffice envelope and sent to him:

Marty,

Here's a prototype of an idea I've been sitting on for a while for the restrooms at the Comedy Warehouse. Guests would really flip their lids over this one. Should I flush it out a little more or should I dispense of the concept?

Tanks,

Kevin Rafferty

The next day I received his red-pen response:

TO Kevin Rafferty

Sit on it a (long) while longer.

MS

I clipped this note to a Mickey-shaped paper toilet seat cover I made and sent to Marty. This was the first of many such silly jokes sent to him over the years. Apparently, this one really bowled him over.

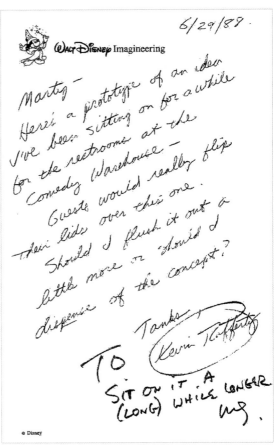

This opened the door to more than twenty-five years of in-person razzing and interoffice gag correspondences between Marty and me. I have an entire drawer filled with all the notes, jokes, and comments he ever sent to me. Among my favorites is a photo I found of a 5,527-pound wheel of cheese. I sent it to Marty with this note: "Marty, I always thought YOU were the 'Big Cheese!'"

For many years, Marty and I exchanged interoffice mail envelopes always containing something ridiculous. I have an entire file cabinet drawer filled with silly stuff like this. (Note what I wrote on the cheese.)

Good thing I already had a job!

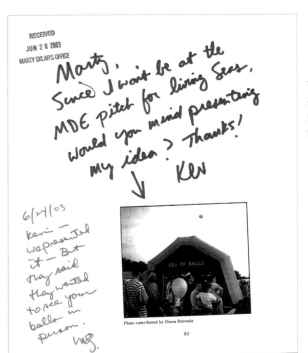

RECEIVED
JUN 20 2003
MARTY SKLAR'S OFFICE

Marty,
Since I won't be at the MDE pitch for living Seas, would you mind presenting my idea? Thanks!
KEN

6/24/03
Kevin —
we presented it — But they said they wanted to see your balls in person.
MS.

SEA OF BALLS

Photo contributed by Diana Schwabe

53

We really had a ball sending these silly things back and forth to each other!

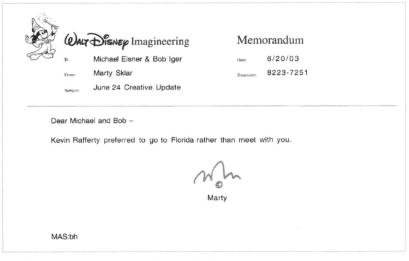

Walt Disney Imagineering

Memorandum

To: Michael Eisner & Bob Iger

From: Marty Sklar

Subject: June 24 Creative Update

Date: 6/20/03

Extension: 8223-7251

Dear Michael and Bob —

Kevin Rafferty preferred to go to Florida rather than meet with you.

Marty

MAS:bh

This is what happened after I told Marty I wasn't going to be able to present a new concept to Michael and Bob because I had to get back to Walt Disney World to finish an important deadline.

The morning after opening night at the Comedy Warehouse I jumped back on a plane to fly home to California to repack my bags, kiss my wife and four-year-old son hello and good-bye, and fly off again to Japan to complete final-phase installation and direct the programming for a new show I was working on for Tokyo Disneyland. Trying to keep my head above water in my rising ocean of global projects was relentlessly challenging, but that's what made it incredibly fun. In the midst of it all, the experience of cooking up my first animated and fully automated dinner show—in a foreign language, no less—was simply out of this world.

PAN
GALACTIC
PIZZA
PORT

COMEDY WAREHOUSE and Typhoon Lagoon

opened a month apart in the summer of 1989. While I worked on them, it helped that they were practically across the street from each other. But two years before that, designer extraordinaire Steve Kirk asked me to join him to develop a new project halfway around the world, which was also scheduled to open the same summer of 1989. Steve (for you Figment fans, he's the man who designed that cute little purple character) started working on projects for Tokyo Disneyland fifteen years before he rose through the ranks to lead the design and development of the epic second-gate park at that resort, Tokyo DisneySea.

The new project in the works was Astrozone, a unique-to-Tokyo Disneyland part of its Star Tours complex, then under construction in Tomorrowland. Astrozone was to include an enclosed skyway bridge that connected Star Tours and a new two-level dine-in restaurant. The story and theme for the restaurant were still up for grabs; and that's why Steve recruited me. He was interested in putting some sort of entertainment experience within view of its double-decker dining area and asked me to cook up a concept for the show.

"They're going to serve chicken paste pizza," he said. "Do you think you can come up with an Audio-Animatronics show around that?" "Chicken paste, huh?" I responded. "You bet!" In addition to the pizza show, Steve had yet another request for me: he was working on the design for an alien character whose purpose would be to entertain guests as they exited Star Tours through the sky bridge and was looking for a story conceit for that as well. I had done a lot of stuff up to that point in a short amount of time, but this was my first foray into the realm of full-scale Audio-Animatronics characters and automated entertainment starting from a blank sheet of paper, or in this case, a yet-to-be-built building.

Thanks to its location, the idea for the pizza show came quickly, almost a no-brainer. What if the restaurant were an intergalactic pizza company's first franchise on Earth? With that as the story hook, I drew story inspiration from the British sitcom *Fawlty Towers* (I love British humor!) and its main character, hotel owner Basil Fawlty, as played by John Cleese (I love John Cleese!). Comedy ensued whenever bumbling Basil tried his best to run his hotel, which only served to make every situation worse and therefore funnier. The main character for the pizza show would be "Tony Solaroni," a stalk-eyed, frizzy-haired Audio-Animatronics chef from outer space trying his best to run an Earth franchise located light-years away from his home base.

Tony's supporting show set would be a giant Rube Goldberg–like anthropomorphic pizza-making machine. In the center of the set, directly behind Tony, would be a matrix of video monitors arranged to create one large screen through which he could communicate "real time" with his wife and boss and play commercials for Pan Galactic Pizza. Everything would be staged to span the length of an expansive ledge located directly above the restaurant's order counter and directly across from the second-level dining area.

In 1987, Steve Kirk, future creative director for Tokyo DisneySea, asked me to come up with an idea for a "dinner show" for a restaurant in Tomorrowland at Tokyo Disneyland. Pan Galactic Pizza Port and Tony Solaroni were born.

The next step was to write the script for Tony, his wife, boss, employees "working backstage in the kitchen," and the Pan Galactic commercials featuring pizza-delivery flying saucers. Imagineering designer and ex-animator Mona Koth designed the saucers and delivery characters that would be animated for the commercials using traditional hand-painted cels. When I was studying animation in college I was a huge fan of the Kurtz & Friends animation studio because I loved their style and storytelling in the animated TV commercials they were producing at that time. Director Bob Kurtz's whimsical work on the Chevron dinosaur commercials really inspired me and further fueled my desire to become an animator. Never would I have imagined then that a few years later—as a result of my own selfish request—I would be working with Bob and his studio on the animated commercials for Pan Galactic Pizza Port. Crazy, I tell you. (This is yet another example of Imagineering providing the opporTOONity for me to actually meet and work with a gifted animator who was a great inspiration to me.)

In addition to designing and modeling the giant automated pizza-making machine, Steve went to work sculpting a maquette from his concept sketch of Tony Solaroni. He was also working on the maquette of the second alien character starting to take shape and, considering the Star Tours story and this unnamed character's location in the sky bridge, I thought it would be fun if the chubby, big-eared blue alien were a uniformed intergalactic customs agent. He would sit behind a desk and welcome visitors from all worlds. While trying to think of a name for him, I happened to be driving to Las Vegas and noticed an off-ramp sign that read ZZYZX ROAD. After that, the character became Officer Zzyzx.

After I had the first-pass show scripts and illustrated storyboards put together for both the Pan Galactic Pizza and Officer Zzyzx shows, I presented them to Steve. He gave the characters and story direction an enthusiastic approval and said the Astrozone show elements were ready to take all the way up to the top. That meant the time had come for me to pitch it to Marty Sklar. Over the course of my career, I have pitched countless ideas to Marty while he was our fearless leader. But this was my very first time presenting to "The Big Cheese." I was keenly aware his "yay" or "nay" could make or break a project, so the pressure was on.

I remember sweating bullets (seriously, they were .357-sized beads) even though it was cold in the conference room because I was so nervous. And that was before Marty even arrived! When the door opened I immediately felt faint. "What have ya got, kid?" Marty asked while stepping into the room. I thought he was asking about my seriously sweaty appearance, thinking I was sick or something. Assuming that, I replied, "Don't worry, I'm not contagious or anything." When he told me that was good news but what he was actually referring to were the storyboards, I felt like an idiot.

Before I learned the importance of kicking off a pitch with a crystal clear descriptive one-liner, I jumped the gun by spewing out something about a Japanese *amminatronics* Italian guy from outer space who runs things, sings things, and does things with *chicken paste*. Those were not the things I wanted to say at all. Marty's eyebrow arched so high it could have lifted a chair off the ground. I was blurting out nonsense to the man whose opinion mattered the most—and all that did was cause me to sweat even more. He knew I was new at this and told me to relax and take him through the show, because it looked interesting.

Once I calmed down and got rolling, I started to have fun with it and I could tell Marty really liked the idea. At the end of my pitch he offered a few solid notes and told Steve and me to keep going because he really liked the characters and the direction. Relieved, happy, and starting to dry off, I promised to get back to him as soon as I had the songs written. He took me by surprise when he said, "You're not gonna sing, are you?" I didn't know if he was joking or serious. Was I not supposed to sing? Was there a rule around here about singing to Marty? Maybe there was a certain protocol to follow when it came to pitching songs I didn't know about yet. Maybe I had stepped over the line with the mere mention of music.

And here it was going so well. "Uh, no," I assured him. "No singing. Well, *yessss* . . . I mean, maybe, there could be." I wondered how the heck I was going to get songs approved by Marty if I didn't sing them to him. By golly, he was gonna get the songs, and that's all there was to it. "Yes, YES!" I confidently replied. "I am going to sing to you. For you. The songs." As he rose to leave he said, "I will look forward to that. I think."

Well, the day finally came when I had the Pan Galactic songs written and ready to sing to Marty. But here's the thing. I can't sing (as an Imagineer I don't like to say "can't," but I really can't sing). I truly believed in the songs, so to encourage myself to sing them anyway I kept repeating in my mind a lyric one of my all-time favorite songwriters, Joe Raposo, wrote in one of his songs: "Don't worry that it's not good enough for anyone else to hear, just sing, sing a song." Marty was at home recuperating from surgery, so he invited me to come over and pitch the songs to him there. I loaded up my cassette player and the tape of the background track I planned to sing along to and drove over to the Sklars'. Marty's wife, Leah, greeted me at the front door and invited me in to set up in their dining room. She told me Marty was on the phone but would be in shortly. The moment Leah left the room I heard perky little doggie nails clicking like crazy on the hardwood floor, indicating a small dog was quickly on its way down the hall towards me. A little white dog soon after ran into the dining room, slammed on his brakes, and sat his fuzzy-little-mutt butt right down in front of my cassette player and me, acting as if he were a privileged one-pup audience waiting for the show to start.

Marty then came in but didn't even acknowledge his dog. He sat down across the table from me and said, "Okay, kid, what have you got?" Taking that as my cue I pressed the PLAY button and started to sing: "Hellooooo, my name is Tony Solaroni from outer space, I run the place . . ." Five notes into the song, Marty's dog spun around 180 degrees and tried to escape as fast as he could; but his little nails were not providing traction and instead he was scratching fast and furiously against the slippery hardwood floor—stuck in gear. The dog was like a top-fuel dragster trying to come off the line . . . and when he finally dug in he shot out like a bullet.

Marty didn't flinch or even move, so I kept going until I finished the song, at which point I asked my boss, "So what do you think?" Marty responded matter-of-factly, "If the dog doesn't like it I don't like it." He sat there in silence for the longest time, keeping me hanging in lyric limbo, until he smiled and admitted he was only kidding and that he liked the song. But ever since that day, any time he walked into a conference room to get any kind of pitch from me, whether it was to include a song or not, he'd be direct: "You're not gonna sing, are you?"

Fast-forward thirty years: I recently received a phone call from my dear friend Marilyn Magness, an executive director for Imagineering Creative Entertainment, our in-house studio that designs and produces live theatrical shows, parades, nighttime spectaculars, and more. In her early years, Marilyn was in the original cast of the Hoop-Dee-Doo Musical Revue in the role of Dolly Drew at the Fort Wilderness campground at Walt Disney World. She has since directed and staged three presidential galas, five Super Bowl halftime shows, parades, Broadway shows, entertainment spectaculars (including live events to launch new Disney Cruise Line ships), and so much more. Marilyn is a live-performance powerhouse.

There is nothing in the world I would not do for her. Or so I thought, until she dropped this doozie of an out-of-the-blue request on me. "Hey, Kev!" she began with her typical firecracker exuberance. "Here's the deal." (She always begins every phone call to me with "Here's the deal," which invariably leads to me asking myself, *What did I just get myself into?*) She continued, "The Disney Family Museum wants you to write a song and sing it live at this huge museum extravaganza dinner show fund-raiser, and they're going to honor our beloved Marty, so your song needs to be about him, or for him, or both. Are you in?"

Before I could say, "WAIT! WHAT?" she said, "Listen, babe, gotta go. But here's the deal. There are going to be a lot of really important people in that audience, hundreds and hundreds of them, all really important, so this is a big important thing. You come up with an idea for the song you're gonna write and sing and the act you're gonna do, anything you want to do, and I'll give you anything you need to do it. Live band, dancing girls, confetti cannons, you name it, and—"

I cut in, "The ACT I'm gonna do?" She interrupted my interruption. "I'll call you on Tuesday, so you have until then to tell me what you're doin'. Love ya!" *CLICK*. This is a perfect example of why, when folks ask me to explain what a typical day is for me at Imagineering, I, of all people, am at a total loss for words.

Marilyn has this magical power to make you forget everything else you're doing, no matter how important it is, to focus on her "deal." Still, in the blinding afterglow of her hyper-hypnotic telephonic trance, I immediately started thinking about the song I would write and sing, especially since, as mentioned, I am not a singer (as Marty could and would tell you). That meant that in order for it to work, it could not be taken seriously. I landed on the big idea, recalling the times when I'd walk into a conference room with a "boom box," indicating I was about to pitch a song to Marty and sometimes his higher-ups, and Mr. Marty Pants would say, "Oh, look. Here comes Frank Sinatra."

Marilyn's offer to provide me with dancers sealed the deal in helping me decide to do a Sinatra parody. On the long commute home that night, I tuned in to the Sinatra channel (Siriusly Sinatra) on satellite radio and Frank was singing "The Lady Is a Tramp." As he sang to that ultra-cool Nelson Riddle arrangement of the Rodgers and Hart standard, I sang right along trying to tweak out a lyric and landed on: "that's why our Marty is a champ." Bingo. When Marilyn called back on Tuesday, it was my turn to say, "Here's the deal," and lay it on her. She loved the idea. "What'll make it great," she said, much to my consternation, "is you will be so vulnerable up there!"

Well, the next thing you know I was in a rehearsal hall at Disneyland learning the choreography with my showgirls and singing as Bruce Healy (longtime music director at Disneyland), who wrote the arrangement especially for me, was accompanying us on the piano. I've experienced countless days in my career that have been, even for me, far too surreal to be believed. But this one was top of the heap, A-number-one. And it was only the first rehearsal.

When the big day for the actual event finally came, I showed up in my rented tux for the dress rehearsal in the ballroom at the Grand Californian Hotel. As Marilyn directed the rehearsal, it dawned on me that I was the only nonprofessional performer in the whole show. Bringing it all home in the finale was Disney Legend Richard Sherman; and hosting the show was none other than Neil Patrick Harris. A half hour before the whole shebang started, the audience began to arrive, including celebrities and other industry notables, Disney Legends even, including Marty Sklar (and all of his family) and Disney family members themselves. John Lasseter, his wife, Nancy, and several directors and executives from Pixar were in attendance. Voice talent from the movie *Cars* and many of the top executives from the Disneyland Resort and Imagineering units were there as well. Everybody that was anybody in my world was there. Holy guacamole—and I'm supposed to dance and sing at this thing? The Imagineering leaders in attendance, including president Bob Weis, had no idea I was going to be onstage, much less perform, so if I chickened out they would never know.

As I was formulating my plan to duck out the back door, Neil Patrick Harris, who did an outstanding job, of course, as singer, dancer, and host, introduced me, saying, "Ladies and gentlemen, here with a special tribute is the best-kept secret keeper on the planet, executive creative director of Walt Disney Imagineering, Kevin Rafferty!" When the spotlight hit me my Imagineering leaders went into shock (but not as much as I was already in) as Bruce's orchestra played me onstage with "He's a Tramp" from *Lady and the Tramp*. I began my act with a heartfelt spoken tribute to Marty that segued into recalling how he always cringed whenever I sang and how on occasion he would accuse me of trying to be Frank Sinatra. With that, I surprised everyone, including myself, when I channeled Ol' Blue Eyes, accompanied by a *swingin'* Las Vegas-y vamp from the orchestra and the dazzling entrance of the long-lashed flashy show-girls from out of the wings. As the girls encircled me to put a drink in my hand, a barstool under my butt, and a black fedora on my head, I said in my best Sinatra, "And now, ladies and gentlemen, with your kind permission, I would like to take this opportunity to *sing* Marty's praises." Then I looked directly at Marty, the music still vamping, and added, "And Marty, this time I have a live combo, so brace yourself." On that cue, the orchestra launched into it and I started singing:

(To the tune of "The Lady Is a Tramp")

> He worked five decades but seems more like eight
> He built twelve theme parks and all of them great
> He never bothers to pay at the gate
> That's why our Marty is a champ
> Fan clubs all ask him to come and expound
> He travels to them the whole world around
> He picks up trash from the Disneyland ground
> That's why our Marty is a champ
> He likes the free fresh blue-sky ideas, especially his
> He's not broke—he's oke!
> He keeps on writing till he gets a cramp
> That's why our Marty is a champ
> Dives into details, says, "Story is king"
> He claims blank paper's "The most frightening thing"
> He always cringes whenever I sing
> That's why our Marty is a champ
> He led the great ones and none of them frauds
> Hung with the Herbies, the Henches and Claudes
> Thinks his commandments are better than God's
> That's why our Marty is a champ
> He loves those free fresh blue-sky ideas, he's such a wiz
> (Pointing to Marty) Don't croak 'cuz you're oke!
> He is the light bulb inside of our lamp
> That's why our Marty, he's such a smarty
> That's why our Marty is a champ!

When the number was over the band played me offstage. I made it back to my table, plopped into the chair next to Bob Weis, and traded my "prop drink" for a real one. A double.

Another "typical" day in the life of an Imagineer!

Here's to you, Marty!

Although I'm not a singer, nor can I read or write a single note (I play instruments by ear and sheer determination), music has always been at the very core of my being and a profoundly important part of my career as an Imagineer. On those occasions in which I've had the oppor-TUNE-ity to write both the music and lyrics for an attraction song—Mater's Junkyard Jamboree and Luigi's Rollickin' Roadsters in Cars Land for example—I first hear the song in my head and then let it out by going into one of our in-house recording studios and singing what I think it should sound like. Then we contract a real arranger/composer to listen to the recording of my singing (not an easy thing to do, so I warn them beforehand) and write the notes as they interpret them on a lead sheet. In the days of developing Pan Galactic, I was introduced to composer George Wilkins, who was once a staff musician at the Walt Disney Studios.

In another cosmic twist of fate, it wasn't long before we started working together that I discovered George was the talent behind many of the TV commercial jingles I knew and loved as a kid, including that song I sang for the creative director at my first ad agency job when trying to talk him into letting me try my hand at copywriting: "New Ajax laundry detergent is stronger than dirt!" George took Madison Avenue by storm in the ad-biz era depicted in the cable TV series *Mad Men* as an advertising jingle writer and singer. While at the top of his game in the mid-1960s, George bought a new red Mustang convertible in New York City, the same year that model made its debut, dropped the top, and headed to Hollywood to seek fame and fortune. He worked with top-name recording industry talent and was also one of the voices heard in some 1960s TV show theme songs, including that iconic one-word lyric *Batman*. Upon landing at the Walt Disney Studios, Wilkins got to know and work with all of the Disney music greats like Lou Debney, Richard Bellis, Buddy Baker, George Bruns, and even the Sherman brothers. These were the music legends that created the instantly recognizable and beloved *sound* of Disney during their golden era. To me, the very heart of Disney when I was growing up was its music, every arrangement and every note in the perfect place at the perfect time to create pure magic. That's why these film, TV, and theme park composers, arrangers, lyricists, and conductors were among my greatest heroes; and I, too, got to work with some of them.

Wilkins and I teamed up as composer and lyricist and wrote a lot of music over the years, including the finale song for it's tough to be a bug!, the Sonny Eclipse ("Biggest Little Star in the Galaxy") lounge act in Cosmic Ray's Starlight Café in Tomorrowland at the Magic Kingdom (Sonny Eclipse, by the way, is a distant cousin to Officer Zzyzx), and the "radio shows" and original songs performed by Disney characters in both Mickey's Toontown in Disneyland and Mickey's Toontown Fair at the Magic Kingdom in Walt Disney World. We also worked together on the original Test Track at Epcot and the updated versions of Walt Disney's Carousel of Progress and Enchanted Tiki Room—Under New Management! at the Magic Kingdom.

Before I teamed up with George, he worked on projects for Epcot, including writing the songs with show writer Scott Hennesy for the brilliant Kitchen Kabaret show in the Land pavilion. This is where George met Steve Kirk, who along with Imagineer Jeff Burke designed Kitchen Kabaret. To keep it all in the musical family, Steve brought George and me together to write the songs and arrangements for all things Pan Galactic. Drawing from his ad-jingle experience, George had a ball writing for the flying saucer delivery commercials.

When we had our act together we took our show on the road to Tokyo to present it to the executives of the Oriental Land Company who, if they liked it, would be funding the project. This was my first trip to Japan. In fact, this was my first trip out of the country. I'll never forget what happened when I arrived in my room on the twenty-seventh floor of the Imperial Hotel (before the Tokyo Disneyland resort had hotels on property). The first thing I did was step over to the window for a bird's-eye view of Tokyo, and when I looked out over the dense cityscape, it appeared as though the distant buildings were rising up and down over a wave that was coming directly towards me! At first I thought I was experiencing what I had heard people refer to as jet lag, but to my disbelief the city kept rising and falling as the buildings continued to ride the wave coming towards me. I rubbed my eyes as if I were seeing things, but when the entire block across the street lifted up and the wave reached my hotel a split second later, the entire building rode up and over it as your body would after you've waded into water that's shoulder-high at the beach.

A moment later I heard a woman outside my door running down the hallway screaming, "Earthquake! Earthquake!" I was born and raised in California, so I know what earthquakes feel like. But this was like nothing I've ever experienced. It was just plain weird. At the precise moment that my hotel room was thrust upward, the built-in nightstand radio suddenly powered on by itself in the middle of a relaxing easy listening version of "The Girl from Ipanema." I switched on the TV thinking there might be a special news report about that unnerving rolling ride, but all I got was an animated show in which a little boy, running while screaming bloody murder, was being chased by a mob of loud, angry girls; to throw them off, he tore off all his clothes in transit, jumped naked onto a birdbath, struck a statuesque pose in all his David-like glory, and started peeing as if he were a fountain. It worked for him. After all that—and after experiencing the crazy high-tech heated toilet with a mind of its own in my room—I couldn't sleep the entire night, not to mention that nighttime was still daytime in my interpretation of time.

The next morning I had to put on a suit and tie, as I was told we had to put on our best clothes and our best behavior for the executive presentation. All "dolled up," I stepped into the elevator feeling very businesslike and was greeted by a white-gloved elevator hostess at the ready. The exquisite wood paneling in the elevator was quite beautiful and exotic, as was the hostess; the combination of both made me feel quite worldly. As I didn't recognize the wood, I wondered which part of Japan it was from. I asked the elevator operator if she could tell me its origin, and she replied, "Oregon." I then asked where she was from and she replied, "Chicago."

It wasn't until I stepped inside the administration building where our Imagineering Tokyo office is located that I was told air-conditioning is allowed only at certain times of the year. This was not one of those times. It was mighty hot and humid, even more so inside than outside. And it got even hotter when the conference room filled up with about thirty dark-suited Japanese executives. There were a few frosted windows on one side of the room, but they were not made to open. The execs sat down in rows of perfectly arranged chairs tucked behind long, thin tables that spanned the width of the room. By the time introductions were politely being made through the interpreter, there was no oxygen left and I was clinging on for dear life. I still had to perform the show and sing the songs, which was why I was there. The whole enchilada was riding on this. I wasn't nervous about doing the presentation. What I was nervous about was passing out. It was so hot in that crowded room I actually began to have cartoon visions of all the execs turning into tie-wearing turkeys and roasting on their chairs.

Just when I was gasping onto what breathable air was still in there, every single one of the execs lit a cigarette at the very same time, as if it were choreographed. This was the signal they were ready for me to begin. But I was ready to keel over. The weird thing is after they lit their cigarettes, they didn't puff them. They just held them between two fingers in front of their faces and sat motionless staring at me and my cassette player, like Marty Sklar's dog did, waiting for the show to start.

Hoping I could hold on, I launched into the show. The thing about pitching a show through an interpreter is that while you have to wait for him or her to translate what you just said in English into Japanese, all the showbiz timing, rhythm, and cadence of your presentation gets literally lost in the translation. It's like stepping on the gas and then slamming on the brakes. Every time I tossed out a joke or line from the show the interpreter would deliver it with the energy and enthusiasm of a sloth. And oh, boy, this was already a tough room. I was hoping the execs would start to liven up, but there they sat, motionless as mannequins, with their cigarettes burning and turning into long drooping ashes—though somehow still staying in place. Blame it on the heat, the lack of air, the lack of sleep, the cartoon kid on the birdbath, the combined smoke of thirty cigarettes and jet lag, but I decided to wake up this post-lunch crowd by having a little out-of-my-country, out-of-my-mind fun. I started performing the character voices and singing the songs with abandon, and challenged the interpreter to step up her game and interpret everything with the same razzmatazz.

I remember at that point Steve Kirk shaking his head. When I got to the part in the storyboard where the little alien pizza delivery guys flew off in their delivery saucers, the interpreter performed the same silly Jetsons-like sound effects I did by making a high-pitched sound while rolling her tongue and vibrating her lips, like a baby spitting out strained broccoli. Now that's more like it! Watching her mimic my sound effects was hilarious because those silly sounds were the same in any language. The executives sprang to life, and reading the room, I could tell they were becoming engrossed with this unexpected, unorthodox pitch and the radical new behavior of their once-timid interpreter.

It was so much fun putting on my tap shoes and bringing the petite, prim, and proper interpreter, who ordinarily worked in high-level ho-hum executive business meetings, right into the presentation along with me. We became an act. Maybe she secretly wanted to get fired, I don't know. But she was a good sport and repeated every crazy sound effect and character voice I tossed out there. She was especially a riot when she performed a character voice for Tony Solaroni's wife, mimicking my falsetto with her own falsetto, not that she needed it. At the end of the pitch I waited for the interpreter to bring home the last line, and when she did, the room exploded with applause, ashes flying everywhere. This meant our pizza chef was getting the dough!

I learned a lot in Tokyo about creating a show for a different culture. While there I met with a local writer who adapted my scripts to better play to a Japanese audience. Upon returning home, I met with Marty to go over the changes. When I told him one of my favorite jokes was changed to something completely different because it wasn't funny in Japanese, he said, "What makes you think it was funny in English?" One of my favorite bits for the intergalactic customs agent was changed as well. The Japanese-to-English translation of the revised line for Officer Zzyzx was as follows: "Excuse me, ma'am, you don't want to get hell ear." I know. It makes no sense. When we recorded the voice talent in Tokyo, I made sure to remember the phonetic delivery of that particular line so I could observe the guest's reaction to it when Officer Zzyzx said it to them. After opening day, when he did say that line, I watched the crowd break into uproarious laughter. What the hell?

Months before that opening day moment, when I flew back to Tokyo from my other gigs in Florida for final-show install—and to direct the animation programming for Astrozone—we started with Officer Zzyzx. Since our character animator had not yet arrived, one of our show-programming technicians, someone who was more technical than creative (but knew how to use all the animation knobs and buttons to give the character motion), temporarily stepped in to help get things moving. He began by animating the character to perform in a silly and almost hyperactive way, which made Zzyzx look quirky in a Captain Jack Sparrow sort of way. But when some of the Japanese construction guys walked through our show space, I watched them to see how they would react. However, they didn't seem to be too enamored with the character. They didn't even stop to look. It was then I realized the quirky animation was disconnected with the dialogue. Funny movements didn't mean a good show. Without regard to the nuances, inflections, and emotions that should jive with the language, Zzyzx's performance was clearly not engaging the local audience; and worse yet, it may have even been disrespectful to them. It became clear that although Zzyzx was from outer space, he had to be Japanese. Since I didn't speak the language, the only way we were going to stay honest regarding the character's body language and gestures relative to his dialogue and emotion was to start over and animate with on-site coaching from an interpreter. After a week of working with interpreters, which included animating several subtle movements and surprisingly no movements at all where appropriate to the dialogue, the construction guys that passed through the area began to stop and watch Zzyzx. One of them even gave me a thumbs-up because the character was not moving simply for the sake of moving; he was now one of them. That's when I learned what you don't animate is as important as what you do. Just because you have a variety of figure functions at your beck and call doesn't mean you should use them all. If you watch an actor, they are not constantly moving, because sometimes not moving can be the most moving thing they can do. If this page were nothing but ink, you couldn't read the words.

Steven "Mouse" Silverstein came over and replaced our technician at the anicon (animation-control console) to work with me and several interpreters to complete the animation for Officer Zzyzx. As a kid, Mouse invented technologies in his family garage that would bring characters of his own design and fabrication to life. In fact, it was Silverstein who designed the state-of-the-art anicon we were using in Tokyo. Mouse was destined to become an Imagineer, and I had the great opportunity and pleasure to work with him early in his career. He is brilliant, so brilliant, in fact, that he mastered the Japanese language in only a few months while temporarily living in Tokyo. And he put that mastery to work in his final animation of the show.

But more importantly, he made going to the bathroom for me a lot easier. When I first arrived at the site, still under construction, the nearest restroom was around the corner from Astrozone in the outskirts of Tomorrowland. On my first day, I stepped into the stall and was shocked to discover there was no toilet, at least not the kind I was used to. Instead there was a ceramic fixture, all right, but it was sunken into the ground. Essentially, there was a hole, flush to the floor, so to speak, with a roll of TP and a what appeared to be a flush handle on the back wall, each only three inches off the ground. When it came to how to use any of this, I didn't know squat. Man, I thought, this is gonna be a long trip.

In the first few weeks before Mouse's arrival, being a creature of habit, I always went into the same stall but never got used to having to be a contortionist. When Mouse finally did arrive and I shared with him how much I loved being in Japan, except for those "ground holes in the stalls," he laughed and suggested I try going into the stall next door. I took his advice and, sure enough, the second stall to the right had an honest-to-goodness, off-the-ground Western-style toilet. Hallelujah! Now the toilets at the Imperial Hotel were similar to ours, off the ground that is, but I wasn't in my room enough to take full advantage of that because I was working at the site most of the time. For those of you who have never been to Japan, heed this warning: never plop yourself down on the pot in your fancy hotel room and, out of curiosity, start pushing the array of buttons mounted to the side of your bowl, or you will suddenly experience upward-spraying jets of warm water, coming from who knows where and everywhere, zeroing in with pinpoint accuracy on strategic targets on your front side and underside. You don't want to get "hell rear."

Tokyo can get bitter cold. Mouse and I were working in the sky bridge before the section we were in was fully enclosed on either side, open to the elements. Icy gusts of wind from Tokyo Bay blew through our show space with such force that my windbreaker could not live up to its name. Poor Mouse was shivering while his frigid fingers tried to turn the frozen knobs on the anicon. Seriously, he was as blue as Officer Zzyzx. Mouse, the perfect example of an optimistic happy-to-be-here Imagineer despite all of the challenges, weather-wise and otherwise, worked crazy long hours with me and never once complained.

My instincts to protect my dear friend kicked in, and I went on a scavenger hunt to find some building material, which was easy in the restaurant space because the show set was still under construction. As Mouse soldiered on, I made several trips back and forth with my scavenged bits and pieces of cardboard, plastic, and wood scraps, enough to erect a temporary windproof hut around him and our equipment. The thing I learned in my first experience "in the field" is that you become very close with your team members, like soldiers do when they serve together and watch out for each other. Most Imagineers will tell you that while working on-site to deliver a project, which in all cases is a demanding, stressful, and trying time, you start out as colleagues and finish as family. I experienced that feeling for the first time far away from home in Japan. Although he has long since moved to Florida with his lovely wife (an interpreter he met while we were in Tokyo) and family, Mouse is still my family.

When the show-set installers came up to the sky bridge to see what I was doing with their scraps, they got a big kick out of Mouse's "fort" being under construction and helped to shore it up. Some of them were from Toho Studios, famous for the Godzilla movies. Working with them was a group from Tokyo Disneyland that I called "the blue-shirted can-do crew." All of them were dedicated and tireless workers, and when they realized Mouse, our colleague Blake Ostrowski, and I had been working two days straight without a break, they decided not to leave the site until we did. But we decided not to leave the site until they did. We didn't want them outworking us. After all, we were The Strong. The Proud. The Imagineers!

While working to outwork each other, another crew came in to install a frozen yogurt machine. After they left, I found some paper cups normally used for paint, learned how to use the machine, and started handing out frozen yogurt to the Japanese crew. At first they were reluctant—they thought they'd get in trouble. But they gave in and really seemed to enjoy it. After that I started ordering pizza and sodas for them from Domino's. Before long we all became buds, even though we didn't speak one another's languages. They taught us some Japanese words and phrases and we returned the favor by teaching them some American slang. I taught one of them to say "Hey, buddy, gimme twenty bucks" and motioned for him to tap Blake on the shoulder and say that. He had no idea what it meant but did it anyway. As deliriously tired as we all were, we laughed about that until, using sign language, we decided to call a work truce and always leave at the same time.

The clock was ticking down to opening day, so we worked many nonstop days on the site but still needed help. Although he was a show writer, Michael Sprout was gracious enough to fly over to jump back into his old role as figure animator to bring Tony Solaroni to life. One early morning, around 2:30, as Michael and I were focused on the show programming for Tony and his pizza machine, I heard a familiar voice behind me. "How ya doin', kid?" I turned and it was Marty. "You've lost a lot of weight. Are you okay?" Recalling my first sweaty pitch to him, I responded, "Don't worry, I'm not contagious or anything!" We were sure happy and surprised to see Marty's friendly face far from home on our site in middle of the night. But that was Marty. He continued, "You're not gonna sing, are you?" I laughed, "Don't have to. Pull up a chair and maestro Michael will ask Tony to do all the singing." Michael set into sound and motion the parts of the show we had completed and Marty took it all in. "Not bad," he said, "for a Japanese animatronic Italian guy from outer space."

In the weeks prior to opening, after having worked on-site for more than three months with only two days off, I was homesick and really missed my wife

On the set with Tony Solaroni at the Pan Galactic Pizza Port in Tokyo Disneyland.

and son. The project had come together beautifully, but I was more than ready to go home because I couldn't wait one more day to see them and was anxious to get back to work on my other projects. Still, after all this, I knew it would be difficult to leave my other family: my team, the show-set construction crew, and the Tokyo Disneyland maintenance and operations folks I had come to know, respect, and admire so much. On my last morning there, prior to the park's opening, as I was walking all by myself through Tomorrowland in a light rain, I turned around to take one last look at what had been my home away from home, the now completed Astrozone. What I saw stopped me in my tracks. I did not expect it, and I will never forget it. There, on the second level exterior balcony of the Pan Galactic Pizza Port, were about twenty of my blue-shirted Japanese pals, the ones I had worked alongside day and night, served gallons of frozen yogurt to, and fed countless boxes of Domino's delivered pizza, all lined up side by side facing me and standing at attention. The moment my misty eyes met theirs, they slowly and respectfully bowed together and remained in that position until I was gone.

THE DISNEY-MGM STUDIOS EXPANSION

THE MORNING I returned to my office in Glendale I didn't have a minute to settle in before I was called to help brainstorm new ideas for the proposed expansion of the recently opened Disney-MGM Studios in Walt Disney World. In its initial concept, that park wasn't actually supposed to be a park at all, because it was originally intended to be a land in Epcot. Michael Eisner always had a keen interest in how things were made, and his original request to Imagineering was to create a large pavilion or land that would provide a place in which guests could learn how movies were made. Before long the concept outgrew the proposed site in Epcot and evolved into a separate "half-day park" with only enough content to entertain guests that had other plans for the evening or were heading back to the airport later in the day.

On opening day, however, the Disney-MGM Studios offered more things to see and do than was previously planned, which ended up working out well, because the park was instantly popular. But it still didn't offer enough entertainment opportunities to meet the demand or stretch the day into a late night. The other huge motivator for us to get going and growing was the new Universal Studios park in Orlando, which was under construction at the time and scheduled to open in June 1990.

Fueled by Michael Eisner's competitive spirit, under the leadership of Bob Weis, Tom Fitzgerald, Eric Jacobson, and of course Marty, Imagineering jumped at the chance to get to work creating more attractions to expand the park, offer more variety, and extend the guest experience. Taking into consideration that most of its opening day studio-themed attractions were designed to be long-duration experiences, such as the Backstage Studio Tour featuring Catastrophe Canyon (tram tour) and Inside the Magic—Special Effects and Production Tour (walking tour), our mission was to come up with shorter-length shows and attractions to add to the park menu. We called this next-phase effort the "Studios Expansion"; it went into full swing in 1990 and continued throughout the busy decade. As a sidenote, Disneyland Paris, the second Disney theme park and resort to be built outside of the United States, was under construction as well at that time, so Imagineering had a lot going on.

The first thing out of the chute for the Studios Expansion project was Muppet*Vision 3-D. As opposed to a ride-through attraction that requires a lot of development time for sophisticated ride-and-show systems, a film-based show presented in a theatrical venue could be delivered more quickly. In addition to continuing to brainstorm ride-based attractions, we joined forces with Jim Henson and Jim Henson Associates as they were called then to help us develop a 3-D experience featuring the highly entertaining and beloved Muppets. Gratuitous 3-D gags and Muppets—it's the perfect combination! Michael

Sprout and I were invited to participate with Jim Henson and key members of his team, including writer Bill Prady (who later became co-creator and executive producer of The Big Bang Theory), to develop the story and related gags for the attraction. Although I added some bits that made it into the show, including Miss Piggy as the Statue of Liberty, I received more from those story sessions with the good Henson folks than I contributed because I spent most of the time closely observing them, their creative development process, and especially Jim Henson himself. Jim was blessed with a gentle and honest spirit, and if he didn't like your suggestion or idea, he let you know it in a way that didn't hurt your feelings or embarrass you in front of others. In fact, he had this uncanny way of letting you down that at the same time lifted you up.

One of my Imagineering colleagues, another wise and gentle character, the late, great John Kavelin, used to call that sensitive method of disagreement or course correction "The Oreo Cookie." If you want to draw someone's attention to something they are saying or doing wrong, or that you don't agree with, you begin by saying something nice and complimentary to them or about them related to the topic at hand, then slather 'em with the stuff in the middle to make your point, and finally bookend it by saying something nice to them (or about them) again, all in truth and with sincere care and respect. But even Jim Henson's "stuff in the middle" was filled with nothing but goodness and somehow, he still made his point with gentle persuasion.

I learned a lot in my short but valuable time with Jim about how to inspire, respect, and get the most out of creative people; and I continue in my role as a creative leader today to be guided by his indelible example and wisdom. Before Muppet*Vision 3-D was filmed, the world lost this gentle genius, who demonstrated on TV and in the conference room at Imagineering that there was far greater power and influence in being a kind and respectful leader than in the oppressive opposite, which oftentimes rears its ugly head out of insecurity.

My mentor and friend, the man who brought me into the creative division, vice president of creative development and show writing, Randy Bright, was a lot like Jim Henson in that regard. Randy was a passionate showman who led with contagious enthusiasm and vision. In a terrible turn of events, we lost Randy to a bicycle accident only two weeks after Jim Henson's passing. That really hit me hard.

Shortly before the accident I was at the Disney Studio meeting with Michael Eisner and a small group in the conference room next to his office. Michael was called out of our meeting to take an important call, and when he returned he told us the caller was Michael Jackson. Michael J called Michael E to tell him he had been invited to be part of the upcoming grand opening event for Universal Studios in Orlando, and didn't know what to do, especially since he had such a strong allegiance to Disney and a great love for the Disney parks. He was really stressed out about it. Michael E thanked Michael J and essentially told him he would honor and respect whatever he chose to do. Randy Bright's funeral service, which Michael Eisner attended, was held a few days before the grand opening of Universal Studios in Orlando. After the service, a group of us went to Randy's favorite roadside burger stand, in rural Yorba Linda, California, to honor his memory. As we were about to raise a toast in the restaurant's patio, we were interrupted by a TV broadcast of a special report: Michael Jackson had been admitted to St. John's Hospital in Santa Monica complaining of chest pains. I didn't want to assume, but knowing what I knew it seemed to me the "King of Pop" was "calling in sick" to Universal's grand opening!

I'll always consider that brief but profoundly influential and inspiring time spent with showmen Jim Henson and Randy Bright—at the most delicate and formative period of my professional career—one of Imagineering's great gifts to me. But the greatest gift Imagineering ever gave to me was the rare opportunity to dream up, pitch, and sell ideas for new attractions when it was time for those dreams to come true. The early nineties were a great time to plant seeds for new ideas because the need to grow the Disney-MGM Studios provided us with fertile ground. The first major ride-through attraction story and name I ever "planted," pitched, and sold, The Twilight Zone Tower of Terror, was born out of a request by our management to add some thrill to the park. In this particular case, the idea for the type of ride came before the story and it also came before my involvement. The original concept team's mission was to explore the creation or adaption of some sort of free-falling ride system. Then they let the story "fall" out of that. But it fell a little short.

Although I was in the room to present another idea altogether, I was not part of the team that developed and pitched a "Haunted Hotel" concept to Michael Eisner and Frank Wells in which a murder mysteriously occurred in the basement swimming pool, causing the elevator to begin to operate in a strange manner. But there was no explanation or solid connection between the murder, the pool, and the elevator. The hotel manager was the number one suspect among those present in the hotel at the time of the murder. The complicated story, which tried desperately to shoehorn in the desired free fall experience, seemed to take its cue from the board game Clue. After taking our top execs through the long attraction story, the team suggested that the legendary horror movie actor, Vincent Price, play the role of the hotel manager. "Vincent Price?" questioned Michael Eisner with a twisted expression on his face. "Frank," he asked Frank Wells, "is Vincent Price still relevant to today's audience?" Frank answered, "Well, he certainly had his day, but he hasn't done anything in a long while." Michael continued, "Well, it doesn't really matter anyway because, I'm sorry guys, it's not all that compelling, and I don't get the story." Michael's putting the kibosh on the idea disappointed the concept team and left a sour vibe in the room. And I was up next. Mind you, this was during a time when you could walk into a conference room and pitch your idea for a new attraction to Michael and Frank knowing full well you could walk out of the room with a green light. Or not.

My show producer, Cory Sewelson, helped me hang our storyboards, and I started pitching the idea for a large theatrical presentation on the same scale and complexity of The American Adventure called The Creature's Choice Awards Show. To start the pitch, I tossed out this one-liner: "This show is the equivalent of the Academy Awards but for movie monsters, including tonight's Lifetime Achievement Award honoree, the biggest star in the genre, Godzilla." At that Michael burst out laughing and exclaimed, "Home run!" There's nothing better than already having the boss on board before you even pitch the show, which I did starting with the lobby preshow. In the lobby, guests would stand beside a snack bar featuring such monster munchies as "Buttered Fingers." Four Egyptian sarcophagi were prominently staged in the four dark cobwebbed corners of the lobby, and the preshow began when their ancient lids creaked open to unleash the doo-wop harmonies of the singing group known as the Sarcopha Guys. (If I were pitching this show today those musical mummies would probably be "wrap" artists.)

After their song, done in four-part disharmony, which I wrote as the setup to the show, the theater doors would open and guests would enter to enjoy a seventeen-minute multimedia and special effects extravaganza in which famous movie monsters would step up, fly up, or crawl up to receive their "Screamy Award." Of course, all kinds of things would go terribly wrong in a funny, surprising, and sometimes epic way throughout the show, given the nature of the award recipients. For example, in the "Best Aliens from Outer Space" category, Martians laser-blasted their way into the theater and landed on the stage in their flying saucer to accept their award. Throughout the show shots from a "live" camera would update the audience as to the progress and whereabouts of Godzilla, who was on his way to the theater from Tokyo. When the big star finally arrived in the finale he would literally bring down the house!

The show was weird, way too big in scale and scope, and seemed impossible to do; and that's what Michael loved about it. But Frank sensed it would be over-the-top expensive and we had other attractions being developed at the same time, all drawing from the same bucket of money. Still, Michael was

Lifetime Achievement Award winner, Godzilla, stomping through Walt Disney World on his way to the Creature's Choice Awards. When he arrives, he brings down the house. No, really, he does.

interested in the show, so he asked that we further design and develop it to the point we could better define its actual scope. "Then," said Frank, "we'll check in again and see where we are."

To begin our research for Creature's Choice, Cory and I hopped on a plane for New York City because, as fate would have it, there was a "Weekend of Horrors" convention, sponsored by *Fangoria* magazine, happening in town. Now I must admit horror magazines and movies are not my cup of tea. (Nor are bugs, roller coasters, or falling from high places, but that never stopped me from helping create and deliver attractions that featured all of those things.) While on the plane to NYC, I recognized a famous singer sitting in front of Cory and me. I couldn't remember her name and I didn't ask Cory because, being in the industry, I was too embarrassed to admit I didn't know a celeb's name. Not being able to come up with it was driving me nuts the entire flight. When we arrived at the gate and were given the signal to unfasten our seat belts, I stood up in the aisle at the same time she did. While grabbing mine and Cory's bags in the overhead compartment, I shot Cory a terse question. Unfortunately, I asked it at the moment I was face-to-face and locking eyes with the celebrity: "Ready?" That was it! Helen *Reddy*.

The next morning Cory and I were standing in a line that wrapped around a long city block waiting to get into the convention. In front of us and behind us were hundreds of growling, grunting ghouls and zombies; there were also guys with chain saws stuck in their bloody heads, women with their fake guts oozing out, all kinds of creepy clowns, and even a few Freddy Kruegers tossed in for bad measure. It was a costume and makeup horror fest for the freakish fans waiting to get in. Cory and I were dressed as our usual everyday business casual, clean-cut selves and stood out in this brawly bunch like Herman Munster's normal-looking niece, Marilyn. An elderly couple strolled down the sidewalk towards us, cautiously steering clear of all the creeps. When they reached us, the nice little old lady stepped over to us, drew us into a private huddle, and whispered, "What are you fellows in line for?" I told her we were there for a Helen Reddy concert, waiting with her biggest fans. But then I told her the truth. At that, the couple jaywalked through traffic to the other side of the street. "Huh," said Cory. "There are hundreds of people in line. Why do you suppose they asked *us*?"

As Creature's Choice evolved over the next few months, we met with all kinds of horror movie experts and celebrities, including Cassandra Peterson, aka Elvira, Mistress of the Dark. Although, as mentioned, horror is not my genre, I did love watching *Elvira's Movie Macabre* on TV because her late-night program featured the best of the worst cheesy B-grade horror flicks, the ones that were so bad they were good. During her show, in which the comedy far outweighed the creepy, she would interrupt the movie and play back certain scenes and comment about them. Sometimes she was interrupted herself by a phone call from a character named "The Breather," who would tell her weird jokes. Talking about weird, "The Breather" was played by John Paragon, an actor and writer who later became an Imagineer and friend!

Cassandra Peterson is gorgeous and hilarious, and I was big fan of hers. So, it was a real treat to meet with her about our show. Naturally, I wanted to feature an Audio-Animatronics figure of Elvira in Creature's Choice. Who wouldn't?

As we started to cast other actors for the show, Jeffrey Katzenberg, who was making big deals with movie stars at that time, suggested to me that Eddie Murphy play the part of our Audio-Animatronics Frankenstein-like monster host. Eddie's participation in our show would be part of the bigger movie deal Jeffrey had in mind. In fact he had already set up a time for me to pitch the show to Eddie the following week, so I had to quickly rewrite the part of the "Monster Host" to be Eddie Frankenmurphy. Jeffrey, Eddie, his wife, and two Godzilla-sized bodyguards met me in a conference room in our bowling alley building. I've done a bunch of them, but this was one of the most memorable presentations I've ever done at Imagineering. The pitch began with me doing an imitation of Eddie Murphy to Eddie Murphy performing as Eddie Frankenmurphy doing an imitation of James Brown singing "I Got You (I Feel Good)" as the show opener.

Creature's Choice Awards Show presenter, Elvira, about to get laser blasted by Martians in a flying saucer.

"APPLAUSE" SIGN. CURTAIN OPENS ON ELVIRA. ORCHESTRA PLAYS A
SEXY "BLUES IN THE NIGHT". SHE IS HOLDING AN AWARD WHILE
RECLINING SENSUOUSLY ON HER VELVET BOUDOIR SETTEE. THE
CREATURES IN THE AUDIENCE GO CRAZY WITH SCREAMS AND CAT
CALLS.

                    ELVIRA
          Oh, stop! I swear, you're all
          such monsters! Now bend an ear,
          my darlings, the nominees for
          Best Alien Invader are: The
          Invaders from Mars...

                    EDDIE FRANKENMURPHY
          Agents. What are you gonna do?
          And now to present the Award for
          the Best Alien Invader is my
          favorite mistress of the dark,
          the lovliest creature known to
          creaturedom - Elvira!
               (smoke pours out of
                Eddie's ears)

Creature's Choice Awards Show host, Eddie Frankenmurphy, as depicted in a storyboard panel. A real cut-up, he was going to keep everyone in stitches.

Can you imagine? As I was performing, Eddie's bodyguards up and left the room because they were laughing so hard—at me, not with me, I'm sure. But Eddie was totally on board with the show. After the pitch, Jeffrey invited me to join them for the dinner he had catered in the bowling alley. Listening to Eddie and Jeffrey converse about the industry and life was both fascinating and a ton of fun. Eddie: "So Jeffrey, how are your babies?" Jeffrey: "When I went in to tuck them in last night they started crying." Eddie: "Can you blame them?" Afterwards we went into the actual bowling alley part of the building and bowled a few games. I mean, who gets to do this stuff?

On that subject, it was great fun in those days to be privy to the private conversations and discussions that occurred behind closed doors—with me actually being on this side of the closed door—between the top three leaders of The Walt Disney Company: Jeffrey Katzenberg, Michael Eisner, and Frank Wells. I really did like the three of them very much, but whenever I was with them for a meeting or presentation, I'd wonder what in the world was I doing there. (I wonder that even today whenever I'm with Bob Iger.) When I was a dishwasher at Disneyland, I was in awe of the supervisors at the Plaza Inn. Now here I was actually hanging out and working with the top leaders of the entire company. How the heck did that happen? My journey had taken me from the dish room to the boardroom, so to speak, and because I never felt worthy or talented enough to deserve to be there, it was a humbling experience, and still is, each and every time.

Soon after he began to come to Imagineering, Jeffrey suggested bringing over some screenwriters from the studio to contribute to our projects. But his grand experiment didn't work. It's not that they weren't exceptionally talented writers; it's just that they didn't understand the real-world limitations, operational mathematics, and practicalities of our dimensional form of entertainment, the type that takes years to understand and master. You can write a scene in which anything can happen in the movies, but trying to write a scene in which anything can happen in a brick-and-mortar attraction, and happen every few minutes all day every day for years and years, is quite another story. Case in point: at the end of the experiment one of the studio writers pitched his "test challenge" to us, which was to write something new to add to The American Adventure. "And then," he pitched dramatically with arm extended, palm up, "the mighty eagle spreads his powerful but graceful wings, swoops down closely over the heads of the audience, and then, with a piercing cry, disappears high into the sky." Well, that's all well and good, I thought, but how does the eagle do all that? Is it attached or tethered to some kind of suspended rolling show-controlled mechanism? Would there be a track opening that is visible in the ceiling, which would be bad because guests would be looking up and therefore notice it? Does the crying bird have a built-in speaker or an overhead line-array of speakers? Is the bird hydraulic or electric? How does it reset for the next show cycle? If it breaks down and stops flying halfway across the audience space would the show go "101" (shut down)?

All of the other outside writer presentations went to the same place—doable in the movies but in our shows and attractions, not so much. It's really hard to do what Imagineers do. But we wouldn't have it any other way. Something good did come out of that exercise, though. It helped Jeffrey better comprehend what Imagineers understand about writing and designing to impossible parameters and physical challenges, and it gave him a whole new appreciation for the type of unusual, problem-solving thinking we must do to do what we do. I'll tell you what we *don't* do: we don't write and design for one movie shot. We write and design for the long haul.

The Creature's Choice Awards Show was coming along nicely, but it wasn't a white-knuckle thrill attraction, at least not in the visceral sense. With everything else going on, I couldn't stop thinking about the elevator idea that got the shaft. There was something there. But what was it? Several weeks had gone by since the pitch to Michael and Frank about the murder in the basement pool, which they pulled the plug on. One day I was leaning in a chair against the wall directly across the desk from designer Steve Kirk, whose upstairs office was on the 1401 Flower Street window side, two doors down from John Hench's (and the same office I'd later move into and reside in for more than ten years). Steve was working on other aspects of the Studios Expansion. I was silently thinking and Steve was silently sketching, but what, I don't know. I broke the silence by bringing up the hotel thing that was nagging me to no end. "Too bad that hotel story got stuck in the basement." Steve nodded in agreement and asked, "So what could the story be?" Of course, that's always the question. "Maybe," I suggested, "we zoom out and think about how it would best fit into the story of the park. The park is about movies and television. Let's think about movies with haunted stuff." Steve offered, "Something like *House on Haunted Hill*. But we turn it into *Hotel on Haunted Hill*."

"But that movie starred Vincent Price," I reminded him. "And we know where that went." We discussed many movies, but none of them sparked anything. "What if," I asked, "it's inspired by a creepy TV show like *Outer Limits* or *Twilight Zone*? I love *The Twilight Zone*!" I had Steve's rapt attention so I kept going with that. "What if our guests get to star in their own episode of *The Twilight Zone* in a story we totally make up? It would be exclusive to that park. And somehow, we connect it to Hollywood, so it also complements the park. Isn't there a Hollywood Tower Hotel?" Steve affirmed there was. It was starting to get juicy. "What if it's The Twilight Zone Tower Hotel?" I suggested. Then suddenly, BING, there it was. "No, wait," I suggested, "what if it's . . . The Twilight Zone Tower of Terror!" Saying it for the first time sounded right and felt right. "By Jove," said Steve, "I think you've got it."

Charged with adrenaline, I dashed out of Steve's office and jumped in front of my computer to start working on the story treatment, which evolved into the very attraction you can experience at Disney's Hollywood Studios in Florida today (it's the only one of the multiple versions in which the elevator car exits the vertical shaft to travel horizontally prior to its thrilling drop, which was one of its selling points. And there isn't a raccoon anywhere in sight). Here's my first-pass treatment from 1990:

> Witness if you will a Hollywood Tower Hotel that stretches up toward the vastness of space, through the void that is the sky, beyond the limits of your imagination. For the tower is host to a most uncommon pair of service elevators, just as the hotel is host to a most uncommon pair of residents: Science Fiction and the Fantasy of Terror. It has been said that science fiction is the improbable made possible and fantasy is the impossible made probable. If you should dare check into this hotel, you may find yourself impossibly lost within the hidden corridors of the improbable. Lost inside a dimension between light and shadow, between science and the supernatural, between the pit of man's fears and the summit of his knowledge. But don't worry. There is an escape. Simply step into one of the elevators and press the button on the panel marked "13th Floor." This button is easy to find. It is the only one. Next stop . . . *The Twilight Zone.*

Yikes! Digging out and reading this treatment almost thirty years later makes me want to do another take and polish it up! Although it captured the *spirit*, it didn't really commit to actual story beats. Following this somewhat vague treatment, Michael Sprout and I got down to the business of doing the hard work of figuring out the story sequence and actual experience in detail, and how exactly it connects to the elevator drop. After landing on the story that's still there today, I wrote the first-pass preshow and ride scripts and then pitched the attraction experience and name to Bob Weis, Tom Fitz, and Marty Sklar. Marty gave the go-ahead to develop concept art and storyboards so I could get it in front of Michael and Frank. I should have been scared to death to present another take on the hotel idea Michael had nixed, but my confidence in and excitement for this solid new story far outweighed my fear. When the time came for the big pitch, I set up the concept art and boards in the bowling alley building's conference room and was joined by Bob, Tom, and Marty. Michael and Frank entered—and it was time to drop the one-line description on them. Only this time, I thought I'd take a chance and begin by simply saying the attraction name instead.

"So, what are we seeing today?" Michael asked. I responded with a playful hint of foreboding in my voice, "The Twilight Zone Tower of Terror. *Mwaaa ha ha ha haaa!*" I had the legendary TV show's musical theme cued up on my cassette player and pushed PLAY. Michael smiled and over the continuing iconic theme said, "I love the name and the alliteration," he said. "What's it all about?" This is exactly the way I *love* to start a pitch. Supported by the new storyboard art, I took Michael and Frank, as if they were walking through the front door of the hotel, through the attraction experience, from the preshow TV in the library on which Rod Serling sets up the story of that fateful night long ago, to the ride experience in which guests become "lost in the story" themselves. Michael and Frank were totally on board that elevator, especially when I pitched that it "breaks free" of the vertical shaft only to travel horizontally across the floor into the . . . BUM BUM BUM . . . *Twilight Zone.* "Did you hear that, Frank? The elevator leaves the shaft. No one will expect that. This is really great. Home run!"

Michael and Frank had a conversation after the pitch. Michael: "Frank, do you think *The Twilight Zone* is still relevant?" Frank: "Are you kidding, Michael? It's iconic. It's timeless. They still have *Twilight Zone* marathons. Yes, of course, it's relevant. Everyone knows and loves *The Twilight Zone.* It's an American institution!" Michael: "Should we do this?" Frank: "All it takes is money." Michael: "Then let's do this!" Michael and Frank thanked us and left the room as calm and collected as if they had just purchased a vacuum cleaner. It was just another day for them at Imagineering (notice I didn't say "typical" day). But this was a huge moment for me, so I reacted quite differently. I wanted to jump up and down and hoot and holler, but Marty was staring at me. Since this was my first major E-Ticket-level ride-based attraction pitch to Michael and Frank, and they went for it, it all seemed like a dream. Needing validation, I asked Marty, "What exactly did Michael mean when he said, 'Let's do this'?" Marty chuckled. "What do you mean what did he mean? We're doing this." I still couldn't believe it. "So, we are actually going to do this attraction? As in *build it*? As in . . . so people can *ride it*?" "Yes," Marty said emphatically, "as in build it so people can ride it. What are you waiting for? Get going!"

Actually, I couldn't wait to get going. We immediately started planning research trips to explore and experience all the ways you can drop. Our first step was to experience a free fall–type attraction. I warned my fellow free-fallers—Steve Kirk, artist David Duran, and Michael Sprout—that I wasn't going to be a very good faller. I knew I had to do it, but I didn't want to do it. I was terrified waiting in line with my colleagues watching that ride vehicle drop over and over again with screaming people inside; one of them was about to be me. Our time came to board, and as I was about to chicken out the guys dragged me on. And before I knew it, the shoulder harness was on—and had me trapped. Up we went and down we went, and I can guarantee mine were the loudest screams heard that day.

I like to think my fears make me a better designer because I don't take any thrill, spill, or chill for granted. In fact, I don't take them at all if I can help it. When the ride was over, I jumped out of the vehicle faster than I traveled in it. After we regrouped, Steve asked Michael to share what the experience felt like to him. "That's easy," Michael responded. "It felt like I was attending mass." "Mass?" Steve questioned. "Why mass?" Michael answered, "Because all the way up to the top Kevin kept whispering, 'Jesus, Mary, and Joseph! Jesus, Mary, and Joseph!'"

This rare moment (of me on a thrill ride) was captured after falling quickly straight down. From left to right, Steve Kirk, me, Michael Sprout, and David Duran. Afterward Michael said riding it felt like attending mass all the way up because I kept screaming, "Jesus, Mary, and Joseph!!"

The next thing we did was arrange to meet an executive from the Otis Elevator Company, who agreed to host us in one of their state-of-the-art elevator cars that had recently been installed in a new fifty-story building in Los Angeles. We met him in the ground floor lobby and he invited us to step into the new elevator. After pushing the button to take us to the top, he spoke into his walkie-talkie to a technician who was standing by somewhere, awaiting instructions. Per our request, the instructions given were to crank up the machinery to send us down the shaft at the fastest possible speed. "Ready?" the Otis exec asked. Given my fear of falling and not knowing what to expect, I braced myself in the corner as best I could like some kind of elevator car contortionist with suction cups on his shoes. "Okay, I'm ready," I said. The exec let out a big laugh. "We're almost back down on the ground!" Before I could respond to that, I heard the "ding" signaling we had arrived on the ground floor. We didn't feel a thing. It was as if we hadn't moved at all. "Was that the fastest it would go?" Steve asked. "That was the fastest," the exec proudly responded. "But," Steve continued, "we didn't feel any sense of dropping." I added, "Not even the tiniest of tummy tingles." The exec looked surprised. "Oh, you wanted to *feel* the drop?" he asked, realizing what our objective was. "We've been working for over a hundred years to perfect our systems so you don't feel anything!" We realized the only way we were going to get the drop effect on this thing was to challenge our ride engineers to "rise" (and fall) to the occasion. And they most certainly did!

In the meantime, while the Creature's Choice Awards Show attraction was continuing to evolve, I found myself on the early development teams for four more projects proposed for the Studios Expansion: Dick Tracy's Crimestoppers, Baby Herman's Runaway Baby Buggy Ride, Roller Coaster Rabbit, and a simulator-based attraction I'd devised called Toontown Transit. The last three attraction ideas mentioned were intended to be part of a new land extension called Cartoon Studios. Working on six attraction concepts simultaneously was quite daunting. There wasn't a minute in the day in those days to stop and take a breath because each one of those six concepts, which each deserved full-time focus, also seemed to have their concept-development meetings at the same times. The good news is the story and vision for The Twilight Zone Tower of Terror was established, approved, and heading into the production phase. So, even though I love to take an attraction all the way through to opening day, I chose to step away from Tower so I could spend more time on the Creature's Choice Awards Show, which needed further development. (Okay, so the truth is I stepped away from Tower so I wouldn't have to ride it a lot!) Besides, I was certain Creatures would progress into production and it would be more than enough work to bring that monster home.

But I was wrong. The show ended up being so big and sophisticated—with all of its show-action equipment and large cast of Audio-Animatronics characters—that its estimated cost ultimately was even more frightening than its cast. It came down to a corporate choice between Tower and Creatures. The park needed more rides, not shows, so the choice was clear. The good news is I was able to clear my plate even more and focus on the development of only four remaining proposed new attractions.

One was tied to *Dick Tracy*, the 1990 Touchstone Pictures film starring Warren Beatty. It opened to mixed reviews but was a hit at the box office. Picking up seven Academy Award nominations, the movie won in three categories, including Best Art Direction thanks to its bold and colorful comic book look. The whole thing seemed like a fun fit for a Disney attraction, so the idea for Dick Tracy's Crimestoppers was born. The concept was way ahead of its time because it married interactivity and targeting with a thrilling and unpredictable ride system. Designed to look like 1930s-style gangster cars, the ride vehicles had toylike tommy guns mounted to the passenger windows. Essentially, it was a rolling shooting gallery. It's important to note that the targets were not bad guys or good guys; the targets were only visible on inanimate objects such as crates, barrels, flowerpots, and other things that would react and animate with a shooting gallery–like gag when hit and then add points to the guest's onboard score counter. As you can imagine, the facility required to house such an attraction was massive, because several cars driving around town take up a lot of real estate. And the nighttime cityscape sets were enormous.

The whole thing seemed way too big and impossible, but I learned that was the kind of stuff Michael Eisner loved. I couldn't wait to pitch this idea to him and Frank Wells. That is, until I was warned by several colleagues that they had heard Michael hated guns. "Good luck pitching that one, Kev," they'd say. The concept art was great, the storyboards were great, and the experience seemed like it would be tons of fun. But there were those tommy guns. As pitch day drew near, I started to panic. I had a pretty good track record with Michael and Frank so far. Would the idea to use tommy guns be the thing that shot down my career? Meanwhile, the warnings kept coming. "Man, you are crazy to be pitching guns to Michael," one would say. Or from another, "Hey, Kev, I heard you're pitching *Dick Tracy* to Michael tomorrow. ARE YOU CRAZY?" I tossed and turned the night before worrying about Michael's reaction to this pitch. In fact, when I finally did get to sleep, I had a vivid dream that Michael was dressed like Dick Tracy and he and Madonna were tossing my guns into the river and me into the hoosegow (certainly better than the other way around).

My pitch was scheduled for 5:00 p.m., so I had all day to worry. When the time came, I carefully set up the idea for the attraction: its giant scale, its gangster-car ride vehicles, the thrill of the chase around city corners. And before I revealed the gimbaled gun, I told him guests would be given the opportunity to interact with the experience. "Really?" he asked with great interest. "How?" I balked. "Ha-how? Well, uhhh . . ." Up to that point I had the concept art covered with black cloth. But it was time to do or die, so I uncovered the art of the tommy gun mounted to the windows of the car and continued, "It's . . . it's—" Michael completed the statement for me. "A GUN?" I jumped right in to defend the premise. "But it's a fun gun," I argued. "I mean, it's very toylike and it doesn't hurt anyone because—" Michael interrupted. "Did you hear that, Frank?" Frank nodded and Michael continued. "Did you hear that? He's talking about a . . . gun!" This, I thought, is the moment my luck runs out. It was do-or-die time, and I guess I'm dead. Michael looked straight at me with wide, crazy, piercing eyes. "This," he said, "is FANTASTIC!"

We immediately went to work, creating a full-sized mock-up of some of the street scenes, art directed to look like they did in the movie, in a giant warehouse space in North Hollywood. We also purchased a 1931 sedan to serve, or in this case, swerve (as in around corners), as a stand-in for our proposed ride vehicle. Concept engineer and all-around brilliant crazy guy Chris Brown fixed up the car for maximum speed, installed safety belts, and designated himself as stunt driver for our upcoming proof-of-concept ride-through with Michael Eisner.

The mock-up turned out to be spectacular in a jaw-dropping way. It was beautifully staged, scenically painted, propped-out, and theatrically lit as if it were a real section of the proposed attraction. When Michael showed up all by himself, we had the gangster car positioned and ready to go. I don't think he expected this mock-up to be so impressive. Driver Chris even dressed the part in pin-striped suit and fedora. Michael happily hopped into the back seat, and I slid in next to him. We had Imagineers dressed like characters from the movie waiting in strategic locations on the set to shout out lines from my attraction script, and we had crates, barrels, trash cans, and other animated props with visible targets ready to react to our mock "shooting." After Chris made sure our seat belts were fastened good and tight, he fired up the old car, jammed it into gear, and hit the gas pedal, squealing the rear tires and sending us fishtailing forward on the slippery warehouse floor into the show. At the first intersection of the city block, a staged obstacle forced Chris to swerve wide around the corner causing Michael's side of the car to slide and slam into a stack of crates and me to slam into Michael. Chris, who in his personal life is a thrill seeker—the kind of guy that bungee jumps off bridges and takes on the most dangerous type of white-water rapids—was in his element. He floored it and skidded around the

Artist Benn Tripp's take on Chris Brown (top), me (middle), and Cory Sewelson during a Creature's Choice team meeting. I like to believe that's why all three of us usually happy-go-lucky Imagineers look so scary!

next corner, slamming us into a stack of barrels and slamming Michael into me this time.

If the mock-up is this much fun, I thought, the real deal is going to be phenomenal. But even though Michael loved it—we all did—alas, Dick Tracy's Crimestoppers went the way of Creature's Choice. Requiring a show-controlled facility big enough to house a city, the attraction ended up being just too huge and expensive to justify. I totally understood why it got shot down.

This decision whittled my project list down to three still in the running for the Studios Expansion. The proposed new Cartoon Studios, inspired by the movie *Who Framed Roger Rabbit*, featured three new attractions: two smaller Roger Rabbit–themed rides and one major new ride I proposed inspired by the cartoon world depicted in the movie but not related to it, so definitely not a "book report." The first, Baby Herman's Runaway Baby Buggy Ride, was a Mr. Toad–like dark ride romp in a baby-buggy vehicle that's broken away and is being chased by a mad maternity nurse through the unpredictable corridors of a cartoon hospital. The second, Roller Coaster Rabbit, inspired by the 1990 short film by the same name, was an indoor/outdoor gravity coaster (as its name implies), but with a few wackier-than-normal twists and turns. And the third, the anchor attraction for the land, had a fresh new story but no known technology to support it. I'll tell the story of that story in its own chapter because it was one of my favorite attraction concepts that didn't happen. And afterwards I'll tell you what happened as a result of it not happening.

YOU CAN'T ALWAYS GET WHAT YOU WANT

TOONTOWN TRANSIT, the anchor attraction for the proposed Cartoon Studios land at Disney-MGM Studios, was based on a story I cooked up about a Hollywood city bus named Gus who really wants to be a movie star. Designing Gus to be able to take guests on a wacky and unpredictable ride through the animated world of Toontown, we planned to mount him on a motion-base simulator and marry him to a yet-to-be-invented wraparound projection technology that would provide an out-of-your-peripheral view through all of his side and front windows. This was all totally made up and unproven stuff and it sounded impossible to do—even in theory. But we kept going. I always loved this attraction concept, so whenever I'd occasionally reorganize or move my office over the years, which usually meant getting rid of copies of concept art and treatments that continued to stack up, I could never part with my Toontown Transit binder dated April 1991.

Here's the original treatment:

Gus the Bus works for the Toontown Transit Line. It pays the bills but Gus's true ambition is to be a movie star, much to the chagrin of his boss who tells him to stop dreaming and start driving! Gus drives us through the Toontown Tunnel on his regular route where on the other side we are greeted by singing flowers and trees and many other cartoon characters that have gathered to welcome us. Suddenly, Benny the Cab cuts Gus off to inform him that auditions are being held at the Cartoon Studios right now. This could be the big chance Gus has been waiting for! Benny tells Gus to follow him because he knows a shortcut. He floors it and we follow Benny, speeding over the cartoon countryside and around high and perilous mountain curves.

Gus can't keep up with Benny and skids off the road, and we splash down into the Toon River. After taking a wild white-knuckle, white-water ride on the rapids, we are caught in a whirlpool and pulled underwater. After the bubbles clear we find ourselves inside Monstro the whale with Pinocchio. Monstro sneezes, sending us high into the sky, and we crash-land back on the road directly behind Benny as if we had never left! The roller coaster-like road filled with lots of twists, turns, and surprising gags takes us on a rollicking route that leads us into the heart of downtown Toontown.

Turning the wrong way on a one-way street, Gus drives directly toward two big trucks, approaching side-by-side. Benny is able to get through the middle of them but Gus is too wide to drive in between. He holds his breath and makes himself thinner at the last minute and

The first "grab 'em" image on the storyboard for Toontown Transit.

Here's a view from inside aspiring actor Gus the Bus in this early-concept art for Toontown Transit.

we manage to squeeze through the middle of the trucks. But we come out the other side only to see a long fire truck speeding towards us with Roger Rabbit clinging to the end of its ladder. To avoid a head-on collision, Benny scissor-lifts over the fire truck and Gus follows his lead. But Gus doesn't quite lift high enough and we snag Roger from the ladder, causing him to crash-land on Gus's roof (we see Roger's physical imprint protrude through Gus's interior). Roger jumps onto Gus's hood (as we see through the windshield) and begs Gus to p-p-p-please help him save Jessica from the top of the burning fireworks factory straight ahead.

Gus gallantly accelerates up a ladder to the top of the burning factory, avoiding wayward exploding fireworks all the way up. We crash though an upper-story window where Gus steers to help Roger, still holding on to his hood, reach out and save Jessica from the flames. But as Roger grabs her, Gus can't stop in time and pushes them both out the window. Finally coming to a stop on the window ledge, Gus teeters downwards to reveal a view to the ground far below where we see that Roger and Jessica have been safely caught in the fire department net. Just as we are about to go over the ledge ourselves, one of the wayward skyrockets crashes through Gus's dashboard (physical animated prop) and lodges itself in the floor directly in front of us. We watch helplessly as the fuse burns down.

KA-BLOOIE! The explosion sends us flying up above the clouds into outer space, where, reaching the apex of our ascent, we happen upon a confused cow that says, "A bus? Up here?!" We nose downward for a view of Earth below. Rapidly falling towards earth, we can see we are approaching the United States, then Hollywood, and finally the Cartoon Studios. Gus crashes through the roof of the very soundstage where it so happens the auditions are being held. And cut! What an entrance! What a talent! The director loves Gus, begs him to star in his next picture, and offers him a movie contract on the spot. It was a tough road to stardom, but Gus's dream has come true!

Our core concept team for Toontown Transit included designer Greg Wilzbach, concept artist Scott Sinclair, producer Janny Mulholland, and me. As we had to invent a bold and risky new projection system that included a bus-sized seamless wraparound screen, we contracted a visual effects company we found in New York that was earning awards and quite a reputation for developing innovative new show technologies for movies, concerts, and theater. For example, they helped pull off the animation and visual effects for Audrey II in the movie *Little Shop of Horrors*. They also dabbled in developing supersecret, high-tech military stuff for the government (which makes me think that if our country ever gets into trouble man-eating plants will suddenly appear and chomp up to our rescue).

This unique company, Associates & Ferren, was led by a risk-taking, technotheatrical filmmaker, photographer, madman/scientist inventor, and visionary named Bran Ferren. Bran is a lovable and charismatic character, a jolly Santa-like man with a Santa-like beard; only Bran's beard is bright red, looking like Santa's would should he ever wash his white beard in hot water with his Santa suit. But unlike his famous red-suited cousin from the North Pole, Bran is from the Northeast, so his suit is khaki pants, khaki utility vest, black polo shirt, and black Nike shoes. That's what he wore every single day with no exception; well, except for that one time he and I were minutes away from pitching Test Track to some GM executives who were visiting Epcot and he showed up in his usual outfit but with the addition of a too-short bright red tie hanging from the never-before-buttoned collar of his black polo shirt. "So," he said pointing to his tie, "what do you think?" I answered truthfully, "It's not you." At that he yanked off the tie, which was easy to do because it was a clip-on, and tossed it into the trash can. After our presentation to the GM execs that day, we walked them backstage and bid them farewell, and Bran and I hopped into his rental car, which was a Lincoln Continental, a product of the Ford Motor Company.

Arriving at that realization I slumped down into the seat so I wouldn't be visible to the GM executive entourage and mentioned this embarrassing over-sight to Bran. His excuse was putting on a tie for the first time threw off all of his power to reason. A couple of weeks later, when I shared that story with Disney president Frank Wells, Frank told me that when he recently traveled to Detroit to meet with GM, he pulled in front of their company headquar-ters building in a Lincoln limo. Suddenly realizing this faux pas, he grabbed the phone to call his support person to ask that she exchange the Ford product with a GM ASAP. But this is how good she was—before Frank made the call, she had already double-checked to see what brand of car was sent to pick him up and quickly arranged the swap! A big black Cadillac pulled alongside the Lincoln close enough for him to make the stealth slide across.

That reminds me. One day while at the studio in a meeting with Frank and Michael Eisner, Frank mentioned he had to catch a plane because he was conducting some important business with a major American company that will go unnamed. "Frank," asked Michael, "when you go to those places do you talk with the top people?" "No, Michael," Frank responded facetiously, "I talk to the first schmuck that pops out into the hallway. Of course I talk to the top people!" I loved that man.

Bran's small but mighty company was located in East Hampton, New York, where he also has a humongous house in the woods that he claims is not a house at all but rather a five-thousand-square-foot addition to his mother's tiny house in the woods. When you walk in the front door you'll see a portrait of his father drawn by his father's onetime roommate: Picasso! Bran had more surprises up his sleeve than he had pockets on his vest, and he was, more than anyone else I've ever known, the personification of the advice my dad was famous for imparting to me: "Son," he would say, "if you can't dazzle 'em with brilliance, baffle 'em with bullshit!" I immediately took to Bran and truly enjoyed every minute I ever spent with him.

When Janny and I made our first trip to the Hamptons to meet with Associates & Ferren, Bran, as much a salesman and schmoozer as he is an artist and scientist, escorted us to his R & D laboratory where he introduced us to a car wash–sized machine. Next to the massive mystery machine was a small screen on which there was a computer-generated (CG) design for a small doorknobby doohickey sporting concentric rings. This type of CG thing was unheard of at that time. "Observe," said Bran as he pressed a computer key, which brought the big machine to whizzing, whirring, clinking, and clanking life. A shoe-box-sized chunk of metal clunked into a front-end bin and the noisy machine had its way with it, tossing it up and down and all around like a tennis shoe in a clothes dryer until it disappeared, only to appear again in the machine's last bin as a small exact representation of the object we saw on the screen. It was hilarious to me that this colossal machine worked so hard to spit out this tiny object. It reminded me of an old cartoon I once saw about an enormous factory that loaded a giant redwood tree–sized log at one end of the machinery and at the end popped out just a teeny, tiny toothpick as the finished product. On the bottom of the little knob's built-in stand was a plaque on which was inscribed my name. Janny got one, too. They were "homemade" welcome gifts from Bran.

The next thing you know, Janny and I are buckled into Bran's Range Rover, bouncing and trouncing across the Long Island countryside on our way to get ice cream. Going to get ice cream is more important to Bran than anything else. I can imagine him getting an urgent hotline phone call from the government informing him of a national emergency in which they need him to unleash his man-eating plants or the entire world will cease to exist in thirty seconds. Bran's response: "Of course. After I get ice cream." When we returned to get down to the actual business of planning the mock-up of Gus the Bus, Bran introduced us to his right-hand man, a young Tom Cruise-y–looking Long Islander by the name of Bruce Vaughn. Bruce was our charming host for a dinner in town that evening, where the vino and the stories flowed until we closed the place at 2:00 a.m. It was the beginning of a long and beautiful relationship between Imagineering and Associates & Ferren.

Several weeks later, when Bran and his clan had the mock-up and its projection system nearly ready to rock and roll, I hopped on a plane back to New York to check in with them. In those days, all Imagineers flew first class, and when I took my seat I noticed I was the only passenger in the cabin. Five minutes before takeoff I was still the only passenger in first class. Although I was happily thinking the in-flight service was going to be incredible with three flight attendants attending to one me, it was a little disconcerting, and just plain weird, to look around and see that every seat was still vacant. Then it happened. About three minutes before departure I heard the squelch of a walkie-talkie behind me. When I turned to look for the source of the sound, I could not believe my eyes. A representative from the airline was escorting into the cabin the Rolling Stones! Apparently, the Stones had booked the entire first-class cabin with the exception of one seat. Guess whose that was? This is one of my all-time favorite examples of my pre-Imagineering past cosmically connecting to my Imagineering present. My high school band used to cover Rolling Stones hits (or at least we tried) because I was a huge fan. Now here I was with the Stones themselves, all to myself in one small place for the next five hours. Who says "you can't always get what you want"?

As the band took their seats all around me, they appeared to be in quite a jovial mood. Keith Richards noticed me as he was passing by. He stopped, lowered his face to face mine, and asked, "Who are you then?" "I'm . . . uh . . . Kevin?" I nervously answered the question with a question like I wasn't even sure of my own name. "Everyone!" proclaimed Keith to the empty-except-for-me-and-the-Stones-cabin, "This is Kev!" All together everyone exclaimed, "'Ello, Kev!" He could have chosen any seat, but Mick Jagger sat directly across the aisle from me within arm's length. His companion, supermodel Jeri Hall, joined him in the neighboring center seat. After we took off, Mick asked, "Why are you off to New York then, Kev?" I explained that I worked for Disney and was heading to the Hamptons for a meeting related to a project I was working on. "Everyone!" Mick proclaimed, "Kev 'ere works for Disney!" "What do you do for Disney?" I heard someone ask from somewhere among the seats but couldn't see who it was. But I was pretty sure it was drummer Charlie Watts. "Well," I responded, "I'm an Imagineer." Charlie then asked, "What's that then?" "Imagineers," I responded, "are the lucky ones that get to create all the fun rides and stuff for the Disney theme parks." Charlie said, "'Ow fun is that? Hey, do you want to trade jobs with me?" I said, "I'd love to, but I don't play the drums." They laughed. "I do, however," I continued, "kinda play guitar." Ronnie Wood said, "Then trade jobs with me!" I responded, "'Ow fun is THAT?" This got another laugh from the group.

One of them said (and I can't remember who because the question shocked me into a mindless stupor), "Speaking of fun, Kev, why don't you blow off your silly meeting and come with us into the city when we get there?" Everyone agreed that was a great idea. Hold your *wild horses*! The Rolling Stones are invit-ing *me* to go with *them*? Did I hear that right? Was this really happening? Just to be sure I wasn't in the *Twilight Zone*, I looked out the window to see if that gremlin was on the wing; you know, the one that freaked out William Shatner in *The Twilight Zone* episode "Nightmare at 20,000 Feet." Only this wasn't a nightmare at all. This was turning out to be a pretty darned good dream. And in it there was a supermodel paging through a Frederick's of Hollywood lingerie catalogue!

"You . . . you want me to go with you to New York City?" I asked, still incredulous. "As in . . . *go with you* go with you?" They nodded and agreed among themselves it would be the best thing for me to do. "Thanks," I answered, "that is really a great offer, but I'm only in New York for one day, so I really do have to go to my meeting. It's really important and I'm really responsible." Someone in the seats said, "Dedicated lad you are. Disney is lucky to 'ave you." At that, everyone settled back down and all the excitement and conversation stopped. I unfolded my Sunday paper, and I'm not kidding, the first page I opened featured a large photo of Mick Jagger with a related article about an autograph shop and the big money they were getting for certain celebrity autographs. Mick's took in six hundred bucks!

I looked across the aisle at the man with the golden hand and noticed he was noticing my newspaper. "It says here," I said excitedly to Mick, pointing to the article under his photo, "that this shop recently sold your autograph for six hundred dollars." He reached across the aisle openhanded and said, "Give me something to sign then." I snapped the pen out of my shirt pocket and grabbed the first papery thing I could get my mitts on from out of my briefcase, which was my Disney travel folder. In those days, the cover of the folder featured the words WALT DISNEY TRAVEL COMPANY under the image of Mickey Mouse standing in a ta-da pose with arms open wide. Mick signed above Mick, handed it back, and said, "You're not going to sell that, now are you?" I answered, "Not for less than six hundred bucks I'm not!"

After we pulled up to the gate at the airport upon landing, I heard the familiar squelch of a walkie-talkie approaching the first-class cabin. A representative from the airline came to escort the band. As I was about to bid them a fond farewell, Keith said, "Come along with us, at least till we get out of the airport," and gestured for me to follow them off the plane. There I was, walking right in the middle of the Rolling Stones, being escorted through the back corridors of the terminal. When our airline host opened the door out to the curbside where the limos were waiting, so were the paparazzi—and they swarmed me, and started taking my picture (like I was somebody)! But by the time they realized I was nobody, the band members had escaped into their limos. A black rear window went down and I heard a voice from inside say, "Last chance, Kev. C'mon then!" I thanked them profusely, but once again declined their gracious offer. Off they went into New York City in their stretch limos, and off I went to Long Island in my compact rental car.

Everyone I share this story with tells me I must have been crazy not to go with the Stones. Maybe so. But that's how crazy dedicated I am to my Imagineering life. After I returned home from that short trip, I was certain the whole thing was a dream. That is, until I unpacked and found my six-hundred-dollar autographed travel folder. To this day I wonder what would have happened had I cast my responsibility and suitcase to the wind and jumped into the back of the limo that night. I know it's only rock 'n' roll. But I like it.

A few weeks later producer Janny Mulholland joined me on the next trip to East Hampton. But Disney Travel had a problem finding lodging for us there. A big wedding event had taken over the town and all of the local accommodations were booked solid, with the exception of one hotel, which strangely had all of their rooms available. This raised a warning flag with Disney Travel, but we wanted a place to stay that was close to Associates & Ferren. Even though it wasn't recommended, we convinced Travel to book two rooms at that hotel for the two nights we were going to be in town. (The hotel will remain nameless to protect its identity, even though it didn't protect Janny and me, as you are about to discover.) Our flight was delayed so we didn't get to town until almost midnight. We were fortunate to happen upon the old hotel, because it was not well lit. As a matter of fact, the only source of illumination was a single naked bulb over its small front porch, under which stood a tall, lank, Ichabod Crane-looking man straight out of central casting. Bags in hand and ready for bed, Janny and I approached the man on the porch. In a low and slow voice that sounded eerily like Lurch from *The Addams Family*, he said, "You are late." Before we could apologize and explain why, he said, "Come," and we followed him through the front door of the smaller-than-life-sized six-room hotel that was built in the 1700s.

Inside the dimly lit snapshot-of-history parlor, there were at least two hundred ticking wall clocks. I know we stepped in at precisely midnight because we were greeted with an unsettling cacophony of chimes striking the hour. After we checked in, the man of few words handed us each a skeleton key and pointed down the dark hall for Janny and up the dark staircase for me. I couldn't help but ask him if there were any other guests staying in the hotel. He silently shook his head. Before we retired to our rooms, Janny and I made plans to meet there in the parlor when all the clocks struck 7:00 a.m. I turned to thank the man before heading up to my room, but he had vanished without a trace.

At the top of the stairs was a short and narrow hallway, at the end of which was a short and narrow door. Another naked light bulb flickered in the hall, but the ceiling was so low I had to step around it. The top of my room door was at chin level so I did the limbo to enter. The moment I stepped in and straightened out I was confronted by two centuries-old portraits of George and Martha Washington on the opposite wall. Their eyes were fixed on me. The dusty, musty room had an unsettling vibe to it and sent a chill through my bones. I tossed my small suitcase on the bed and unzipped it with my back to George and Martha. But I knew they were watching. I quickly pivoted around to see what they were up to—and they had not taken their eyes off of me. I tried to lose them by doing the Soupy Sales shuffle back and forth across the tiny room, but their eyes followed my every move. When I stepped over to my suitcase to unpack, the zipper I thought I had unzipped was zipped. *Hmmm.* I unzipped it again and hung up my clothes. Returning to the suitcase to retrieve my bathroom supplies I found it zipped again. A pair of my socks was on the bed. I had not taken them out. I don't believe in ghosts, so I convinced myself there must have been some logical explanation. But George Washington begged to differ. And he doesn't lie.

There was nothing modern in the room. No phone, no TV, not even a toilet; just a ticking clock. I had to limbo again under the only other short door in the hall outside my room to find the toilet. There was no shower next to it, only a Barbie Dreamhouse–sized claw tub. No kidding, the scale of the 220-year-old hotel's second floor was only slightly bigger than a dollhouse, one which I was starting to think belonged to Chucky. Returning to my room from the water closet, I found the door wide open. I had closed it when I left the room. The open door perfectly framed George and Martha as I approached. They knew what was up. I sternly said to them, "I don't believe in this paranormal poppycock, so I am going to bed!"

As exhausted as I was, I couldn't get to sleep with all those goings-on going on; plus, there were the clocks downstairs and their spy disguised as a windup alarm clock in my room tick-tocking, which was driving me cuckoo. I covered my ears with my pillow. Turning over on my left side had me facing the short door. Under it was a wide gap through which light poured in from the bulb in the hall. Suddenly, I saw a moving shadow under the door and I heard the floor-boards creaking as if someone or some*thing* were approaching. Quietly sliding out of bed so I could sneak up on whatever was sneaking up on me, I gripped the doorknob like a victim in a horror movie would at the moment the audience is saying to themselves, "No! Don't open the door!" And I opened the door.

But there was nothing. I closed the door and the floorboard creaking imme-diately started up again. Once more I opened the door and saw and heard nothing.

I jumped back into bed and pulled the covers completely over my entire self, feeling like a scared little kid with no mommy to call out to for help; well, except for Janny (producers are like mommies), who was downstairs somewhere probably sleeping like a baby, so I didn't want to disturb her. I switched the nightstand light on. George and Martha were clearly enjoying every bit of this. The moment the wind started howling outside the window I felt a tug on my eyebrow. As I was reasoning that it was a sleep-deprived twitch, it happened again. I sat up with the spring action of a switchblade and fired a warning to the Washingtons: "Call off your friends or you're both flyin' out the window!" It occurred to me that I had not yet looked out the window, so I got out of bed to see what was out there. In the moonlit median between two lanes of a desolate road was a long thin ribbon of land upon which were old crooked tombstones.

My room was next to an old cemetery! No wonder grim grinning ghosts had come out to socialize with me. Because of that I did not sleep a wink, so I heard all of the clocks strike every single hour until 5:00 a.m., at which point I got out of bed to go wedge myself into the Barbie bathtub. By that time, I was so angry and cranky I didn't care if the ghosts saw me as naked as their stinking light bulb. I just hoped they weren't going to tug on anything else.

When Janny and I booked our rooms, the hotel demanded full payment for the two-night reservation prior to our arrival (gee, I wonder why?). But I was not going to stay in that place one more creaking night. At 6:00 a.m. I stuffed everything back into my suitcase, gave George and Martha a sustained raspberry, and ducked under the short door to *amscray*, more than happy to wait outside for an hour for Janny. But when I turned to step down the stairs, Janny was already waiting at the bottom, staring up at me with suitcase in

Oh, no. Nope. No sir. Not a ghost of a chance I'm staying another night in this haunted hotel!

153

hand, very much in a stiff and stern Mary Poppins posture. But she didn't look like Mary Poppins. She looked like a wreck. There I was, at the top of the stairs staring down at her, and there she was at the bottom of the stairs staring up at me, neither one of us saying a word amid all the ticking clocks but both knowing what the other was thinking. I knew she knew what I knew, and I knew she knew that I knew what she knew. After perhaps a full fifteen seconds of our silent somber stare-out, we both drew a sharp breath and spoke at the very same time, stating the very same thing: "How was your night?" I was the first to respond. "Let's get out of here and I'll tell you." There was no sign of Ichabod Crane or anyone else around as we both flew out the door and jumped into our escape vehicle.

Wary of picking up any hitchhiking ghosts, I floored the gas pedal to speed past the long cemetery. Then, once in the clear, we shared our long night's experiences. Compared to Janny's night, I got off easy. Neither one of us got any sleep or proper grooming, so when we arrived at Associates & Ferren we were a mess. The receptionist, Susan, greeted us by asking a question that was actually more of a statement: "You stayed there, didn't you?" We nodded. She continued, "I can't believe you did that, especially since everyone knows that place is haunted." Susan helped get us rooms for the night at a normal (as opposed to *paranormal*) hotel in Sag Harbor. I've taken thousands of trips for my job over the years—and never once have I had any of my expense reports questioned. Except for one. This one. A few weeks after I returned from New York I got the call. "Hi, this is Mary from Corporate Travel. We were just wondering why you have charges for two different hotels in two different towns on the same night." I answered matter-of-factly, "That's because one of them was haunted." There was a long pause and then Mary ended the call by saying, "Okay. Well, um. Thank you."

Despite the sleepless night before, the mock-up we were there to review looked promising. Bran's team had created a multi-camera rig and mounted it to the top of a van. They drove the van around town and projected the captured footage on a screen that wrapped around both sides and the front of the wooden mock-up of Gus the Bus. The onboard projection system, mounted out of view on top of Gus, provided a seamless, out-of-the-periphery image as seen through the bus windows. There were also subwoofers on board, so when the mock-up began, it sounded and felt like Gus was starting his engine. The crude motion base under the whole thing was programmed to choreograph with the action on the screen. It was like experiencing Circle-Vision, only better, because with no mullions to divide the screen and no frame to define the screen, it felt like we were traveling on a little bus through East Hampton. This was all very exciting, and because of it I was confident about moving the project forward. Its success meant we could invite our leaders, all the way up to Michael Eisner, to come to East Hampton to experience the mock-up.

When they arrived, Bran jumped on the opportunity to present a lot of other fun, interesting, and most-impressive stuff he and his associates were working on in their facility. Michael Eisner quickly became enamored with Bran and his company, and soon they were doing other innovative projects for Disney. Before long Michael invited Bran to come out to Glendale to head up Imagineering Research and Development. When he moved to California, some of his associates followed, hoping to land a job at Imagineering as well. One of them was young Bruce Vaughn.

A few days after Bran arrived, he called me and said, "What are you doing?" I was under the gun trying to knock out an important deadline so I responded in a "leave me alone" tone of voice: "I'm working like crazy." "Never mind that," he said. "Meet me out front in five minutes." Five minutes later I was walking out the lobby door as Bran pulled up in his gleaming new red Corvette ZR-1. I gasped. He got out, leaving the driver's-side door open and engine running. "You're driving!" he said. I couldn't believe it when I slipped behind the wheel, because I had never been in a Corvette. That's because I could never afford one, so why put myself through that pain of sitting in one knowing it could never be? But I'd had a lifelong love affair with the legendary sports car ever since my dad took me to a Chevy dealer in 1959 and there, on the showroom floor, was a shiny new red one with her top down. I named her Ruby right there on the spot. Yes, it is possible to fall madly in love when you're only four years old. I excitedly assumed we were there because Ruby was going home with us. But then we went home in a stupid station wagon. I never forgave Dad for that. And I never gave our station wagon a name, either.

I joyously pushed in the clutch as Bran switched the control over to "Sport" mode with a knowing smirk on his face. I put the six-speed manual into first and off we screeched onto Flower Street, speeding past the place where I'd had my interview while thinking about how far I'd come since driving down that street for the first time in Old Unreliable. Little did I know when I rocketed onto the freeway and slammed her into sixth gear that before long General Motors would invite me to drive their special souped-up Corvette at top speed on their proving grounds track in Michigan when my research would begin for Test Track. Bran would later join our Test Track team. After tearing up all the streets of Glendale and a few more in Burbank in his growling animal ZR-1, I told Bran I had to get back to work. "Never mind that," he said. "Let's go for ice cream!" For years to follow I'd often get a phone call from Bran, always at one of the busiest times of my day. "What are you doing?" really meant "We're going for ice cream." Ice cream and Corvettes on company time. Two of my all-time favorite things and two more not-your-typical-workday reasons I loved my crazy Imagineering life.

When Bran left Imagineering to establish another company, wicked-smart Bruce Vaughn took over as head of our R & D. A few years later he would take an even bigger step up to become the head creative honcho of Walt Disney Imagineering. Bruce's rise to power was a fascinating thing for me to witness given our long history together. At one time, Bruce was working for us. The next thing you know we're working for Bruce! Had I never come up with the idea for Gus the Bus, Bruce probably never would have come to Imagineering, much less become its leader. (Always be nice to everyone you work with because you never know who's gonna end up being your boss!)

Alas, Toontown Transit and Cartoon Studios did not come to fruition because the Roger Rabbit franchise was fading fast and Imagineering was establishing new and different goals. Although the projects I was working on for the studio expansion were canceled, I didn't consider it a loss. I had a lot of fun with them, learned a lot from them, and took comfort in the fact that a lot of good came out of them. We may have lost Roger and Jessica, but we gained Bran and Bruce. And, as is usually the case, things that are designed for projects that get canceled often find their way into later concepts. The wayward skyrocket with the burning fuse that crashed into Gus the Bus's interior reappeared as a wayward storm-stopping missile that crashed into the storm-diffusing aircraft interior in SeaRider at Tokyo DisneySea. At least The Twilight Zone Tower of Terror rose to the top and opened in 1994 to elevate the level of thrills at the Disney-MGM Studios, which was the primary goal of our Studios Expansion effort.

I was never, in my entire creative career as an Imagineer, in need of work. Projects came and projects went: some got built and some didn't. That's the nature of our business. Gus the Bus had barely been laid to *rust* before I suddenly found myself on several more new projects in the early- to mid-1990s with even more on the way, including Mickey's Toontown for Disneyland; the Carousel of Progress show refresh, a New Tomorrowland push, a Snow White's Scary Adventures refresh, and Sonny Eclipse, the Biggest Little Star in the Galaxy, for the Magic Kingdom; the creation of Blizzard Beach Water Park; and the most important new attraction of them all, the joyous arrival of my second son, Bradley Alexander. Brad came out of the Studios Expansion effort, too, thanks to my wife tagging along on a few trips to the romantic Hamptons. I consider Brad as my turning point and good luck charm because after he was conceived almost every attraction I worked on got green-lit. They all made it

from the spark to the park. Also at the time, unable to quell the anxious animator trapped inside my Imagineer body (and being up most of the night anyway
with baby Brad), I did some moonlighting for Disney TV Animation in 1992 as
a writer on the CBS Saturday morning show *Raw Toonage*, starring Bonkers D.
Bobcat. For that I unexpectedly received an Emmy nomination.

Another unexpected surprise came when I was invited to write Michael
Eisner's on-camera introductions to the *Wonderful World of Disney* on ABC on
Sunday nights. Man, I was living the dream! Hanging out with the Stones, lick-
ing ice cream cones, staying in haunted zones, and cruising in Corvettes without
taking loans. It just couldn't get any better. Well, actually, it could. And it did.

NONSTOP
'90s

THE ORIGINAL Carousel of Progress is, in my humble opinion, one of the greatest theatrical presentations of all time. The version that debuted at the 1964 World's Fair in New York and was moved to Tomorrowland in Disneyland in 1967 will always be one of my favorite Audio-Animatronics shows. This innovative combination of a theatrical venue and rotating ride system is the perfect example of Imagineering showmanship at its best. The writing was spot-on brilliant; the timing impeccable; the characters and sets charming, believable, and relatable; and the optimistic and beloved song, "There's a Great Big Beautiful Tomorrow," is one of the Sherman brothers' very best.

One of my favorite memories as a kid (not just one of my favorite memories at Disneyland, but one of my favorite childhood memories period) is sitting next to my father in the Carousel and hearing him sing that song louder and with more gusto than the show's "Father" (voiced by Rex Allen, who had plenty of gusto himself) as the entire building rotated like a giant wheel to move the audience progressively from scene to scene. As an employee of the Southern California Gas Company, Dad brought home tickets to Disneyland once a year for the "Gas Company Night" private party. During that time in the 1960s, many new neighborhoods featuring "Medallion" homes started to spring up all over Southern California. Medallion signified the homes were all electric and furnished with General Electric appliances, not gas, which made GE the gas company's competition. In one scene from Carousel, when his dog, Sport, barks at an audience member, Father scolds him. "Now stop that!" he says. "He may be a good customer of General Electric." After that line, the gas company audience would always boo. Except for my dad. He'd tell everybody to pipe down, "or I'll give ya something to boo about!" Dad loved the Carousel of Progress as much as I did, so it was a must-see whenever we went to Disneyland. With all that love for the show and personal history that goes along with it, imagine my surprise and delight when Marty Sklar and Bob Weis asked me to take a stab at updating the Carousel at the Magic Kingdom in Walt Disney World.

The Disneyland show was closed in 1973 and moved to Walt Disney World, where it opened in 1975, one year after America Sings! moved into the rotating building in Disneyland's Tomorrowland. When it reappeared at the Magic Kingdom, it featured a new song written by the Sherman brothers called "The Best Time of Your Life," performed by the new voice of Father, Andrew Duggen. In 1992, when I stepped in to give the show a refresh, a new generation of guests had never heard "There's a Great Big Beautiful Tomorrow." Both songs were optimistically wonderful and appropriate, of course, but because I wanted to change the name of the attraction back to Walt Disney's Carousel of Progress, it seemed only fitting that we bring back the song the Shermans wrote as a

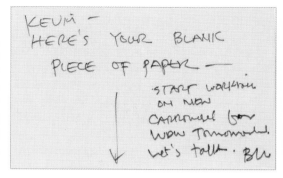

With a fun nod to Marty, Bob Weis left this note stuck to a piece of paper in my office asking me to work on a revised show for the Carousel of Progress at the Magic Kingdom in Walt Disney World.

tribute—unbeknownst to him at the time—to Walt Disney. I also thought, in the spirit of change, it would be fun to celebrate a special time of the year for each scene, such as Halloween and the Fourth of July. I asked my musical partner, George Wilkins, to jump in to bring the Shermans' original theme song back and to arrange it, with his own special twist, in the time periods and seasons depicted.

Bob Weis and I went to the Magic Kingdom to see the last show before we closed it down to start working on the next version. Afterwards Bob had a great idea, which he is known for from time to time. "Ya know who would be great in the role of Father?" he asked. "Jean Shepherd." Yes, of course! I was crazy about Bob's suggestion because I loved American storyteller and humorist Jean Shepherd. I can't tell you how many times I read his book *In God We Trust: All Others Pay Cash*. He turned one of the stories in that hilarious and heartwarming book into the screenplay for the holiday movie classic *A Christmas Story*. He also narrated the movie as the adult voice of Ralphie. Jean Shepherd was the perfect choice for the role of "Father" in this beloved all-American Disney show! And as a nod to Father's original voice, we cast Rex Allen for the role of Grandfather.

I always looked up to this man as a father figure.

Jean and his wife, Leigh Brown, lived in Florida, so I flew out to meet them and be their host on a grand tour of Walt Disney World. They were both, as expected, warm, wonderful, and genuinely funny, folksy folks. It was such a pleasure to have the opportunity to spend time with and get to know Jean because he shared the stories of his life with me in the same "smile in his voice" narrative style he brought to *A Christmas Story*. Wherever we were around Walt Disney World, Jean had a wonderfully engaging story to tell related to the place, time, or subject. He talked extensively about growing up in America's Heartland with his "Old Man," his tour of duty in the army in Korea, his fish-out-of-water arrival in New York City, and life there with his roommate, poet Shel Silverstein. Another one of his "cut from the same cloth" friends was Earl Hamner Jr., the man who created and narrated, very much in a Jean Shepherd style (albeit not comedic), *The Waltons*. This prime-time network television show was about a loving family that pulls together in hard times, as narrated by the eldest son, a writer, and every episode of *The Waltons* always touched and greatly inspired me. The thing about being a productive creative person is, in order to keep delivering the creative goods you have to constantly feed your creative mind, heart, and soul. (Input = output.) As an artist, to do your very best, you have to stay energized and inspired, whether it be with a great book; movie; song; live theatrical, musical, or storytelling performance; art show; dog show; car show. Basically, whatever nourishes your noodle.

I wanted to give Jean Shepherd a Red Ryder BB Gun, but I didn't want him to shoot his eye out, so I gave him this official Walt Disney Imagineering cap instead. He said it would have made his old man proud.

Spending time with Jean Shepherd, who came to my house to hang out, sip his favorite Maker's Mark whiskey, and talk about life, his inspiring friends, and his many adventures and misadventures, fed my creative being to the brim. His own personal story about how a shy, picked-on kid from Indiana became a fearlessly vocal radio personality, author, screenwriter, and host of public television's *Jean Shepherd's America* was the stuff of legend. Jean used to broadcast baseball games live on the radio when he was not even present at those games with all the play-by-play excitement he'd have if he were really there. The trick was he'd interpret alphabetic symbols as they would come out of a ticker tape machine as transmitted from someone actually at the game. For example, LF meant left fielder, and since Jean knew every name and position of every player in baseball, that's all he needed. On one occasion, halfway through the first inning, the ticker tape machine jammed, so Jean, still live on the air, totally made up the rest of the game.

Jean came to California for our recording session for Carousel and my family and I took him and Leigh, both of whom had simple tastes, to a hoity-toity restaurant. When our waiter asked if he wanted sun-dried tomatoes, Jean responded, "What's with you Californians? Where I come from we call those rotten tomatoes!" Directing Jean Shepherd in our recording studio at Imagineering was truly a career highlight. That is, until we got to the singing part. When you bring talent into the studio to record dialogue, and there is also singing involved in the session, you keep your fingers crossed that that person can actually sing. Well, Jean could not. Not by a long shot. The first note out of his mouth was so awful I thought he was joking at first. But he was not joking as he continued singing with great enthusiasm all the way through to "Just a dream away."

"Ho, boy, that sounded great, eh?" he said proudly. Music director George Wilkins shot me a wide-eyed "Holy sour note! What do we do now?" look. "Stand by, Jean," I said. "We're going to get you some hot tea while I talk to George." As George and I stepped out of the studio he grabbed my arm and said, "He's off-key, off tempo, and off his rocker if he thinks he can do this!" "So," I said, "does that mean you can make this work?" George shook his head. "I'm a musician, not a miracle worker." "Okay, Jean," I said upon returning to the studio. "Let's knock out the rest of the song." "Oh, ho!" exclaimed Jean, striking a pose like Pavarotti behind the mic. "I'm ready!" It was obvious we weren't going to come out the other side with any usable material, so we recorded everything in one take. To that Jean said, "I'm even better than I thought!" We covered the base by later bringing in Jess Harnell, a talented character voice actor and singer who has the gift to mimic anyone's voice in song.

Jess sang in Jean's style and voice as it might sound in a perfect world and nailed it. When we reopened Walt Disney's Carousel of Progress in 1993, I invited Jean and Leigh to come see the finished show with my fingers crossed that he wouldn't be too hurt that we replaced his singing with that of another performer. When Father started to sing "There's a Great Big Beautiful Tomorrow," Jean slapped me hard on the leg. I thought the jig was up and I was in big trouble until he exuberantly proclaimed, with his hands flailing about in his excitement, "Holy cow, I really knocked that singin' out of the park, didn't I?" "Calm down, Jean," I said. "Or you'll put my eye out!" On my birthday that year, Jean gave me an autographed copy of *In God We Trust: All Others Pay Cash*. Inside he drew caricatures of the two of us and wrote:

Kevin Rafferty,
A great left fielder on his birthday. WALT DISNEY LIVES . . .
Jean Shepherd

I grew up listening to the reassuring deep gentle voice of singer, songwriter, and movie actor Rex Allen. Known as "The Arizona Cowboy," Rex found fame in the era of acting and singing cowboys. His records were often spinning on our home phonograph and his voice was often heard on our TV on Sunday nights as he narrated many Disney movies and shows featured on *The Wonderful World of Disney*. Rex Allen, Disneyland announcer Jack Wagner, and Thurl Ravenscroft (also the voice of Tony the Tiger, and who in his later years lived in a retirement community two blocks from my childhood home) were the vocal soul of the sound of Disney, as their unmistakable voices were immediately recognized as such. Of course, Rex also performed as the Audio-Animatronics host of the Carousel of Progress during that time when those Disney voices were all at the happy heart of that classic Disneyland soundscape. Having the opportunity to direct Rex Allen for our later version of the Carousel show was a humbling experience.

One thing I discovered over the years is every time legendary talent comes to our Imagineering recording studio, they bring along their personal stories; stories you have never heard or read. Or even if you have, you get to hear them directly from the source. That means at least half of the time allotted for a recording session is taken up by storytelling, prior to the session and between takes. But I wouldn't have it any other way. When I told Rex what an honor it was for me to be directing him since I grew up hearing his voice, he started reminiscing about his own childhood. He told me that when he was old enough to leave his life on the ranch to come to California and follow his dream to become an entertainer, his father didn't embrace that idea too well at all. After finding fame, Rex bought a ranch-style house in California's San Fernando Valley and invited his dad to come visit. But he refused. Rex had to bribe him with the promise to buy him a new pickup truck if he'd honor the invitation. After Dad drove his new truck from the Valley dealership to Rex's house, they celebrated his visit with a backyard barbecue by the pool. Afterwards, Rex asked his rancher father, who had never stepped booted foot out of Arizona, "Well, pa, what do you think of California?" "Son," he responded, "I just can't get used to how you California people do all your eatin' *outside* and all your shittin' *inside*."

Rex Allen was a longtime friend of Roy E. Disney. When Roy found out he was coming to Imagineering for a recording session, he called to ask that I let him know when his old friend was there because he wanted to come over and surprise him. Rex was a smoker and we didn't allow him to light up in the building. So, between takes, he'd go out back to our loading dock for a cigarette. When Roy arrived, I asked him to wait in the small visitor's room a few doors away from our studio while I went to fetch Rex who was outside having a smoke. Not pleased that he had to put out his perfectly good cigarette to follow me in, Rex entered the visitor's room shocked to discover Roy puffing on his own cigarette. "Roy Disney," Rex said sternly to his old friend, "why do you get to sit there and have a smoke inside when they make me go outside?" "Well, Rex," Roy answered as he took a long deliberate drag on his cigarette, "My last name ain't Disney for nothin'.'"

Our refresh of Walt Disney's Carousel of Progress was actually part of the bigger revamping of Tomorrowland at the Magic Kingdom. Tomorrowlands are always the toughest lands to create or change because by the time you build one with the intent to showcase the future, the future has already become the past. Led by Paul Osterhout (who also performed the son's voice in the final act of the Carousel), the future we landed on for the New Tomorrowland was a playful version of the "future that never was." In this whimsical machine-age-meets-early-sci-fi-comics future, robots cut your hair and walk your dog, and

Carousel of Progress—some assembly required!

citizens live out in the hoverburbs. With the real future being showcased and changed out regularly in Innoventions at Epcot, we invented a fantasy "Community of Tomorrow" where the attractions and other elements all became part of the neighborhood. The ExtraTERRORestrial Alien Encounter attraction, for example, took place in the Tomorrowland Convention Center, and Space Mountain was the community spaceport. To tie it all together, the Tomorrowland Transit Authority (TTA) transported citizens around the community to see its many sights from great heights. I thought it would be funny to give the smallest shop in the land the longest name. It was a kiosk, really. I named it Ursa Major Minor Mart.

After our work in the land was complete, Executive vice president Eric Jacobson called me in my office back home in Glendale. "Hey, Kev, guess what?" Eric began. "Thanks to you a baby was almost born in Tomorrowland today." Well that certainly got my attention! Eric continued to tell me there was an emergency situation in which a woman went into labor and almost didn't get the help she needed in time because of me. When the security cast member called for help on his radio while the poor woman was screaming with labor pains in the background, the dispatcher immediately went into action asking for his location. "We're next to the . . . the . . . uh, you know, the . . . Minor . . . the Major . . . the Minor Major . . . no, that's not it. . . . No . . . we're next to the Major Ursa . . . we're at, *ummmm* . . . Ursa. . . . Something about Ursa . . . you know, that Mart, that . . . Ursa Mart place. WE'RE BY THAT LITTLE SHOP THAT SELLS FILM IN TOMORROWLAND! HURRY!"

Not far from the Ursa Major Minor Mart, in the spaceport spirit of the community of Tomorrowland, I changed the name of the Tomorrowland Terrace Restaurant to Cosmic Ray's Starlight Café. Similar to Pan Galactic Pizza Port at Tokyo Disneyland, Cosmic Ray's is an intergalactic restaurant franchise on Earth. Appearing "live" in its main dining room is "The Biggest Little Star in the Galaxy," Sonny Eclipse, an intergalactic lounge act who sings while playing the Astro Organ. Prior to his gig at Cosmic Ray's, Sonny performed at mall openings, bar mitzvahs, and weddings all over the galaxy. He's a big deal on his planet, but on our planet he's really down to earth. Honestly, I don't know how I ever sold the idea for Sonny Eclipse. He doesn't bring in any extra cash or even have a tip jar, which would help justify his existence, and he's too small to be marketable. But somehow—maybe it was my threatening to hold my breath until I turned as blue as Sonny's cousin Officer Zzyzx—Cosmic Ray was able to hire the intergalactic entertainer.

George Wilkins and I wrote eight original songs for the character. I thought it would be fun for Sonny to sing different types of music, from ballads to rock to blues to "Bossa Super Nova," so we wrote in all those styles. I penned the lyrics and jokes to reflect Sonny's outer space perspective. George performed most of the instrumentation for the new tracks and we recorded everything in his garage studio in Sherman Oaks, a section of Los Angeles. Sonny is voiced by Palm Springs, California, blues singer Kal David, who also laid down some string-bending blues riffs on his guitar for the song "Gravity." We recorded all of Kal's vocals in George's laundry room where the microphone was propped up between the washer and dryer. (Yes, dear project management friends, I know how to keep a project under budget!)

When Sonny first appeared at Cosmic Ray's Starlight Café, he rose to the occasion on a lift that carried him to the stage. I can't tell you how thrilled I was the first time I saw guests responding to him with their fingers snapping and toes tapping—and some of them even danced to his musical stylings. Imagine my surprise when I read a newspaper article about two Disney park fans who fell in love while dancing to "their" song, "Bright Little Star" by Sonny Eclipse! Sonny introduces that song by telling the audience how much he misses his girlfriend and that he wrote it with her in mind:

> O bright little star, though I'm light-years away from her now
> I can't help but to feel that somehow we're both wishing on you
> I imagine your light in her eyes as she gazes up into the skies
> At this moment, does she realize you are in my eyes, too?
> O bright little star, is she wishing the same wish as me
> That somewhere out in space there may be a nice planet for two
> Where someday we'll be all alone in our own galaxy
> Dancing under a star canopy and our favorite is you
> Someday somewhere I will find her in the universe up above
> Tell her, little star, I'll surround her with all my love
> Good night, little star, watch and keep her till we meet again
> In the glow of a love without end shining brightly like you do
> And every night as we gaze at your loving starlight
> We will know that when wishes are right they will always come true.

After singing that song about love, Sonny, who is big and green, performs a blues number about the second strongest earthly force:

> Gravity you've got a hold on me, yes you do, yes you do
> Gravity you've got a great big hold on me, oh, yeah
> I can't see ya, can't even feel ya, and now I know you will never set me free

Since the world is round, must be people upside-down
What's keepin' them from falling off and floatin' all around?
All those people down under are beginning to wonder
If you would ever cut the juice and set 'em loose, good-bye!
Hello, gravity, mean old gravity
I am green but gravity you're giving me the blues
Gravity set me free, you're a magnet of course, a famous earthly force
Yeah, gravity let me be
If it weren't for you I wouldn't weigh what I do
Gravity you're weighin' heavy on my mind all the time
Gravity why do you treat me so unkind? I never did nothin' to you!
I can't see ya, can't even feel ya
But I'm green and gravity you're giving me the blues.

During the same time Sonny and all of the New Tomorrowland work were going on, my old pal Joe Lanzisero, who was leading the design and development for a new land in Disneyland called Mickey's Toontown, asked me to jump in and work on overall gags for his project, which included partnering up with George Wilkins to create the "Toontown Radio Show." When completed, the "live radio program" was broadcast over two toon-themed radios; one was in Mickey's house and the other was in the garage-themed load area of Roger Rabbit's Cartoon Spin. The call letters for the radio station were W-A-C-K-Y. Writing the "Wacky Radio" program, which included news and advertisements for local Toontown businesses (including the ad jingles and songs sung by some of the characters), was a joy because it was right up my alley. My favorite ad jingle was for the Three Nephews from Duckburg Catering Company:

Three nephews from Duckburg will help you if you're stuckburg
If you don't have the time to fix a meal
They'll do all the cooking without you even looking
Call them for a booking, what a deal!
Your guests, they will love ya, they'll put you high above ya
Their taste buds will shout out "ooh la la!" (ooh la la!)
So, put on your favorite tux, leave the cooking to the ducks
Three nephews from Duckburg
Try Huey and Dewey and Louie's ratatouille
Their Swedish meatballs really hit the spot—yeah! (plop!)
If it's catering you want make your home a restaurant
Three Nephews from Duckburg!

From left to right, fellow show writer Art Verity, character voice actor June Foray, and me. I grew up hearing all of June's voices, from Rocky the Flying Squirrel to Natasha Fatale. We were recording material for Mickey's Toontown that day.

Throughout the radio show there would be breaking news reports about the weasels and Dip to shill the story of Roger Rabbit's Cartoon Spin. Fellow show writer Art Verity and I wrote the story setup for that attraction featuring fiendish plans being devised by the weasels as overheard in the queue. This effort provided a glorious opportunity for me to get to write for and direct a legendary cartoon voice talent I adored my entire life: June Foray. I think my mom's was the only other female voice I heard more through the years. June was the voice of Rocky the Flying Squirrel, Natasha Fatale (from Boris and Natasha), Cindy Lou Who, and too many more to list.

And speaking of talent I adore, the designer who created the layout and show sets for the attraction was a fresh new face to Imagineering who would later become my longtime creative partner in crime, Rob't Coltrin. But I didn't know Rob't then because I had not yet worked with him, and I didn't work with him directly on Roger Rabbit's Cartoon Spin because I was focused primarily on the show in the queue, the layout of which he had already designed.

Rob't and I were also working on Snow White's Scary Adventures for the Magic Kingdom at that time; but again, not together. He was the show designer and I was the show writer. As we were both taking separate direction from senior designer Brock Thoman, Rob't and I, strangely enough, never collaborated with each other. Brock's assignment was to bring Snow White to the Show White attraction. This sounds weird, I know, but when Snow White's Adventures opened in Fantasyland at the Magic Kingdom in 1971, Snow was a no show. The thing is, *you* were supposed to be Snow White. All of the characters played to you, in your ride vehicle, as if you were her. For example, the old hag held the apple out to you, dearie! But over the years many guests reported their disappointment that they didn't get to see Snow White on her own attraction. Well, that reaction is certainly understandable. By the time I came to the project Brock and Rob't had the show set package almost completed with Snow White already staged.

My job was to bring the show to life with script, recorded dialogue for all the characters, and musical soundtracks. By that time, Rob't had moved on, so he and I never even saw each other on that project. I always thought it odd that the two of us worked on two projects together but without personally collaborating on either one. But that was about to change.

The Many Adventures of Winnie the Pooh at the Magic Kingdom in Walt Disney World was the very first of many attractions to come in which Rob't and I were close creative compadres. When designers Rob't and his sister, Lori (both now executive creative directors), were ready to bring a show writer on to their project, they asked me to join the Pooh team because Rob't had put two and two together: we had previously worked together—well, sort of. Working with Rob't and Lori on that attraction would forever change the way I approached dimensional design and the art of Imagineering. When it comes to theater and showmanship, which is what Imagineering is all about, those two are a focused force. We three clicked instantly. (Today, when the two siblings wrap me in a hug—me the hot dog, them the bun—they give me fair warning beforehand: "Here comes the Coltrin Sandwich!") Watching Rob't, a master at up-front design and story, and Lori, a master at "take it to the finish line" theatrical production, was like watching an Olympic relay race. Pure perfection.

I wrote the script and directed the voice talent for The Many Adventures of Winnie the Pooh. Rob't, Lori, and I were honored to work with Disney Legends Buddy Baker and Richard Sherman on the musical score and with the talented cast of characters. Buddy adapted his same arrangements of the Sherman brothers' score for the 1977 movie of the same name to fit precisely into the length of each of our attraction scenes. It was sort of the *Reader's Digest* condensed version of musical arranging. And Buddy was the best in the business. When it came time for the recording session, Buddy made sure the orchestra was made up of the very same players, as many as were still available, that performed for the original movie score. They also brought along some of the not-so-typical instruments they played for that score. One of the things I love to do most while working on an attraction project is to sit in the recording studio with the orchestra as they perform all of the cues live.

From:	Coltrin, Robert A.
Sent:	Friday, September 25, 1998 9:18 AM
To:	Rafferty, Kevin P.
Subject:	whole lotta pooh goin on

kev
i don't want this to get too mushy, but thanks for all your help, advice, wisdom, and friendship in the last year...i appreciate you enduring all my rambling chats, pontifications, and other unscheduled wastes of time i burden you with...it should be no surprise that everyone around here wants to work with you...i know you won't wanna hear it, but i think you're a truly creative genius and a warm, genuine human being...i am certainly a better person for having known you...
thanks again...
did that get too mushy?

Rob't. Coltrin
Walt Disney Imagineering
Concept Design

This first of many wonderful and thoughtful notes I would receive from Rob't through the years. I am certainly a better person for having known him!

Truly, it was a remarkable opportunity for me to be seated among the many members of the orchestra that played for the movie score while the same maestro, Buddy Baker, conducted them. The icing on that honey cake was having Richard Sherman in the house as well. It was as if I had gone back in time to 1976 and was present at that original session.

A few bars after Buddy began conducting the cue for "Heffalumps and Woozles," Richard stood up and interrupted the orchestra. "Hold on, everybody," he said while waving his hands as the whole studio suddenly went silent, except for one lone trombone that hilariously improvised the sound of a flying Heffalump coming in for a crash landing—which was, of course, accentuated at the end with an improvised cymbal crash. Richard continued, "Something important is missing." Bewildered, Buddy lowered his baton and blurted, "Missing? What's missing?" Richard smiled that magical Richard Sherman smile and answered with one word: "Kazoos!" "Of course!" realized Buddy. "Did anyone bring a kazoo?" Richard added, "We need at least two." "Two?" I asked. "Why two?" "Because," Richard answered with a wink, "two are funnier than one!" No one in the orchestra had brought a kazoo. Richard promised Buddy he'd bring

Our "Pooh Crew," the team that designed and delivered The Many Adventures of Winnie the Pooh for the Magic Kingdom in Walt Disney World, sent Buddy a heartfelt thank-you letter as written by Pooh himself. This was Buddy's response back to Pooh (us).

two kazoos with him to the session the next day, which he did. And when the orchestra performed the "Heffalumps and Woozles" cue, Buddy and Richard stood side by side in front of the microphone humming joyously into those two funny kazoos.

Here were two men who had done so much to bring so much to our lives, together in their element, together in their love for one another. And I was there. What a glorious, privileged, once in a lifetime moment to be present with my two musical heroes as they brought to life that big, funny sound on those two tiny kazoos. "Sometimes," said Pooh, "the smallest things take up the most room in your heart."

Speaking of heroes (I know, I have a lot of them), while growing up, I never missed *The Paul Winchell Show* starring ventriloquist Winchell and his

Here's how Richard Sherman brings a Heffalump to life!

Having the oppor-TUNE-ity to work with my all-time favorite music legends, Buddy Baker, Richard Sherman, Alan Menken, and Michael Giacchino, has to be one of the biggest joys of my career. I'm smiling because I get to be an Imagineer and a songwriter!

two dummies: Jerry Mahoney and Knucklehead Smiff. Paul was also famous for being the bouncy, trouncy, flouncy, pouncy voice of Tigger. While directing the character voice talent for our attraction, one of the most memorable moments of my career occurred during our recording session with the very same Paul Winchell. Before I escorted him into our recording studio, Paul pulled Rob't, Lori, and me aside to let us know that this was going to be his final performance as Tigger. After more than thirty-five years of performing that character's voice, he was going to retire after our recording session. Being informed of that news immediately before our session naturally put us in a somber mood, which is not where you want to be when you're about to record such an upbeat character. Paul sensed our sadness, and staying true to the high-spirited, happy-go-lucky performer he always was, went right to work making the session, as Tigger would put it, "Fun, fun, fun, fun, fun." I was the last person ever to direct Paul Winchell performing the voice of this most beloved character. After he covered all of the material, Paul asked if he could perform one more line for the road. "Of course," I said to the entertainer I admired so much. "The microphone is all yours. And we're rolling." Paul winked at me, took a deep breath, and said, "TTFE. Ta-ta for ever."

Although I did not work on The Many Adventures of Winnie the Pooh at Disneyland, which shares the same name (but is a different attraction experience), that project team did use the music and vocal soundtracks we created for our Magic Kingdom version. In either location, you can hear Buddy and Richard's performance together on the kazoos and Paul Winchell's final performance as Tigger. I consider it a rare gift that I was present at both recording sessions and was able to contribute to the design and development of this timeless attraction honoring one of the world's most endearing characters. Lori, by the way, went on to deliver two more renditions of our Magic Kingdom version of the attraction for Hong Kong Disneyland and Shanghai Disneyland. Helping create the first Magic Kingdom version of The Many Adventures of Winnie the Pooh was an adventure in itself, and thanks to Rob't, Lori, Buddy, Richard, and Paul it was certainly no "bother." "How do you spell 'love'?" asked Piglet. "You don't spell it," said Pooh. "You feel it."

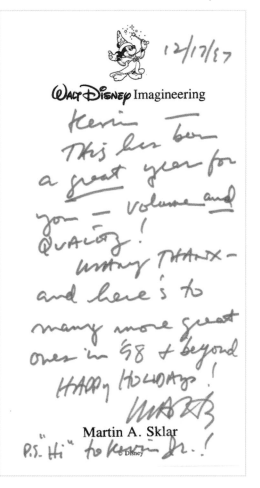

12/17/87

Walt Disney Imagineering

Kevin —
This has been
a great year for
you — volume and
quality!
many THANX —
and here's to
many more great
ones in '98 + beyond
HAPPy HOLIDAYs !
MARK

Martin A. Sklar

P.S. "Hi" to Kevin Jr.!

© Disney

Thanks, Marty! I'll be looking for that raise in '98!

174

The 1990s were a blustery daze of nonstop work—a blur, really. In addition to the projects I've already mentioned in this chapter, it was the busiest chapter in my life because I was also working, sometimes simultaneously, on Blizzard Beach and the Winter Summerland Miniature Golf for Walt Disney World; Mickey's Toontown Fair and The Enchanted Tiki Room—Under New Management! for the Magic Kingdom; a hardcover book, *Walt Disney Imagineering— A Behind the Dreams Look at Making the Magic Real*; it's tough to be a bug! for Disney's Animal Kingdom; Test Track for Epcot; Rock 'n' Roller Coaster Starring Aerosmith for Disney's Hollywood Studios; and Rocket Rods (preshow lyrics) and host Tom Morrow's introduction to Innoventions for Disneyland. It's a good thing I've always had Tasmanian devil–level whirling, twirling energy— much to the chagrin of my wife—who frequently tells me, "You need to learn how to sit down and relax!" Well, honey, I'll have to relax later, because the time has come for the talk about the birds and the bees.

"WALK THIS WAY," said Aerosmith lead singer Steven Tyler to my then ten-year-old impressionable son. "I'm gonna tell ya the facts of life." That wasn't exactly the invitation a dad wants to hear extended to his innocent young child from a longtime rock 'n' roller. But before we rock that birds and bees story, let's talk about the birds from The Enchanted Tiki Room— Under New Management! and the bees from it's tough to be a bug!

There was a time in the early history of Walt Disney's Enchanted Tiki Room when there were fewer things to do in the park, which meant there was more time available to sit down, relax, and marvel at the first-ever Audio-Animatronics show. Then came along more in-park experiences and a new "MTV" generation of easily distracted young guests with shorter attention spans, who had grown up seeing Audio-Animatronics in many different shows and attractions. As a result, guests started to leave the Tiki Room at the Magic Kingdom before the show was over. This initiated a grand experiment to find out what would happen if we shortened the Magic Kingdom version of the show and picked up its pace. It also raised this question: Do we use this opportunity to change the structure of the show by introducing a new character or more? If so, where do we begin? You can begin to tell a story by saying your dog went to go lie down on his bed. But wouldn't it be more interesting to say your dog went to go lie down on your cat's bed—while the cat was still in it? Perhaps it was time to introduce a new bird to the beloved cast; one that could ruffle a few feathers.

The bad guy, Jafar, in the Disney animated feature *Aladdin* had a very vocal sidekick in his pesky parrot, Iago. Given his dominant and opinionated personality, Iago seemed like the perfect bird to drop in and take over the Tiki Room. He would be just the type to interrupt the show, present himself as the new owner, and inform José, Pierre, Fritz, and Michael there would be changes. With all due respect to another of my greatest heroes, composer Alan Menken, I rewrote the lyrics to his *Aladdin* song "Friend Like Me" as I thought it would be sung by Iago to the four existing birds. Of course, I could only do this with Alan's permission, so I met him for breakfast with the hope I would be able to step away from the table with no egg on my face. With a bit (okay, a *lot*) of trembling and trepidation, I presented my revised lyrics to the man I believe is the greatest theatrical and film composer of our time. I remember feeling like I was asking Leonardo da Vinci for permission to draw a mustache on the *Mona Lisa*. But Alan was warm, wonderful, and gracious, even complimentary, and he gave my lyrics his blessing without changing a single word. Here's what Iago once sang to José, Fritz, Michael, and Pierre when he rudely interrupted their show (to the tune of "Friend Like Me"):

Now listen, you birdbrains, if you're gonna keep your jobs you gotta get hip. I know all about hip, see?

'Cause I'm a very famous movie star and all of Hollywood drops my name
Who cares about Aladdin or Jafar? I'm the one with all the looks and fame
I've got a million crackers in the bank and I plan to get a zillion more
And you guys will all have me to thank when they're linin' up at your door
You are boring Tiki Birds, I'm a big cele-birdy
That's why I'm gonna go and change your show
Ain't it great to have a friend like me?
(José) *But señior, we've done this same show*
(Fritz) *Ja, since 1963!*
My, how time flies, get a life, you guys, you are ancient history!
Can your tails do this? Can your wings do that?
Can you bad birds sing hip hop or rap? Can you rock 'n' roll?
Well, listen here
It's a whole new world, so you'd better get hip or your audience will disappear
Here's your showbiz magic lamp, rub me right I'll set you free
You've paid your dues now you birds can't lose
Ain't it great to have a friend, great to have a friend
You can't wait to have friend, wait to have a friend
You ain't never had a friend like me!

Rude? The intent of this song was to establish Iago as a rude, obnoxious, and stuck-up intrusion to the show so the Tiki Birds and the audience would be relieved when the Tiki goddess Uh-Oa appears to cook his goose, save the Tiki Room, and restore peace to Polynesia.

Years later I would have another most welcome opportunity to meet with Alan Menken when we were revising the story and writing a new theme song for Sindbad's Storybook Voyage at Tokyo DisneySea. Alan invited me to his house in upstate New York to meet with him and lyricist Glenn Slater to work out the story direction for the new attraction song, "Compass of Your Heart." It was the first time this California native ever saw the breathtaking fall colors of the great Northeast, which surrounded Alan's home like a warm embrace on a chilly day. Again, I asked myself, "What am I doing here?" The entire day's experience was magical, even dreamlike. You can't even image how thrilled I was to be sitting in Alan's studio next to the man himself and the very piano where he sat and composed his many Tony- and Academy Award-winning songs. Alan's music stirs my soul, melts my heart, makes me appreciate the captivating influence and power of musical genius, and always, always inspires me to do my best.

Alan Menken Office

October 18, 1996

Kevin Rafferty
Walt Disney Imagineering
1401 Flower Street
Glendale, California 91221

Dear Kevin:

I've taken a look at the final changes and they look great. I'd like to convey my best wishes on the new _Improved_, "Tiki Room." Please let me know when it opens. My family and I would love to see it.

Best regards,

Alan Menken

Alan Menken, left, will never know how much his genius and work has inspired me. Actually getting to spend time with him and collaborate with him was a thrill.

The evening I returned home from that trip, I walked into my backyard—2,500 miles away from Alan's house—and heard my neighbor playing "Part of Your World" from _The Little Mermaid_ on her piano. If only she knew who I was with earlier that day!

Iago's feisty takeover of the Tiki Room was softened by his straightlaced business partner, Zazu. A hornbill from _The Lion King_, Zazu is better known as Mufasa's sidekick. Although he is a majordomo, Zazu is not a major star, which raises this question: Do two sidekicks add up to one star? No, not at all, but Iago and Zazu did play well together. Zazu's "voice of reason" role in the show was to warn Iago about the tiki gods. But he ignores the many warnings, and Iago's antagonizing antics ultimately awaken Uh-Oa, the Tiki Goddess of Disaster. (Uh-Oa has always been hidden somewhere under the tropical hideaway, but no one has ever made her upset enough to appear. Until now!) George Wilkins and I wrote an original song for the show sung by Uh-Oa called "Messin' with Me." Backed up by her chanting tiki gods (her "Polynesian Pips" à la Gladys Knight, if you will), Uh-Oa rises from out of the center fountain to sing the song and cast a spell on Iago, threatening to turn him into parrot stew. As she warns him beforehand, "When you mess with Polynesia, the tiki gods will squeeze ya!"

One day I was presenting the show to a group of colleagues in an upstairs conference room in the MAPO building called "The Aquarium." We gave the room that name because one entire side of the room was floor-to-ceiling sliding glass doors that opened onto a narrow balcony above the first floor. At that time, much of that open first-floor space was taken up by the huge scale model of the Tokyo DisneySea park, which was surrounded by a backdrop of concept art. When I got to the "Messin' with Me" part of the show, I sang it out loud and proud in the spirit and choreography Uh-Oa would emote with my gyrating backside poking out of one of the partially open sliding glass doors.

About halfway through the song, I noticed a wide-eyed Kathy Mangum giving me the old finger-across-the-throat motion, indicating I should ixnay on the ongsay. Upset about her interruption, which was ironic because the new show was all about Iago interrupting the tiki birds, I whapped the OFF button on my boom box, stared Kathy down, and said, "WHAT?" She smiled with a smug "I know what you don't know, *neener-neener*" smile and pointed down to the first floor, where the rest of my audience of colleagues now had their gazes fixed as well. I turned around to see what they were all looking at; and what did I see but the entire Disney Board of Directors. All gathered around the new park model but staring directly up at me! I had apparently captured their attention while singing and dancing like the Tiki Goddess of Disaster. And oh, this was certainly a disaster. Standing at the front of the group like the lead bowling pin was actor Sidney Poitier, who slowly raised his hands to me and began to clap with increasing momentum. The rest of the board joined him until the applause reached a fevered pitch. Was I embarrassed? More than I had ever been. But here's the way I looked at it: who else could shake their butt at the Disney Board of Directors and get applause?

I directed Gilbert Gottfried, the voice of Iago, in our studio at Imagineering. When it came time for him to sing "Friend Like Me," I kept my fingers crossed hoping he could pull it off. And boy, did he ever. He even held that last long note until he turned blue. I was glad we rolled tape during his practice performance because he sang the entire song in one fluid, perfect take, the take we used for the show. At the conclusion of our session, Gilbert asked me if he could go to Disneyland. Thinking he meant sometime in the distant future, if ever, I responded, "Sure, just let me know when you'd like to go." He said, "Now. I wanna go right now. Will you take me?" Gilbert happily hopped into my car and off we went to Disneyland where he was recognized by many guests, making me the sidekick's sidekick. (One guest noticed Gilbert and said, "Hey! You're that guy!") This is a good lead-in to the lesson learned in creating The Enchanted Tiki Room—Under New Management! I should have realized sidekicks are sidekicks for a reason. They exist to support the main character in a story as a confidant and for comic relief, and therefore are not meant to carry an entire show on their own. The lovable Sebastian from *The Little Mermaid* is a happy and charming little crab character, but he's not strong enough to be the star of a movie. Iago, on the other *claw*, was not even created to be happy, charming, or even lovable. He was created to be, well, obnoxious, and he could get away with it because he was paired up with a villain. That's why Iago seemed like he would be the perfect bad bird to take over the Tiki Room. But a little Iago goes a long way and as a result his was a limited engagement. When Iago flew the coop, José, Pierre, Fritz, and Michael were able to recoup their show, albeit, as José would say, in a "chorter" version.

As opposed to getting a few bugs *out* of a show, the following story is about getting a few bugs *in* to a show. While I was in a concept meeting for Disney's Animal Kingdom with Michael Eisner, he took a close look at the scale model of and concept art for the Tree of Life and took us all by surprise when he asked if it were large enough to house a theatrical show. The experts in the room discussed this among themselves and agreed it was indeed large enough. But inserting a theater into the space in the tree trunk that was originally designed to be an open walk-though could only be accomplished with major modifications.

Intended to be the "castle" icon (or weenie) of the park, the massive trunk of the Tree of Life was going to be sculpted with an intricate collage of integrated animal shapes so its "show" would be on the outside, not on the inside. "Okay, Kevin," Michael challenged, "go come up with a show we can put inside the tree." I had six weeks to go from blank sheet of paper to storyboard pitch, which was tough enough to do if that's all I had to do. But I had a lot of other projects in the works, each with their own deadlines and demands, including writing Michael's weekly introductions for the *Wonderful World of Disney* TV show. The good news is the idea for the show inside the tree came to me right away—and it seemed obvious. Inspired by the recent release of *The Lion King*, it made sense that the shaman baboon, Rafiki, would be the perfect host for a magical, mystical presentation about the Animal Kingdom. I saw Rafiki clearly in my mind staged beside the tree interior upon which he could draw images that would animate to bring his stories to life. Given his thin legs, I imaged him being attached to a moving support rod hidden behind his torso that would raise and lower him to move exactly like he did in the movie. The message of his presentation would be the value and importance of all of the animals in the kingdom. Perfect, I thought, for the theme of this park. After writing the theme song for the show, I finished a first-pass script and worked with an artist to board the story sequence. In five weeks, I presented the concept to Marty Sklar and then to Michael Eisner the following week.

After my pitch to Michael, he said, "For the Tree of Life, I'd give this show an eight on a scale from one to ten. Anywhere else in the park it would be a ten. But that tree has to have a show that's even better than a ten." Before I could suggest to Michael how I might be able to take the Rafiki show from an eight to a fifteen, he suddenly lit up with an entirely different idea: "Pixar is working on a movie about bugs," he said. "Go up there and find out what they're doing. This show should be about bugs!" After dropping that bug bomb, he dashed out of the room. Stunned, I looked at Marty and asked in my confusion, "Did he really say . . . 'bugs'? Marty nodded. "I HATE bugs!" I said, suddenly feeling the weight of the world on my shoulders. "Why does it have to be bugs? This is the ANIMAL Kingdom, not the BUG Kingdom!"

I'm not kidding, when I walked in my front door after work that night there was a Raid bug spray commercial on our TV. See? That's a sign. How could I create a compelling, entertaining show about bugs when people want them dead? After sleeping on it, I sucked it up and bought a bunch of bug books the next day to begin my research. Doing so meant I had to stare one of my biggest phobias in the face. On top of that, I was trying to justify why I was about to create a show about insects for a park about animals. My respect for Michael flew out the window like a fly as I tried to remain open-minded about his flea-brained suggestion. That is until I opened the first page of one of my bug books and learned to my great surprise, even shock, that there are ten quintillion insects in the animal kingdom and they make up almost 80 percent of the world's species. Hold your horseflies! Bugs are animals? We were going to do an entire park about animals and leave out 80 percent of them? MICHAEL IS A GENIUS!

Trying to land on a story premise, I went to put a bug in Tom Fitzgerald's ear as he is always great with story stuff. "Hey Kev," Tom said, "remember that Disney short It's Tough to Be a Bird!?" "Yeah," I said, "it was an educational film, right? I saw it in school." Tom, who knows every frame of every film that ever came out of the Walt Disney Studios, explained that the educational short featured an animated bird that explained how his fellow birds actually help humans, even though humans have often tried to kill them. He was on to something. Bugs, as much as they creep me out, don't get enough credit for what they do, even though I don't want to see them do it. I wanted to find out more, so I set up several appointments to meet with the top entomologists in the country. But before that, Tom and I flew up to Pixar to meet with another top bug expert, John Lasseter, who was working on his second movie after taking the world by storm with Toy Story. a bug's life was still in early production and Tom and I didn't know anything about it. We arrived early, so we decided to explore Richmond, California, where Pixar had its first studio in a plain, unmarked industrial building. Very Imagineering-like of them, no?

We found a bakery in town; well, actually, our noses did, and we decided to kill some time by having a cookie. But the cookies in this bakery were the size of pizzas. Tom and I each had one (and ate the whole thing). It was probably the equivalent of eating a dozen normal-sized cookies in one sitting. Why we did that I don't know but we were both as green as the Army Men characters in *Toy Story* when we arrived at Pixar. We were escorted to a small conference room, where producer Darla Anderson came in carrying a giant tray stacked with those giant cookies! "You guys just have to have one of these," she said. "They're from the best bakery in town." Just when I was about to toss my giant cookie, John Lasseter stepped in. This was my first trip to Pixar and the first time I met John. I never imagined then I would be flying to Pixar countless times over the next twenty-two years to work with John and his team on several future projects. John graciously took us through the story and concept art for the movie, though they were still in early development. The only character designs he had approved were Flik and Hopper. *a bug's life* was scheduled for release six weeks after opening day of Disney's Animal Kingdom and the premiere of it's tough to be a bug! So Flik and Hopper would be introduced to the world in our show. John gave us permission to run with them and agreed they would be animated by Pixar. But his animation studio would not be able to support us with anything else because they were totally absorbed in making their next movie. *Toy Story* would be a hard act to follow so they had to remain focused. That meant it would be up to us to create the story and supporting cast of characters for it's tough to be a bug! Several entomologists came to Imagineering with live creepy crawlies. These were not my favorite research days! But the day I'll always remember is the day I was surrounded by a panel of entomologists who inspired all of the show's characters and the subject for the finale song, all based on real stuff bugs do. "Okay, everyone," I began, "this is going to be a 3-D experience, so I'm looking for bug 'acts' that'll really get in your face. Any bugs out there that jump or spray stuff or throw stuff?"

The group became energized like the smart kids in the class who know the answer and beg to be called on by the teacher. "Ooooh, oooh, oooh!" exclaimed one of the entomologists. "There's a termite called the soldier termite who sprays acid." "Perfect!" I said. "He can be the Termite-ator!" Another entomologist offered, "There's a Chilean tarantula who tosses poison quills." I was getting excited. You can't make this stuff up. "Keep 'em coming!" I encouraged. The panel of experts suggested a long list of possible "entertainers," from stinkbugs to jumping spiders. I've never had such a love-hate relationship with a theme for a show. I could see all these acts in my head, while at the same time fearing they would appear in my bed!

The final challenge I gave the experts was a tough one. "I have thirty seconds at the end of the show for the grand finale," I told them. "If you could use that small window of opportunity to communicate to millions of people the key points they need to know about bugs, what would they be?" Their answer was unanimous. If insects were not around to pollinate and to eliminate waste, mankind would not be long for this earth. In other words, without insects we'd be toast (because there wouldn't be anything to make toast with)! That's a huge message to deliver in thirty seconds. Here's the song I came up with (the bees buzz in from the wings, and . . .):

We're pollinators! We're pollinators!
If you like vegetables, fresh fruit, and flowers
Give thanks to us bugs for our marvelous powers
If it weren't for the fact that we like the taste
You'd be out there wallowing in shoulder-high waste
And if all bugs were wiped off the face of the planet
There'd soon be no humans around here to man it
The best thing about us, you can't live without us
Still it's tough to be a bug!

Thanks to extensive research and to the insect experts who pollinated my mind with fun facts, the show practically wrote itself. Hosted by Flik the ant, it's tough to be a bug! quickly evolved into a variety show performed by a cast of talented bug characters whose real-life "acts" demonstrate their natural survival techniques. Their message to us, the "honorary bug" audience, is being a bug is not easy, but it's a good thing they have these incredible talents to help them survive because if they didn't, we humans wouldn't either. The bugs have mounted their show in the natural interior of the Tree of Life Theater where previous "Off-Bugway" productions have included *Web Side Story*, *A Cockroach Line*, and *Beauty and the Bees*. After I defined the cast and their names, wrote the first draft script, put the storyboard together, and got it all approved by Marty and Tom Fitz, I couldn't wait to get back in front of Michael Eisner to pitch the new show that grew out of his suggestion that at first made me think he was out of his ever-lovin' mind. But I caught the bug!

The actual show length ended up being about nine minutes, but my first script timed out at twelve because it featured one more "act" that didn't make the final cut. Here's why: the day I pitched the show to Michael, everything went perfectly and he was all abuzz with excitement until I got to the part called the Mating Game. For those of you old enough to remember *The Dating Game*, this segment was a parody featuring Flik as the eligible bachelor seated on one side of the divider wall, while on the other side of the partition were three poisonous bachelorettes that, in nature, kill and/or devour their mates: the black widow spider, the praying mantis, and the jumping spider. (Instead of the groovy graphic flowers on the wall as seen on the real *Dating Game* set, these flowers were real.) As "Johnny," the announcer of the *Mating Game* show, I performed for Michael the opening sequence and the introduction of bachelor Flik and the three bachelorettes. For example: "Bachelorette number one likes to hang out in old woodpiles by day and spin strong silk by night. Please welcome the Black Widow Spider." As the game began I performed as Flik asking his first question: "Bachelorette number two. We just had our first romantic encounter. What happens next?" "That's easy," she replies. "I bite your head off and suck your guts out!" Michael gasped and gave me the "time-out" signal, like a football referee. "Wait, wait, wait. Stop, stop, stop!" he interrupted. "We can't do this." I questioned, "We can't? Why not?" Michael answered in a serious tone: "Because an ant would not date a spider." I thought, *Oh, yeah? Well, an ant doesn't talk either!* Michael requested I cut the Mating Game segment out and happily settled back in for the rest of my storyboard pitch. After I finished singing the finale song, Michael said, "Home run! It's more than a ten. This show is perfect for the Tree of Life."

Claire de Room is the name of the stinkbug in the show. During her act, she turns her backside to the audience and lets out a stink bomb you can really smell thanks to a special effect. After challenging our special effects team to come up with that smell, they came to the first meeting with a real stinkbug in a sandwich bag, thinking we wanted to faithfully re-create that odor. We did not, but we didn't know what we were looking, or smelling, for. Week after week they would meet with Tom Fitz and me to let us take a whiff from their latest bottled concoction. We rejected one after another, and when our nose hairs and sense of smell were gone, whenever we'd see special effects coming with another sample, we'd run and hide.

Choosing a scent was a tough call because we didn't want the smell to be so bad the audience would want to leave the theater. But we did want the gag to be fun and believable. Finally, the effects guys landed on a scent that wasn't putrid, but it was, let's just say, obnoxiously organic. I took a slight whiff of the formula in the little bottle and happily passed it along to Tom. We whole-*nosedly* agreed it would work. Joe Rohde, creative lead of the Animal Kingdom park, happened to be walking by and we grabbed him and his schnozzola. As opposed to both Tom and myself, who had learned to take protective little kitten-like sniffs whenever another stinkbug sample came our way, Joe grabbed the bottle and snorted it long and hard like a bull in heat. "*Ahhhhh*, yes!" he exclaimed. "It's earthy!" At last! We had con-*scent*.

As a big fan of *Seinfeld*, I selfishly wanted to give Jason Alexander the role of Weevil Kneevil, the acorn weevil who pesters Chili, the quill-tossing Chilean tarantula voiced by Cheech Marin. When I found out Jason had accepted the role, I was ecstatic. But when he came to our recording studio at Imagineering, he assumed that because the weevil was an animated character I wanted him to come up with a new "cartoony" voice. This could not have been further from the truth. I wanted Jason to perform like George Costanza, his character in *Seinfeld*. But I could not tell him that. "So, I've been playing with several different voices for this little guy," Jason informed me. "Let me try some out on you." The first voice out of his mouth was a squeaky little sound that was cute but sounded nothing like Jason Alexander. No one could have guessed it was him, which defeated the purpose. "No," I said, "that's not quite it." He performed more of his vocal inventions, exploring the highs and lows of his range, and still none of them were even close to sounding like himself. I could see he was getting frustrated, as was I. "Okay," he said, brightening up, "here's a special one I've been saving. It's a little Cockney thing." He dropped his voice as low as it could go and performed like a soot-choked chimney sweep in *Mary Poppins*. Jason could tell by the look on my face that wasn't it either. The poor guy was such a good sport but had run the gamut of everything he had up his sleeve. Finally, he became upset and blurted out, in perfect George Costanza, "I give up, Kevin, I just don't know what you want!" I jumped up from my chair and proclaimed, "THAT'S IT! What you just did. That's what I want!" He shook his head as he realized, "You want George Costanza."

When we recorded Dave Foley performing Flik, we went over to stage 4 at the Walt Disney Studios and piggybacked on John Lasseter's recording sessions for *a bug's life*. I have a lot of fond memories of being over at stage 4, better known as Doc's stage. In 1990, after we had worked with and become longtime friends with the voice of Mickey Mouse, sound effects wizard, and Disney Legend Jimmy Macdonald, he sadly confided to me and Imagineering sound effects master Joe Herrington that he heard the studio was going to clear out all of his sound effects props and gadgets. "Fellas," said Jimmy, who was then eighty-three, "I don't know what to do."

For more than fifty years, Jimmy hand-made all of his sound effects gizmos in his garage on the weekends. They were crude-looking devices, which included wooden canvas-covered drums (that when spun under the canvas would create the sound of the wind) and a large caged drum filled with dry beans (that when turned would create the sound of rain or waves crashing on the beach). One circular gadget, with a single steel wheel that rolled along on a circle of steel track when turned with a handle, created the clickety-clack train sound, not only for Casey Jr. in *Dumbo* but also for Big Thunder Mountain Railroad. Among my favorite effects were Jimmy's brake drums scavenged from a junkyard that wouldn't appear to be anything out of the ordinary to anyone. But Jimmy perfectly "tuned" the drums by grinding and sanding them until he could achieve the thirteen notes of the chromatic scale by tapping with a rubber mallet. Jimmy created the sound of the chimes on Big Ben in *Peter Pan* and the clock chiming midnight in *Cinderella* with those brake drums.

Every one of the hundreds of his clever handmade props served to create most of the sound effects heard in every Disney movie and TV show from the 1930s to the 1970s. All sound effects in those days were created by hand and performed by hand, foot, or voice. But technology came along at that time in which digital libraries were created that were filled with every sound effect you could possibly imagine, right there at your fingertips. All you have to do now is click and "sample" the effect you want and download it into your digital media. Jimmy's hand-painted green props made from common materials were no longer needed, and they looked like junk to someone who didn't know what they were. But to me, Joe, and especially Jimmy, they were worth more than gold.

"Here's the plan, Jimmy," I said to my dear friend with the little white curlicue mustache—a man who made a difference in the lives of every Disney fan, and who continued to make a difference in mine. "Joe and I are gonna go get your effects. But we need your help." A sparkle returned to Jimmy's eye. "I'm in," he said. "What do you want me to do?" I said, "Joe and I are going to get a big van and the three of us are going to drive it over to stage 4 where we'll drop you off. You'll walk in, surprise everyone, and keep them distracted with your stories while Joe and I make off with the goods." Jimmy said, "Hot dog!" We were a SWAT team, and I say that because had we been caught, we probably would have received a good swat. But we didn't get caught. At 1430 hours, we drove the van past security and parked it on the side street in the backstage shadows. At 1435, Jimmy went into action while we found the storage room where the effects were stashed and "*Jimmy*'ed" the lock. To passersby Joe and I appeared like men who were there to clear the storage area. But as we were filling the back of the van, we were fulfilling a promise. By 1510 we had loaded the van and completed our plan. I entered Doc's stage, where I found everyone inside fully engaged by Jimmy and his stories in the very place he had spent most of his career. I winked at Jimmy and said in code, "The eagle's nest is empty." He left the stage with a spring in his step and I belted him in to ride shotgun in the van while I sat on the only available space left on the floor next to him. "Thanks, fellas," Jimmy said, a little choked up as we drove off the studio lot with his life's work. "Thank you, Jimmy," I responded. "For everything."

All of Jimmy's sound effects props are safe and "sound" inside a locked cage at Imagineering. I'm proud and happy to say that Joe Herrington, who is the media designer on Mickey & Minnie's Runaway Railway, the new attraction I'm currently leading, is creating our sound effects for the attraction the old-school way, using some of Jimmy's classic props that we saved from the rumored purge. Digital is the way to go in the industry these days, but Jimmy was the voice of Mickey Mouse for thirty-eight years. This is Mickey's first-ever attraction in our sixty-seven-year history of designing and building attractions, and it's filled with high-tech show technologies we've invented that are sure to daze and amaze. But the sound effects, quite appropriately and lovingly, will be performed by hand and heart.

Bobbie Macdonald, Jimmy's wife, gave me this rare photo of the Disney Studio musicians and animators at play. "Oh, the crazy things they'd come up with," Bobbie used to say. "We all had a ball!" I could write a book filled with the stories told to me by Bobbie and Jimmy Macdonald. That's Jimmy sitting behind the drum. He later became the drummer for the Dixieland band the Firehouse Five Plus Two.

When Jimmy Macdonald passed away in 1991, I was the first one Bobbie, his wife of more than sixty years, called to tell the news. She also asked for my help because she was elderly and had no children or anyone to help her, and Jimmy had always taken care of everything. Joe Herrington and I took good care of Bobbie and she treated me to her wonderful stories about when the Firehouse Five Plus Two, the legendary Dixieland band made up of Disney animators and drummer Jimmy, would spend many a long weekend together in a cabin in the mountains. I heard her personal stories about Walt Disney, stories she had never shared with anyone, such as when she was a nurse during World War II and Walt used to come to her to donate blood for the war effort.

Bobbie Macdonald used to tell me firsthand stories about the early Disney Studio days and her friendship with the animators, studio musicians, and Walt—stories that were never written in any book. Here she is taking care of Walt after his regular blood donation during World War II. Bobbie gave the uniform she is wearing, along with this photo, to my wife, Patty.

Bobbie gave me a one-of-a-kind 1943 photo of herself in uniform taking care of a smiling Walt. But the best thing she gave me was her personal rec-ollections about Walt, the Nine Old Men and their wives (and the dinners she used to host for them and the studio musicians), and about Marion Morrison, her best friend in high school, who used to treat her to sodas at his father's drugstore in Glendale and later changed his name to John Wayne.

There are many books out there about Walt Disney and his studio. But I got to learn about the man and his people, not by reading secondhand stories, but in firsthand accounts from the people themselves, like Jimmy and Bobbie, who were very much a part of that first Disney family. To know where you're going, you have to know where you've been. Getting to know and appreciate the history of The Walt Disney Company straight from those that made that history has made me a better and more appreciative Imagineer. Through my relationship with Jimmy, Bobbie, and others from that remarkable, prolific, and magical time, I felt connected to the people from that first generation of studio staff and Imagineers. They made such a difference in the world because, as I discovered, there was something magical about each and every one of them.

Bobbie and Jimmy had the most beautiful crepe myrtle tree I ever saw in the front yard of their little house in Glendale. I liked it so much I planted one in my front yard. But it didn't survive. Bobbie encouraged me not to give up and to plant another one. When I showed her the newly planted little tree in front of my house she touched it and promised it would be even more beautiful than hers one day. This tree took root and continued to grow, but it never bloomed like Bobbie's, not a single blossom in the six years I took care of her. But upon returning from her funeral, my crepe myrtle was in brilliant full bloom and even more beautiful than I had ever seen hers.

In the final stages of programming it's tough to be a bug!, there was a pause in the show I didn't like. So, I instinctively knew I'd be returning once again to Doc's stage for a pickup session. There's a "save the day" moment near the end of the show when the villain Hopper gets snapped out of the air by the whiplike tongue of a chameleon and disappears into its mouth. But when Hopper breaks out and flies out of sight, I noticed that there was a long—too long—moment of silence on an empty stage. I wanted to fill in that blank spot, but the film was completed and installed, so the only thing I could do was create an audio "hole filler." The only option seemed to be to write some backstage banter, perhaps a reaction to Hopper's abrupt disappearance. So, I added a hidden stagehand bug that asks this question: "Flik, what do we do now?" Flik responds, "Bring out the next act!" The stagehand says, "He refuses to come out of his cocoon." Flik exclaims, "Cue the finale!"

We needed to record this bit right away, so we struck a quick recording deal with the actor, director, producer, writer, and creator of *Happy Days*, Garry Marshall, who at the time was in the building across from Doc's stage editing a movie. We stole Garry right from his editing chair and set him up in front of the microphone. "We only have two lines for you," I said while handing Garry the script. "Thanks so much for doing this." He said, hopefully seriously, "Hey, are you kidding? This is great material." Garry knocked out the two lines in one take. When he performed the line, "He refuses to come out of his cocoon," it struck me as so hilarious I dropped to my knees laughing. "So long, fellas,"

Garry said as he headed out after working for us for all of about thirty seconds. "And somebody help Kevin off the floor, will ya?"

Longtime Imagineer Skip Lange lent his talent to the construction and sculpting of the interior theater space inside the Tree of Life. He really had to jump through hoops when Michael E. directed us to turn the tree interior into a theatrical venue. I'll never forget when the time came, just prior to opening day, when we invited a test audience to see the almost completed show. When the two hundred or so test guests came in and sat down, I spotted Skip in the corner of the room, hiding behind one of the giant tree roots he created. He spotted me, too, as I was standing along the back wall, and he held up crossed fingers. We were in this together and we were about to find out how the audience would react. During the show, they laughed and screamed in all the right places, and at the end they broke into the glorious applause of approval we live for. While the audience was leaving, talking excitedly among themselves, I went around to give Skip a big hug, hoping he wouldn't notice my eyes were misty. That's when I noticed he was shedding a few happy tears of his own.

Imagineers are an emotional bunch, that's for sure. "They loved it!" literally cried Skip. The last two test audience members to leave were a slow-moving elderly couple. As they were stepping through the exit door nearest to us, I watched the man stop and turn to his wife. "I don't know what the hell that was," he exclaimed to her, "but I want to do it again!"

I did the show again for Disney California Adventure, but I didn't work on anything else that was in that park on its opening day, except for naming the hot dog stand on Hollywood Boulevard: Award Wieners—Best Wieners in a Supporting Roll. it's tough to be a bug! opened with the new park, but it was the same show we created for Disney's Animal Kingdom, sans the giant tree, of course. Prior to the opening of Disney California Adventure, my colleague, show writer Dave Fisher, was working on a prime-time TV special, hosted by supermodel Cindy Crawford, to promote the new park. The production team planned to shoot a scene about it's tough to be a bug!, so Dave asked me to join Cindy on camera and tell her about the show. My role was going to be super-easy. This is how the shot was to play out: I was going to be sitting in the theater and Cindy was going to step in, sit down next to me, and casually say her line, "Hi, Kevin, can you tell me about it's tough to be a bug!?" My scripted response was "Sure, Cindy. It's a variety show put on by the bugs themselves to showcase their natural talents." Cindy would then continue to ask a few more questions. Dave and the camera crew arrived in the theater to set up the shot. When they were ready, Cindy was called in. I had never met Cindy Crawford, but I sure knew what she looked like. I took my seat, the camera started rolling, and when the director called, "Action!" I waited for Cindy to sit next to me and ask her first question as directed in the script. Cindy stepped in all right, but she didn't sit next to me. She sat *on* me! Being the fun-loving person she is, she playfully plopped herself down on my lap, put her arm around my neck, navigated her perfect glossy lips an inch away from mine, and said, "Hi Kevin. Can you tell me about it's tough to be a bug!?" I could not. My brain was oatmeal. Cindy Crawford had her entire supermodel self on me, her famous face so close to mine it was blurry, and she smelled so good I slipped into a nonresponsive euphoric trance, like one having smelling salts administered to them, only backwards. I eventually came to and remembered I had to deliver a line, but when I did, it sounded something like this: "*Eeeabwaahoooooohwaahmuwaaahhhh.*" When Cindy's fun performance was over, she took the next take seriously and did what she was supposed to do. But it took me several more takes to seriously remember who I was, where I was, and what I was doing there. It really happened exactly as I described. If you don't believe me, ask Dave Fisher.

Joe Herrington recently reminded me of another most embarrassing moment that happened during our first show of it's tough to be a bug! when it premiered on opening day of Disney California Adventure. He brought it up after I shared with him another crazy thing that happened after I joined our chairman of Parks and Resorts, Bob Chapek, onstage at D23 in 2017 to announce Mickey & Minnie's Runaway Railway to an audience of seven thousand fans. After my presentation, I went backstage to watch the rest of the showcase on a monitor set up there. My back was against a black curtain through which, near the end of the show, Mickey Mouse, Goofy, Chip 'n' Dale, and a few other characters stepped towards to await their call to the stage. I thought it a strange coincidence I was wearing a Mickey tie that day and Mickey himself stood right beside me. The other characters disappeared back through the rear curtain, leaving Mickey and me alone to watch the monitor together. Suddenly, out of my periphery, I noticed a white glove appear through the slit in the curtain directly behind Mickey, who was standing to my right. The glove had an orange sleeve above it, clearly connecting it to Goofy. The Goof reached in further, grabbed and squeezed the left side of Mickey's rear end—the side closest to me—and quickly withdrew his gloved hand back through the curtain. Mickey turned, shot me a look, and shook his finger at me. He thought I was the perp! I was set up by The Goof!

It really happened exactly as I described. If you don't believe me, ask Goofy. When I told that story to Joe, he laughed and said, "Well, that doesn't surprise me. That kind of stuff happens to you all the time." To illustrate his point, he told the story about when he and I were sitting together during the premiere of the bugs show and I got attacked—not by a bug, but by something even more dangerous: an angry woman. At the end of the show we have a gag in which a traveling mechanism hidden under each seat makes it feel like a "bug" is quickly crawling around under your bottom (gets 'em every time!). When that moment happened at the end of that first show, the woman seated to my right thought I was getting fresh with her. She jumped out of her seat and whacked me with her purse! And her purse was studded with sharp little doodads! It really happened exactly as I described. If you don't believe me, ask Joe Herrington.

Even though I learned during the development of it's tough to be a bug! we can't live without insects, I still don't like them, just like I don't like riding on roller coasters. The difference is we can survive without roller coasters. If you ever happen to be walking down the street, or driving in your car—or even flying in a jet thirty-five thousand feet up—and hear a voice screaming, "Save me, sweet Jesus!" that would be me after sitting down in a roller coaster vehicle and spotting a spider in it. Hey, everyone has their phobias, but somehow I ended up turning mine into shows and attractions. It was exciting working on the Rock 'n' Roller Coaster Starring Aerosmith, but the thought of eventually having to take a ride on a vehicle that is catapulted from zero to sixty miles per hour in 2.7 seconds only to career upside down on two back-to-back inverted loops kept me awake on many a long night. But working on the project itself was a blast. I got to fly on the Disney corporate jet with John Dennis, our Imagineering director of music, and producer Paul Osterhout to meet with Aerosmith in their hometown of Boston. We met in a small hotel conference room downtown where there was a large convention in session in the grand ballroom next to ours. When that session let out and the crowd migrated into a large common space, it was at the same time Steven Tyler was returning from the bathroom. Bad timing. I thought he was going to try to sneak unnoticed around the mass of people, but he spotted me standing on the opposite side of the room. "Hey, Kevin!" he shouted across the crowded floor. "This *#&%ing ride is gonna be &$%#ing awesome!"

While in Boston we had a recording session for the band so they could do a few dialogue pickups. When I set the script on the stand in front of Steven, the tech asked for a sound-level check and I leaned into the mic and made the sound of a water drip by tapping my finger against my cheek and forming the sound with my lips. "Whoa!" reacted Steven with surprise. "Teach me how to do that!" I gave him "drip" lessons and he became obsessed with mastering that sound, which took us all the way up to our lunch break. We were recording pickup lines that day to use for the preshow film we'd shot the week before with the band at a soundstage in Hollywood. High-res digital video was not yet available, so we shot the scene with a Showscan camera to better create the illusion that Aerosmith was really on the other side of the glass in a recording studio. Showscan uses 70mm film and moves it past the lens at a superfast sixty frames per second, which is two and a half times faster than standard. The benefit of using Showscan is it eliminates all perception of film flicker and thus creates a more believable image.

The challenge with shooting in Showscan, however, is it requires twice the intensity of light for the image to register on the film emulsion because it's moving past the lens so quickly. There were no film cuts because the scene had to be believable as one real-time, real-scale continuous moment. That meant poor Aerosmith had to hit their marks and deliver their lines—in other words, do the entire scene—in one uninterrupted shot. Our film director, Jerry Rees, had the patience of Job as the band entered the set upon his call to "action" only to squint because of the twice-as-bright light. It was like looking at the sun. "Remember," Jerry kept reminding the band with each take, "no squinting!" The members of the band were troopers, as it took twenty-seven takes to finally get the shot. As we were shooting on Saturday, I brought along my ten-year-old son and sat him in an out-of-the way chair in the corner of the soundstage. After we wrapped, Steven Tyler went over to chat with Kevin Jr. and I was able to take a photo of them together. That's when Steven decided it was time to tell him the facts of life. He grabbed "KJ" and they both stepped away from me for "the talk." I tried my best, but if you can't read Steven Tyler's lips, you can't read anybody's. After it was done Steven shot me a thumbs-up.

"So," I couldn't wait to ask my son on the drive home, "what exactly did Steven tell you about . . . life?" KJ answered matter-of-factly, "Well, he said it's really all about three things." He left it at that, which left me hanging. I just had to find out what those things were, even though I didn't really want to know. "And what three things," I asked apprehensively, "are those?" KJ answered, "Rock and roll, fast cars, and chocolate cake." I smiled with relief and asked one more question, because I wanted to put the whole thing to bed, so to speak. "He didn't mention anything to you about, you know . . . women?" KJ shot me a look. *"Eeew!"* he answered. "Why would he do that?"

Years later Kevin Jr. was at a concert, and before it started he struck up a conversation with the group sitting in front of him because they were talking about their favorite band, Aerosmith. "Have you ever been to an Aerosmith concert?" they asked. "Sure have," Kevin responded, but he didn't tell them Aerosmith had invited us to be their special guests at the Hollywood Bowl. One of the guys bragged that at the last Aerosmith concert he attended, he got to sit only nine rows away from the stage, the closest he'd ever been. "I swear," he

said, "Steven Tyler looked right at me." He then smugly said to Kevin, "I'll bet you've never been that close." Kevin answered, "You're right," as he pulled the photo I took of him with Steven's arm around him out of his wallet. "I was THIS CLOSE!"

While working on-site at the Rock 'n' Roller Coaster, my entire team constantly picked on me because I refused to take a ride. For weeks before opening day, everyone tried talking me into riding with them—and some even went so far as to bribe me, even blackmail me. I would not go. If someone offered me a brand-spanking-new Corvette if I rode the Coaster, I still would not go. My fearless friend and tough Texan, media designer Joe Herrington, whom I've had the pleasure to work with on most of my attractions, sat in the coaster vehicle with his media rig on his lap to mix the soundtrack on board, which meant he had to ride it over and over again without stopping. One day he rode fifty-seven times in a row on it, with a cast on his leg to boot (he had broken his leg outside of work, probably on a bucking bronco), to get the sound just right.

I marveled at Joe as I stood on the unload platform and watched him return and take off again—and each time he'd give me his famous smile and salute before being catapulted instantly out of sight. "You know, Kev," music director John Dennis kept telling me, "after all this work we've done, you're going to have to ride it at least once." To get everyone off my back, I finally promised the team I would take one ride and one ride only, and only on the day Tom Fitzgerald came to approve the onboard sound. That bought me some time to try to figure out what story I would make up when I called in sick that day. But dang it if Tom didn't show up a day early! Everyone held me to my promise. No, really, they held me! Tom refused to ride without me by his side. The audio team put Tom, who will ride anything anywhere no matter how high, fast, or insane, in the front seat of the first car of the super-stretch limo coaster vehicle. Then they caught me (I'd escaped their grip and was running in the opposite direction), wrestled me down, and jammed whimpering, hyperventilating me into the seat next to Tom. Everyone then hopped in behind us. "C'mon, Kev," assured Tom, "you're gonna love this!"

Tom's mission was to listen closely to the sound mix and decibel levels to give the executive approval the sound team had been working and waiting for. My mission was to figure out a way to escape the locked-down shoulder harness and run all the way to Cuba without stopping. I learned at that moment all of my other phobias were small change compared to my fear of riding this coaster. This was proven while waiting for vehicle dispatch by all of the options that flashed through my head of things I would be willing to do to get out of this coaster car: I would go over Niagara Falls without a barrel, walk on the freshly waxed wing of an airplane in smooth-bottomed slippers without a harness, or even let a dozen tarantulas crawl all over my naked body to get out of this.

But it was too late. The vehicle rolled forward and stopped at the launch point. I would have passed out had it not been for the nausea keeping me vomit vigilant. The very moment I was about to throw up, the sudden g-force of the launching vehicle shoved it all back down. The nightmare was real until I slipped into a linear induction-induced semicoma and everything became as blurry as Cindy Crawford's up-close face during our "talk" on bugs. And that's with my eyes closed. Before I knew it, we had returned to the unload platform, where I crawled my shaking, soaking self out. Already on my knees, I kissed the ground as my team cheered wildly. "So, Tom," John Dennis asked, "how did everything sound?" Tom shook his head, pointed at me, and said, "I don't know. I couldn't hear anything but THAT GUY screaming." Steven Tyler got his three "facts" right. After reminiscing about all that rocking 'n' rolling in a fast car, working on Test Track was going to be a piece of cake.

Marty Sklar joined me on opening day of the Rock 'n' Roller Coaster Starring Aerosmith. Just further proof that Marty rocks!

TEST
TRACK

BEING A CAR GUY, you can imagine how deliriously happy I was when ten years after the opening of EPCOT, Marty Sklar asked me to put some thought into how we could update and enhance the World of Motion pavilion. When I first came to WED, one of my favorite things to do was check in on the progress being made on the figures, show sets, and cars during the production of the attraction that showcased the history of transportation, starting with the invention of the wheel to the present day, as presented by General Motors. When I saw our figure-animation team pushing a showroom-perfect, root beer–colored 1955 Chevrolet Nomad into the MAPO building I was giddy. That is until they started taking out the engine and the seats and cutting big holes in its floor. But that's what they had had to do to get the Audio-Animatronics family into the "family car" for one of the show scenes.

I was among the first to get to see the concepts for the scenes because the attraction designers Marc Davis and later Ward Kimball, came to me to have their original concept art dry mounted and matted. I loved World of Motion because it was designed and produced in classic Imagineering style with great sets and staging, delightfully designed and costumed animated figures, clever quick-read visual gags, and even an exclusive theme song entitled "Fun to Be Free." The biggest challenge facing our story and design team, assembled by Marty for the sole purpose of refreshing the existing show, was how to make an already wonderful experience even better. But that was our mission—and an important one, because at the time General Motors was considering whether or not to renew their contract with the park. As we began to present some of our new enhancement concepts to the GM executives, they challenged us with this totally unexpected question: If we gave you the freedom to create something entirely new at our pavilion, what would it be? That's the kind of question Imagineers love to be asked! Sticking with the theme of transportation, we looked at this out-of-the-blue invitation as a blue-sky opportunity to create the first E-Ticket thrill ride at Epcot.

To get the ride rolling, our fearless leader Marty, along with Barry Braverman, then executive designer for Epcot, and Bran Ferren, then vice president of Creative Technology, put together a lean and mean concept development team that included Dan Armstrong, Bruce Johnson, and Al Mirabella from Ride Systems Development and concept designers Tim Delaney, David Durham, Eric Robison, and me. We started with an "anything goes" attitude and our big thinking segued into developing and inventing, albeit theoretically, what Bran articulately called "state-of-the-art-stuff." This stuff included infrared imaging systems, nontraditional audio and media systems, and "instantly changing environments." Taking our inspiration from the pavilion's original theme, our first idea was to invent a "transformer" vehicle that could mechanically turn into any vehicle imaginable. For example, you'd be speeding along in a Formula 1 race car at one moment and then be landing your fighter jet—that same vehicle in a different form—on the deck of an aircraft carrier the next.

"To pull off this big idea," Bran directed, "we'll have to avoid subtlety at all costs." During this early exploratory phase, we invited the GM executives out to ride a mock-up of the Indiana Jones Adventure vehicle Dave Durham had just programmed. They were so excited by this "rolling simulator" vehicle that they asked us to explore the possibility of using a similar system for our "transformer." But how could we use a ground-based vehicle that simulates bumps, road hazards, and skidding in our attraction story? Marty had the perfect answer: "How about a test track?" he suggested. "They're a huge part of the GM story, and they're pretty rigorous. Believe me, I barely survived one while we were developing Epcot." We went to work exploring that very possibility.

"Whatever the vehicle is," directed Bran, "it's got to be different from anything we've ever done. Faster. Smarter. Better. Basically, it has to do a lot more . . . stuff!" Given that incredibly detailed direction, we designed a new ride vehicle that not only looked and behaved like a real car but could zip along a high-speed track that extended for quite a distance outside of the pavilion. It would also be capable of hitting any speed in between the range being set and could travel over any road surface with real tires like an actual car. This incredible go-anywhere, do-anything, supersmart ride vehicle raised the question (yes, it was so smart it could even raise questions), why *simulate* various road surfaces and high speeds when you could really do it? This was radical thinking.

Dave Durham laid out the very first version of our proposed test track and, after doing some research on the subject, I had a first-pass story sequence developed to go along with the layout. We invited the GM execs back to take a look. They didn't only love it, they *loved* it! Why wouldn't they? This concept was the perfect marriage between their real-world story and our attraction story. It was both fun and informative, which made it so Epcot! The excited GM execs invited us out to their test track—also known as a proving ground—in Milford, Michigan, to take a ride in *their* vehicles. I was excited to go for two reasons: it's a car guy's dream, and I knew our experience out there could, and probably would, inspire and inform our overall attraction story and "test" sequence. And that's exactly what happened.

One of the things I've always loved about my job is never knowing what is going to happen next. One day I'm sitting in front of my computer plinking away, and the next I'm sitting in the driver's seat of a gazillion-horsepower

Corvette nicknamed "Mad Dog"—zooming almost one hundred miles per hour—backwards! It all started when Dan, Eric, and I traveled to Milford for a "leisurely" tour (note the quotes there and consider Gilligan's "three-hour tour"). Dan was invited because he was the ride guy; Eric was invited because he was the design guy; and I was invited because they must have found out I drove a Ford and, sensing I was susceptible to motion sickness, they wanted to punish me. "Our cars are really punished," said a Test Track executive at dinner the night we arrived. "They are dunked, sandblasted, scorched, frozen, skidded, rolled, and crashed, as you will see tomorrow when you" (pointing at me) "get behind the wheel." Our host, a GM executive named John, added, "Our vehicles are driven day and night over all kinds of rigorous roads. It's our way of making sure everything goes smoothly when you get behind the wheel in your hometown." I said nervously, "Uh, I thought this was going to be a t-t-tour." John responded, "Oh, it will be. From the inside of a few of our . . . heh, heh . . . test vehicles." I'm not kidding, at that moment, in the restaurant bar, a band began to play "Dead Man's Curve" by Jan and Dean.

The next morning, we met John and Tom at the proving grounds. The four-thousand-acre site was indeed impressive, energized, as I had expected, with dozens of top secret prototype vehicles buzzing here, there, and everywhere like bees in a field of flowers. It was definitely a privilege for us non-car biz types to be there. "We'll start on our off-road track," said Tom. "Jump into the Suburban." The view through the windshield to the off-road course ahead looked like the surface of the moon after an A-bomb explosion, followed by a monsoon, and then by an earthquake. "Buckle up!" instructed Tom. *SCREEEECH!* At that exact moment, my head flattened the foam of the headrest to the thickness of paper. I couldn't help but regret getting GM's money's worth at the all-you-can-eat breakfast buffet an hour earlier.

Now feeling the greasy curse of my self-serve sausage sampler, I focused not on the off-road ahead but on trying to exorcise my brain of that nausea-inducing word "sausage." "Here comes the 'Big Dipper,'" warned driver Tom as he launched the truck high into the air like a rocket. The flying in the air part wasn't so bad. It was the coming back down to the ground that was extremely noticeable. Boulders, trees, mud, Mount Everest—you name it, the vehicle we were in went through or over it. You know how when severe motion sickness kicks in, the last thing you want to think about, besides life in general, is food? As he fought with the steering wheel, Tom said, "You're in for a treat at lunchtime. I'm going to barbecue." Trying to change the subject from food to anything else, I weakly interrupted, "How . . . how about those Detroit Tigers?" Tom said, "I'm a big Tigers fan, but what I really love about going to the games are their big juicy spicy sausages." John commented from the bouncing back seat, "Me, too! I love 'em smothered with peppers and onions and sauerkraut." I wondered if the rest of my team was feeling as sick as I was as we careened over the crevasses of the craters of the moon—or this land that was serving as moonscape. I glanced over at Eric, whose only concern was trying to keep his sunglasses on his face. Dan was just yelling "whoopee!" and "yee-haw!" in typical ride-guy fashion. As for Tom and John, it was just another day at the office. *Thump! Slip! Slosh! Crash! Bang!* Tom, still thinking about sausages, added, "Yeah, with gobs of spicy German mustard." I mustered all the strength I had left to ask, "Tom, uh, is there much more of this?" He laughed and said, "Oh, you want more? Don't worry, there's LOTS more. Just wait'll we get to the rough section and I drop 'er into four-wheel drive!" I must have blacked out, because I don't remember stopping. As I slid out of the Suburban like a slug, I cursed it for being so high off the blessed flat, solid ground. What started out as clean and shiny ended up looking like a giant green-and-black mud-covered hair ball—and that was just me.

We had arrived at the legendary "Black Lake." As large as fifty-nine football fields put together, the vast flat asphalt surface got its name because it looked exactly like a big lake after a rain. Its horizon bowed from left to right as far as the eye could see. "Nothing like it on the planet," Tom said proudly. He respectfully removed his cap, bowed his head, and added, "You can see this from the moon." Eric questioned, "You can see your head from the moon?" Tom ignored Eric and continued, "We do a lot of brake, steering, and general performance testing out here. It's also where we train the Secret Service and the FBI how to drive evasively." I was still feeling extreme motion sickness when he asked what kind of car I wanted to have out there. I mumbled, "Ambulance," which Tom must have interpreted as "Corvette." He drew his two-way radio out from its holster like a Colt .45, spun it around Wyatt Earp-style, and ordered cars to be brought up for Dan, Eric, and me. Suddenly, three souped-up Chevys, like the Blue Angels in perfect door-to-door formation, roared over the distant horizon of the Black Lake and came in for a perfect landing directly in front of each one of us. The driver of my Corvette was the spitting image of mustachioed actor Wilford Brimley. At that time, the real Wilford Brimley was starring in oatmeal commercials. "Oatmeal," I whispered to myself. "I should have had oatmeal." My driving instructor jumped out, introduced himself as C. C., ran around to the passenger side and said, "She's all yours. Hop on in!" For those of you that have never driven a Corvette, when you drop into the driver's seat, it feels like your butt is actually below ground level. Looking at the dash you'll discover the speedometer and tachometer have more numbers than a

New York City phone book. I had no idea what we were going to be doing out there in that astronomical expanse of asphalt, but if all those spirograph-like tire marks were any indication, it was not going to be like taking a Sunday drive to church.

"I have a wife and two little kids," I said to C. C., emphasizing the profound importance of my staying alive. "That's why," he said, "I want you to do exactly what I tell you exactly when I tell you to do it." We buckled up and I put a death grip on the wheel. "Hit the gas NOW!" I floored the pedal and we blasted like buckshot out of a barrel. Before you could say "juicy spicy sausage" we hit 90 mph and were quickly closing in on the back edge of Black Lake. C. C. pointed me onto a long, thin connecting roadway that in the blink of an eye directed us like Secretariat out of the gate onto the high-banked oval track where he said, "Take her up to one hundred miles per hour and then kick 'er in the butt!" *WHOOOOOA!* 125 mph . . . 145 . . . 155 . . . all the way up to the highest of the five severely banked lanes on the four-mile speed oval. The vertical safety rail fence posts, only inches away, dissolved into a blur until they disappeared altogether, making the horizontal rail look like it was floating in midair. C. C. appeared to be calm and relaxed despite the fact his long, droopy white mustache was now wrapped horizontally past his ears and around his head. He never told me, but I deduced "C. C." must have stood for "Cool Cucumber." I, on the other hand, was absolutely petrified driving over 160 mph, my hands tightly gripping the wheel like the talons of a hawk trying to fly off with a bull elephant.

"Now," instructed C. C., "take your hands off the wheel." I laughed nervously, in polite reaction to his stupid joke. "Really," he said, "DO IT!" I didn't do it. I couldn't do it. "Trust me," C. C. said calmly. "Nothing is going to happen." I argued, "What if a UFO lands on the track in front of us? Then what?" In the time I uttered those words, at the speed we were going, we probably did ten laps. I could tell he really wanted to prove something to me so, confident I had my living trust in order, I slowly released my grip from the wheel. C. C. was right! Nothing happened. "Centrifugal force," he said. "We could stay up here in this lane all day long. That is, unless a UFO lands in front of us. Sheesh, you Californians."

With both hands back on the wheel, we shot back over to Black Lake, where off in the distance, I could see Dan's and Eric's cars zigzagging across the surface. "See that mile-long wet spot ahead?" pointed out C. C. "Yeah," I responded while watching Eric's car spin around and around. "I'll bet that came from Eric!" C. C. didn't get the joke. "Nope, it's a chemical mixture that simulates ice on the road. I'm going to show you the difference between regular brakes and antilock brakes." Before I could fire off a Hail Mary, C. C. flipped the

NON-ABS switch on the console—and at 80 mph, we hit the edge of the "ice," two wheels on, two wheels off. "Brake as hard as you can," commanded C. C., "NOW!" "*AAAAaaaAAAAaaaAAAAaaaahhhhhh!*" Let me just say, I now know what a banana feels like in a blender. We instantly did at least eight 360-degree spins. I was not expecting that as much as I was not expecting Cindy Crawford to jump in my lap.

"Another lap!" cried C. C. as he switched back over to ABS. When he told me to brake hard again, I braced, assuming we were going to spin again. But the active antilock brake system kept that Vette moving as straight as an arrow. After all that spinnin' and grinnin', C. C. was chillin' like he was relaxing in a beach chair in Maui. But he did have to scrape me off the headliner like gum under a church pew. Then, over the next hour, C. C. taught me several evasive driving techniques, like collision avoidance, steering while braking, skid recovery, and barfing breakfast safely out the driver's side window, a special maneuver that was not on the official agenda.

We finally rolled to a much-needed, blessed stop. Who knew being an Imagineer would teach me how to be a better, safer driver? But man, I was so glad all that Black Lake lunacy was over.

"And now," exclaimed C. C., "for the grand finale!" From the passenger side, he shifted the automatic transmission into reverse. "Ever do a one-eighty?" he asked. I answered, "A one-eighty . . . *what?*" He instructed, "Punch the accelerator all the way to the floor and hold it there NOW!" *SCREEEEECH!* The car was literally screaming (or maybe that was just me) like a crazed banshee as it blasted backwards. Suddenly, all I could see through the windshield was pure white smoke pouring in from both sides of the car over the contours of the pronounced fenders and hood until the front end was completely engulfed in white. I knew at any moment that blinding cloudy whiteness would dissolve, like a scene change in a movie, to reveal the pearly gates. C. C. yelled, "Slam your brake hard NOW!" *SCREEEECH!* "Okay," he shouted out, "turn your wheel hard to the left until it locks NOW!" At the high speed we were traveling backwards and then hard braking, turning the wheel hard left whipped the front end of that Corvette around 180 degrees faster than a finger snap. C. C. pulled the tranny out of R, shoved it into D, and shouted, "Step hard on the gas NOW!" From 75 mph to . . . 95 . . . 105 . . .125 . . . and counting.

"You did it!" he praised. I had no idea what the hell I had just done. All I know is when I finally opened my eyes, we were speeding in the opposite direction from where we started and my wallet was on the other side of my pants. It was then I spotted a ribbon of thick black smoke, the type you see after a horrific crash, billowing high into the air. "Oh, no!" I cried, thinking the worst,

The cover of the winter 1999 *WDEye* magazine.
Note I'm in an Autopia car and costume!

"Dan and Eric!" C. C. smiled. "Yep, it's them," he said, "and the rest of 'em, too. Looks like Tom has fired up the barbecue and he's cookin' up his favorite. Hope you like sausages!"

The good GM folks were marvelous hosts. They set up a shade tent and a barbecue on the Black Lake to serve us up a home-cooked meal. Over lunch, Dan's driving instructor boasted how Dan had broken the test-track record for the most consecutive nonstop 360s in a row. Well, sure, he's the ride guy. My instructor, C. C., told everyone how he joked with me about taking my hands off the steering wheel on the speed oval. "And he actually did it!" he proclaimed. After lunch, our research continued. We experienced various road surfaces, brake tests, potholes, water trenching, sandblasting, scorching heat, freezing cold, and anechoic chambers—and watched barrier tests, where they crash new cars manned with sensor-equipped crash dummies against thick concrete walls. By the end of the next day we had seen and done just about everything at the Milford proving ground. After I had learned to steer like an FBI agent, speed like Dale Earnhardt, and brake like Fred Flintstone, I had a newfound appreciation for everything GM does to test and prove the more than fifteen thousand parts that go into every new car. And I had gained much respect for GM's bottom line: dedication to safety and performance. Some of what I did out there was definitely crazy, but they actually do every bit of it for a reason.

Driving back to the airport a much more skilled and safe driver, Dan, the new 360-Degree King, was gushing about our experience at the test track; and rightfully so. We got to see and do what a lot of car guys only dream about. Proudly adjusting his new GENERAL MOTORS PROVING GROUND cap, he said, "If only we could capture in the new World of Motion just a taste of the thrill we had out there, we'd have a home run attraction." Eric agreed: "Oh, man, the place would be packed. We'd have to design a queue area the size of Black Lake." "Imagine," I said, "a queue you could see from the moon!"

Our experience in Milford did indeed inspire and inform our attraction story sequence. Every "test" featured in the attraction is based on a real test we personally saw or experienced at the proving ground. When we presented Test Track to Michael Eisner, he commented, "When guests get off the ride, they should be asking themselves, 'Was that just a great ride? Or are they really doing automotive testing here?'" To maintain the automotive legitimacy of our design, we brought in two new members to our team who were automotive designers before they became Imagineers: Albert Yu, who designed our vehicle body, and Orrin Shively, who became our show producer for the project. When Orrin found out we were changing World of Motion into something else, he worried it was going to be something like "Favorite Hubcaps from the Past" or "The Happy History of the Vega." But when he found out we were going to tell the story of a test track, he instantly understood, by the name alone, what it was and where we were going. The name perfectly and instantly communicated the attraction story and experience. That's why I was shocked and surprised to receive an invitation from GM to take part in a "naming charette" to change our working title, Test Track, to a "real" attraction name.

"What the heck is wrong with Test Track?" I questioned Orrin. "It says what it is and it sounds fun." Orrin insisted, "You should go to the charette." Orrin came from the auto industry and seemed to have great insight about such things. Besides, I had to go. The company GM hired for the naming exercise was flying all the way from New York City to Los Angeles just to meet with me.

I have personally named a lot of attractions over the years but never in an all-day session with a room full of people whose only expertise is naming things. I didn't even know there was such a thing. My experience in coming up with names is they just come to me, and when they sound and feel right, that's it. No overthinking, no muss, no fuss. One day, Bob Zalk, who was the creative producer for the Disney Cruise Line, came into my office, as a lot of Imagineers do when they need a name for something. "Kev," Bob said, showing me a concept sketch, "here's a new waterslide we're designing for the *Disney Dream*, and it needs a story and name. Can you help us?" The name came in an instant. "How about 'AquaDuck'? We can connect the story with Donald and the nephews." "Done!" exclaimed Bob, and he happily went on his merry way. Coming up with names for stuff is one of my favorite things to do.

Another example is when I was working on Blizzard Beach, I had to name a snack shack, which, considering the story of the park, came to me quickly: "Avalunch." That's an example of a name that can also inform the facility design, and it did. I just couldn't see the necessity of fifteen "professional namers" traveling across the country to lock themselves in a room with me to come up with a name, especially since *Test Track* sounded and felt right. But apparently that's how it works in the automotive field and other industries that don't have Imagineering show writers on staff.

The naming session took place in the large conference room of a fancy hotel in Los Angeles. I was the first to arrive. When the entourage entered the room at precisely the correct scheduled time, they were perfectly groomed and very well-dressed, like models from *Glamour* and *GQ*, making me feel out of place in my jeans and Hawaiian shirt. None of them acknowledged me at first but sat with their backs to me facing double doors like hungry dogs waiting for their masters to get home. Suddenly, the doors burst open and a tall slender silver-haired, steely-eyed, black-suited, stiletto-shod woman entered into the room with all the calming presence of a Sherman tank. The group went silent and snapped to attention. This woman had the demeanor of Gloria Swanson meets Maleficent. She made Meryl Streep's Miranda Priestly in *The Devil Wears Prada* look like Snow White. She didn't even look at me when I stepped over to introduce myself to her. "Everyone!" she proclaimed to her royal subjects and me, "sit!" I sat. "Now," she commanded, "give to me swift animals. Swift, swift animals! Come, come, come . . ." Her people started shouting out suggestions like "gazelle" and "cheetah." "Cheetah!" she repeated. "Yes, yes, cheetah. Everyone repeat after me: *cheeeetaaaaah!*" Her minions quickly wrote all of the fast-animal types being shouted out on the blank paper wall that encircled us. "Now," Gloria continued, "give to me forces of nature! Nature, nature, nature! Come, come, come . . ."

On it went like that for the rest of the day until the huge pile of once-juicy Sharpies went dry. It was by far the weirdest brainstorming session I had ever attended, and all for one name. At the end of the day, there were thousands of words like BRISK, SPRINGBOK, SAILFISH, and even WHIRR written on the paper wall by members of the group, and they were instructed by Gloria Maleficent to return to NYC and organize them in terms of those that best "evoke"—are you ready for this?—"a world of motion." I KNOW! I

Over the years, I've enjoyed the opportunity to provide names for many different things in the Disney parks, including this snack shack for Blizzard Beach. Its name came before the concept design of the facility, making this a great example of how a name can inform the actual design!

couldn't believe it myself. The company packed up and informed me they would soon send out their top recommendations for the new attraction name, which I fully anticipated would include such gems as *The Brisk Springbok Adventure*, *Whirr of the Cheetah*, and *Gazellebration!* Well, you know what we ended up with, which goes to show, when it comes to naming attractions, *cheetahs* never prosper.

On my flight home from that grueling but worthwhile research trip to the GM proving grounds in Michigan I tried to calm the elderly gentleman sitting next to me, who was clearly upset by the terrible air turbulence. Compared to the "turbulence" I had just experienced at the proving grounds, this plane ride was a piece of cake. I had survived every conceivable road rigor and sausage they could toss at me and came out the victor, so I was as laid-back as a bank on Sunday. "What do you do for a living, young man?" he asked, trying to keep his mind off the bumpy flight. "I'm a writer," I responded. "Writer, eh?" I nodded affirmatively. "For the life of me," he wondered, "I don't know how you writers can just sit there in front of one of them computers all day long."

"ASPIC!" INTERRUPTED

Tom Schumacher, then head of Disney Feature Animation, while I was pitching the concept for a scene in Mickey's PhilharMagic, where Donald Duck is the "guest" in the Beast's dining room and the camera travels over the table towards the translucent jiggly dish I referred to as "gelatin." "It is aspic, not gelatin," repeated Tom. "Do you," he continued, "know what aspic is?" "Yes!" I shot back semi-emphatically. "It's a . . . kind of . . . gelatin." I wanted so badly to get it right because Tom was head of a major department and it was important to get him on board with our attraction concept that radically turned his art form upside down by inserting Donald Duck into some of the most emotional and most beloved musical moments from Disney Animation. I was pitching a "fish out of water" attraction story, but in this case, the fish was a duck. And I didn't want our concept to be a sitting duck. We needed Tom's blessing.

My fallback plan, should Tom understandably disapprove Donald disrupting classic scenes from his forte, feature animation, was to blame Michael Eisner, who was not in the room. Michael, who as our CEO clearly pulled rank on the head of Feature Animation, suggested Donald be the instigator of the commotion throughout our story because he reasoned it would make the show much more interesting and funny than going with our first choice for the mischievous role, Tinker Bell, who we thought would look really cool flitting and flirting about in front of our noses in 3-D. I convinced myself I would pull that Eisner card if—and only if—I could not win Tom over with an articulate and thoroughly convincing non-argumentative explanation. "Would you explain," Tom asked, "why in the world you would even think about putting Donald Duck into our classic scenes?" "IT'S MICHAEL EISNER'S IDEA!" I couldn't help it. It just came out.

"I see," he said, realizing his opinion had been painted into a corner by the big brush of the boss. While I had him there captive, I jumped into action explaining why Donald was critical to the show. "You see, Tom, prior to the concert, Maestro Mickey warns Donald not to put on his sorcerer's hat. But being Donald, he can't resist. The moment Mickey leaves and Donald dons the hat, the instruments in the orchestra magically come to life, gang up on him, and sweep him away into your iconic animated worlds. But the elusive hat keeps getting away from Donald, and he knows he needs to get it back to the concert hall. That makes for a really great story thread, doesn't it? And who else but Donald to make off with Mickey's hat?" Tom saw the logic, smiled, and graciously approved. As we say in the pitch biz, "Whew!"

It all began on opening day of Disney California Adventure, a few weeks after Tom Fitzgerald suggested we think about doing another "Mickey show" in the very theatrical venue that housed the Mickey Mouse Revue, an Audio-Animatronics stage show that was one of the original opening day attractions in Fantasyland at Magic Kingdom. The show closed in 1980 and was moved to Tokyo Disneyland to be one of its opening day attractions. Tom thought it would be fun to create a new musical show reprising Mickey's role as the conductor of an orchestra but in a fresh and bold new way. Following the grand opening ceremony at Disney California Adventure—and shortly after my purse whack-ing in the first bug's show—instead of attending the media events and festivities scheduled throughout the day, Tom, George Scribner, Marianne McClean, and I stole away to the roof of the Grand Californian Hotel, gathered under the shade of an umbrella, and began to brainstorm Mickey Mouse Revue 2. Tom and I had already worked closely with Marianne, our media producer and visual effects expert, on it's tough to be a bug! and other shows; and George, who directed the Disney animated feature *Oliver & Company*, had recently come over to join us at Imagineering after many years at Feature Animation.

Soarin' Over California (an attraction produced by George's brother, Alec Scribner, with a film produced by Marianne, and a show directed by Rick Rothschild), was Tom's brainchild. I was blown away Tom was so excited about brainstorming the new Mickey show that he shuffled us up to the roof instead of sticking around to listen to guests' comments. I actually enjoy eavesdropping on our guests, but I'm glad he chose to do what he did because the four of us enjoyed a fun and fabulously fruitful rooftop brainstorm. We were so focused and in the zone that by the end of the day we had landed on a solid attraction idea and opening sequence for the show.

Here's what we dreamed up: after guests put on their 3-D "opera glasses," the curtain rises to reveal there are no musicians, only a pile of abandoned instruments. At a loss about what to do, Maestro Mickey whistles to "someone" offstage. From behind us there suddenly appears a magical little light (special effect) that traces along the theater sidewall and up to the stage. The little glow flies over the instruments, showers them with pixie dust, and they magi-cally come to life. The glow then flies up to our faces, revealing it is none other than Tink, who gives us a wink! She flies back to make another pass over the orchestra as Mickey happily begins to conduct the overture, and showers it, and Mickey, with too much pixie dust, causing musical mayhem. Musical notes start to fly off the pages and the instruments play faster and faster until they work themselves into a frenzy and begin to whirl around the theater. The whirlwind of enchanted instruments—and the conductor—blow close by us as Tinker Bell tries desperately, but unsuccessfully, to get everything back under control. The orchestra turns on Tink and chases her until she is swallowed by the tuba, which turns and swallows us! Now in total darkness, we see a match being lit, and the flame from it lights Lumiere's wick. The enchanted candelabra begins to sing "Be Our Guest" to Tink. With that, we ended the presentation and our grand afternoon at the Grand Californian. But we still had a lot of work to do.

Tom, Marianne, George, and I regrouped in Glendale to meet when we could between our other projects until we had a rock-solid show structure, including all of the places we would go in the show, including Ariel's grotto; the Pride Lands from *The Lion King;* Agrabah; and London, where we soar between buildings, tall ships, and down along the surface of the river Thames before swooping dramatically upward towards the full moon. Silhouetted against the brilliant moon we see who we think are Tink, Peter Pan, Michael, John, and Wendy. But as we draw closer, the silhouettes become more clearly defined and are actually the enchanted instruments performing the score with Maestro Mickey still conducting in midair, à la *The Band Concert*. The movement of instruments fills the frame and we become caught in the middle of the orchestra's biggest and most dramatic movement. Mickey motions with his baton and we all begin to fall. On the final downbeat, we "crash" to the theater floor and the instruments and Mickey crash safely onto the stage. The last thing to fall is Tinker Bell, who drops out of the sky and comically crashes on a cymbal. Maestro Mickey turns to take a bow. As the curtain drops behind our conductor, Tinker Bell flies out from under it to take her final bow just beyond our noses. She then flies all around, showering us with pixie dust, which we can feel. As we are sprinkled, our seats become enchanted and begin to rise. Tink's pixie dust washes over the entire theater creating a magical sparkling effect. She flies back under the closing curtain in the nick of time before it hits the floor.

After George sketched that storyboard sequence, he used his "pitch fork" from his days at animation (a real fork that extends out to three feet like an antennae) and pitched it to Michael Eisner as we heckled from the sidelines. Michael thought the show was great but quickly tossed out Tinker Bell. That's when he suggested Donald Duck be the disrupter, and we changed the story accordingly. (Tink lands a dazzling pixie-dusting role after all, as she kicks off the "You Can Fly" sequence.) George mysteriously ducked out the day we were to pitch our revised show to Tom Schumacher, so I got duck duty.

It ended up getting approved and we went into production. Having become close friends with Jimmy Macdonald, and hearing his many stories of working with Pinto Colvig (the original voice of Goofy) and Clarence "Ducky" Nash (the original voice of Donald), I became obsessed with my self-imposed challenge of creating a "classic" sound for Mickey's PhilharMagic by building Donald's entire vocal track out of existing recording sessions of Ducky Nash through the decades. To do that, I acquired all of Ducky's sessions from the forties, fifties, and sixties from the Disney Studio. All in all, I was able to collect almost nine hundred individual recording sessions, and in each there were hundreds of lines performed, including many outtakes. I combed through each and every recorded take, which took hundreds of hours of listening, to pull the ones I could use to build Donald's part in the show.

There are only three spoken lines by Donald in Mickey's PhilharMagic that are not performed by Ducky Nash, plus a musical bit where Donald hums along to "Be Our Guest." The humming and new lines I needed that were not in the Ducky Nash sessions were "Where's my hat?," "A pie?," and "Thank you." (Hard to believe that Donald never once said "thank you" in more than thirty years-worth of recorded material.) These new lines were performed by the current longtime voice of Donald Duck, and dear friend, Tony Anselmo.

At that time, my ground floor office was located on the executive "Gold Coast" of Imagineering. My next-door neighbor was then president Don Goodman; and on the other side of Don was Marty Sklar, who always used to stop by my office on his way in from the parking lot in the morning to chat or playfully bug me (or both). Listening to the Ducky Nash recordings in my office one day, Don Goodman appeared at my door. "What the heck are you doing in there?" he asked quite seriously. I explained I was essentially "mining" through decades of recordings to dig up priceless "gems" of classic Donald-speak to use for the new show. "I wish you would have asked me first," he said sternly. I thought I was in trouble thinking all of my decibel-inducing ducky doings were probably disturbing him next door. I felt terrible for being so inconsiderate. "Sorry, Don," I apologized. "It won't happen again." He said, "You better believe it won't happen again, and do you know why?" I assumed he was either going to move me out or knock me out. "No," I responded. "Why?" He took a deep breath, I ducked for cover, and out of the side of his suddenly scrunched-up mouth came the most perfect Donald Duck vocalization you've ever heard say, "Cuz I can do Donald's voice for you!" Don really gave Ducky and Tony a run for their money! Who knew? My crazy Imagineering life!

Before we landed on a name for the show, Tom Fitz asked me to submit to him my usual long list of name options from which to choose and use. This is how Tom and I have worked together for thirty-plus years of naming countless things—from restaurant menu items to major attractions—for our parks around the world. Although I generated a long list of possible names for him, my favorite, the one I bolded at the eye-catching top of the list, was Mickey's PhilharMagic. To me, the choice was obvious. It sounded right, it felt right, it WAS right. What the heck else could it be? I was certain Tom would think so, too.

But to my surprise, he didn't bite. "I dunno, Kev," he said coming into my office with my list in his hand. "'Mickey's PhilharMagic.' It's really good but feels like it needs something else at the end, you know, 'Mickey's PhilharMagic . . . *Something*.*"* Shocked and disappointed, I asked, "You mean 'Mickey's PhilharMagic' on its own isn't enough?" He argued it needed something else. Rarely have I ever disagreed with Tom. But on this one I did. We went back and forth about it until one day I marched into his office and told him point-blank how strongly I felt about the name, the only name it could be, and that it didn't need that something else at the end. Tom held his ground. I am not a squeaky wheel, so on the rare occasions when I do squeak, people know I mean business. Every time I saw Tom after that I squeaked about it. I pestered him in the parking lot, cornered him in the cafeteria, hunted him down in the hallway, rattled him at a red light, and even bickered with him in the bathroom until he finally cried uncle. When the show was a few days away from opening, I gasped when I saw a Walt Disney World transportation bus drive by with MICKEY'S PHILHARMAGIC rendered across the side of its entire length. It was beautiful. And since it stretched from front bumper to back bumper, there was no room left for something else at the end.

Like music to
my "ears"!

More than any other theatrical show I've ever helped bring to life, Mickey's PhilharMagic helped me to realize the enormous power a show has over an audience once they are under its spell. About a month before opening, George Scribner and I were in the theater working on final-show programming. There's a scene in which Mickey's sorcerer's hat—the one Donald has been frantically chasing after the entire show—drops out of the sky and lands upright on the back of Aladdin's flying carpet. Seeing it, Donald happily flies his own carpet close to Aladdin and Jasmine's to finally get the hat. But then suddenly, at the moment Jasmine places the hat on Donald's head, Iago silently swoops in and knocks it off. "Do you think Iago's entrance reads on its own visually?" questioned George, who was afraid the pesky parrot's stealth dive into the scene might go unnoticed. He continued, "Maybe we should give Iago a loud audio cue, like he yells as he flies in so people don't miss him."

It seemed fine as it was to me. "Let's wait and see how our first test audience reacts," I suggested. When we brought in our test audience, which happened to be about two hundred unsuspecting guests walking through Fantasyland, we went directly into the theater, George and I agreed to sit among them about a dozen rows back in the center section. That way we could watch their reactions, if any, to the Iago moment in question, maybe even talk to a few audience members afterwards. After we took our seats, I noticed a boy, about six or seven, using crutches to help him walk over to the center front-row seat. When the moment came and Iago swooped down out of the sky, the boy stood up on one leg, knocking his crutches to the floor with a bang, and yelled, "Look out, Donald! Behind you!" After that we didn't change a thing. Well, except for taking out the aspic.

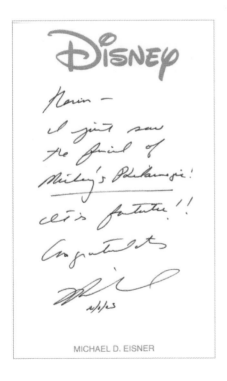

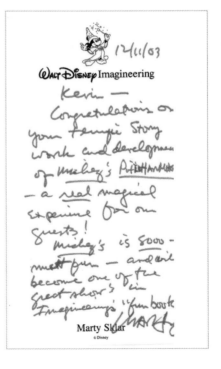

OCEANS
OF FUN

IT BROKE MY HEART the Submarine Voyage

remained closed at Disneyland for more than five years. When the subs were gliding gracefully across the colorful lagoon, they added stunning aesthetics and kinetics to the park—and it was a must-do literally immersive ride (not to mention Disneyland was able to boast about having the eighth largest submarine fleet in the world). The Tomorrowland favorite was the perfect example of a major attraction that offered guests an opportunity to enjoy an experience they may not otherwise have had. Marty Sklar knew this well, and he wanted the subs back so badly he threatened to lie down on Harbor Boulevard until they were returned to operation.

I promised Marty if he ever really did that I would lie on the busy boulevard alongside him, as long as he was the one on the side of the oncoming traffic. Tony Baxter was in the same boat, so to speak, in that he never gave up coming up with compelling ideas to try and bring the subs back. Among his ideas were an interactive hunt for undersea treasure and an adventure inspired by the Disney animated feature film *Atlantis*. Alfredo Ayala, resident genius from our R & D studio, was inventing a new "dry for wet" technology that created the believable illusion of generic animated fish swimming around in real water, mostly because it was real water. I was also independently trying to come up with a story hook strong enough to save the subs. So, there we all were, working in our own little "sub groups" looking for the answer. All of this momentum-gaining independent thinking going on by different people in different buildings around our Imagineering campus was a strong indication it was time for the subs to relaunch.

Unrelated to the subs, in March, 2003, I took my family to the IMAX theater in Irvine, California, to see James Cameron's *Ghosts of the Abyss*. In this fascinating film, the director bravely mans a tiny submarine and dives into the dangerous dark depths of the Atlantic to explore the *Titanic* in its final resting place. Cameron's film was captivating and visually stunning, and it naturally turned my thoughts once again to our own Submarine Voyage. Tony's take on *Atlantis* was a great and worthy idea, but it featured a sub-shaking attack by the giant Kraken from the film, which I personally felt would be too scary for kids. I loved his undersea treasure hunt idea, truly big thinking and more family friendly, but it would have required major modifications to the existing subs. This most likely would have required too deep of a dive into our corporate treasury to justify project approval.

We had to do something. But what else could it be? If only we could come up with an idea solid enough to get everyone on board.

As I was leaving the IMAX theater with my family, two men were wheeling in a large lobby display for the upcoming Pixar film *Finding Nemo*. They stopped directly in front of us to unload it from their cart. The display featured beautifully detailed dimensional versions of Marlin and Dory with a wide-grinning Bruce the shark looming ominously behind them. The timing was impeccable, if not strange, because the new big idea for the Submarine Voyage, like Marlin, Dory, and Bruce, was staring me right in the face. Why hadn't I connected *Finding Nemo* with the Submarine Voyage before? I had seen the executive rollout at the Disney Studio two years before, which introduced us to the cast, character designs, and certain scenes from the work-in-progress film. And prior to that, I was part of a most fortunate group that was treated to director Andrew Stanton's pitch of the film's story. Andrew's unscripted telling of the story—sans teleprompter—was one of the greatest pitches I've even seen in my life. He stepped onto the naked stage of the El Capitan Theatre in Hollywood, while a bunch of us executives were there for project updates, and without any visual or audio aids, brought the entire story of the movie to life from beginning to end. His mesmerizing one-man performance had us hanging on his every word.

Why didn't I think of this story and character connection for the subs at that time? Could it be I wasn't even thinking of the subs back then because the time wasn't right? I'll never know, but I believe that spark was waiting for just the right time to ignite, and it ignited in the form of a cardboard and plastic lobby display that happened to be unloaded and set up directly in front of me as I was walking out of the theater after watching a movie featuring a submarine that got me thinking about the Disneyland submarines. Coincidence?

As it was late Sunday afternoon, I raced home from the theater, grabbed every index card my wife had stashed in her desk, and started to sketch "fish stick" figures to create and lay out a rough-attraction storyboard sequence. All I had to go on was what I remembered from the movie rollout, including the concept art and rough animation of the characters—and Andrew's unforgettable storytelling. By eleven that night I had a first-pass storyboard, albeit crudely sketched on index cards, covering our kitchen table. The voyage would start out as it had in the past with the captain as our narrator. Only our new captain would be Australian. Instead of going under a polar ice cap, as was the original destination, our new destination would be the active undersea volcano that the original submarines also visited on their voyage; only it would be Mount Wannahockaloogie from Nemo's world.

But how do we transition from our world to Nemo's? The answer came right out of the original Submarine Voyage script, which I knew by heart because I had been a passenger on that wonderful voyage countless times from the impressionable age of four to the impressionable age of almost forty. "The fish world has always been considered a silent habitat," said the captain since 1959. "But now thanks to remarkable advances in marine technology, we can use instruments such as our sonar hydrophones to actually hear the fish talk." In the original show, what you heard after that line was a bunch of bubbly underwater-y ambient noise with added high-pitched sounds picked up from a distant dog trying to yip and howl with its mouth stuffed with socks. I never asked him (and I wish I had), but my guess is this was the sound effects work and voice of Jimmy Macdonald. I would bet the writer or director of the show called him and said, "Say, Jimmy, I know this sounds fishy but we need you to make fish-y sounds." I'm glad they did because that "sonar hydrophone" setup was the perfect segue for our new show, because Nemo and his friends really can talk! After our Australian captain wraps up that very same statement by saying, "To actually hear the fish talk," we would immediately hear Marlin call out, "Nemo! Where are you son?" Jumpin' jellyfish, this was gonna work!

First thing Monday morning, I grabbed my rubber-banded stack of index cards and left home at 5:00 a.m. so I'd have enough time to pin them up on a board and wait for Marty to stroll in from the parking lot. If for some reason he didn't stop at my door and toss in his usual Marty-ism to start the day, my plan was to head him off at the pass and kidnap him; even wrestle him to the ground if I had to. I was really excited about this and I had high hopes he would be, too. After I finished pinning the sequence of sketches on the board I turned my chair around to face the window to watch and wait for Marty. By the time he arrived, I was so anxious I was about to explode, so I stood outside my door like an over-caffeinated traffic cop to whirl my arm and redirect him in. He stepped into the Gold Coast corridor carrying his usual heavy stack of papery stuff in his arms, and before he could say a word, I directed him into my office and plopped him down in the awaiting chair. "What's this about?" he asked. I answered, "It's about ten minutes. Well, no, maybe twenty."

Marty, I'm sure, appreciated my honesty and agreed to stay put. "What have you got, kid?" "I think I've got an idea that'll keep us both off of Harbor Boulevard!" I put the stack of stuff he had had on his lap on my desk, swiveled his chair around in barber-like fashion so he'd be facing my rough but ready storyboard, and dove in, starting with the proposed attraction name I had hand-printed with a Sharpie inside a sketch of a submarine porthole. At the end of my fish-stick figure pitch I asked Marty what he thought. "You had me," he chuckled, "at Finding Nemo Submarine Voyage."

When I finally released my "kidnaped victim," he told me to get with Tony Baxter, who he knew had been working on other ideas for the subs, as soon as possible to take him through the storyboard. He further suggested I continue

Here's a sample of the rough "fish stick figures" I drew on three-by-five-inch cards to pitch to Marty Sklar a *Finding Nemo*–themed show for the restored Disneyland subs attraction.

to work with Tony to get "this one going." After I met with Tony, he brought in Chris Tietz, one of the most talented dimensional designers Imagineering has ever had, to start working on a large-scale model of the entire attraction. At the same time, I brought in my favorite "good luck charm," storyboard artist and designer Chris Turner, to join the team to create some *real* storyboard art. Plus, Kathy Mangum came on board as our producer. Within a couple of months, I had the attraction script written, Chris Turner had his beautiful storyboards completed, and Chris Tietz finished his stunning overall attraction model. Using the model and storyboards, Tony and I presented the concept to Michael Eisner (one of the last pitches to Michael prior to his departure), Bob Iger, Jay Rasulo, and Tom Staggs. We were cleared to set sail!

Kathy and I had worked together on many projects after we did the Blast to the Past Submarine Voyage in 1988, but I loved that she and I were sailing full circle back to the sub lagoon almost twenty years later. Only this time, it would be with an attraction that was certain to last longer than one summer. Since we were having oceans of fun working to bring the Nemo characters into the submarine lagoon, Kathy and I also dove into yet another underwater project together. (It's a good thing we get along swimmingly!) Concurrent with the subs effort, we set our periscope on Epcot to bring the same lovable cast of fish characters to The Living Seas pavilion. Although the two attractions featured different types of ride systems (one featuring real submarines, and the other "Clamobiles" that travel on a continuous Omnimover track), the stories were similar. The exciting thing about both The Seas with Nemo & Friends at Epcot, which opened in January 2007, and Finding Nemo Submarine Voyage, which opened only five months later, is we designed certain scenes in which we presented the animated characters as they would appear in real water.

In the finale of The Seas with Nemo & Friends, the characters, all singing "Big Blue World"—the attraction theme song written by Bobby and Kristen Anderson-Lopez of *Frozen* fame—appear as though they are swimming with the real live fish in The Living Seas pavilion aquarium. When I was working on show installation and programming in that particular scene with a view through the glass into the 5.7 million-gallon aquarium, I made a new friend—a dolphin. Every time I stepped into that scene, the dolphin appeared and came swimming up to the glass next to wherever I was to hang out with me. Even though there were others working in that scene, the dolphin, for some reason, was only interested in me, and what I was doing. As I walked back and forth, he swam back and forth with me. When I stopped, he stopped. I showed him the pictures I have of my family in my wallet and he seemed to like that. I also showed him a concept sketch of Peach, the starfish character from *Finding Nemo*, and he seemed to like that, too. (Peach is voiced by Allison Janney, and as a big fan of hers, I was thrilled to have the opportunity to write her script and direct her for this attraction. My stomach was sore for a week after our recording session because she made me laugh so hard.)

Allison Janney came to our Imagineering studio to record Peach the starfish. Peach is featured at the end of The Seas with Nemo & Friends at Epcot.

While working on The Seas with Nemo & Friends at Epcot, I made friends with a dolphin. He was always happy to see me when I arrived and made a big splashy deal about it. As I was telling animation director George Scribner about my new friend and how we went everywhere together, he drew this.

My best dolphin friend and I really hit it off for some reason—so much so I started to feel like Bud from the sixties TV show *Flipper*. Our friendship lasted for several weeks. We started playing a game where I'd hide around the curve where the glass ended and he'd pretend to look for me. Then he'd hide in a similar manner and I'd pretend to look for him. When we'd "find" each other, slowly peeking past the edge of the glass in perfect face-to-face synchronization, like Lucille Ball and Harpo Marx did in an episode of *I Love Lucy*, I would laugh and he would shake his head up and down with that ever-present smile on his face. We had a ball, Dolphy and me. When the project was completed and I was ready to return to California, I was genuinely sad to leave my perky pal. When I returned home and told this story to George Scribner, he whipped out his animation sketch pad and drew a picture of me driving my rental car with my best amphibious buddy riding next to me, his head sticking out the window like a happy dog. I miss Dolphy. When this book comes out I'll have to send him a copy. He'll like that.

One of the very best parts of bringing the Nemo characters to Disneyland and Epcot was getting to know and work with Pixar director Roger Gould and producer Liz Gazzano. I had worked on two Pixar-related attractions prior to Nemo, including it's tough to be a bug! and Flik's Fun Fair at Disney California Adventure, but that was long before Pixar had established a separate theme park group to support all of our Pixar-themed projects. Roger and Liz—both in actuality Imagineers trapped in Pixarian bodies—were the founding father and mother of Pixar's theme park group, which has since grown into a large and busy sub-studio (and I don't mean that as in "submarine," although that's where it started).

Since that time, I have worked closely with them on several more projects, and those two wonderful friends have become family. We've done a lot, traveled a lot, and have been through a lot together. When Roger and Liz came to Disneyland one morning for a walk-through of the Submarine Voyage show building, we set out on the narrow and precarious catwalks that had a lot of overhead steel cross bracing, which you had to duck under to get by. They weren't yet used to wearing bright orange safety vests, safety glasses, and hard hats. As we were stepping carefully though the show building, I followed closely behind Liz to make sure she would be safe. All went smoothly until she turned to me to ask, "Why do we have to wear hard hats in here?" When she turned back around she bonked her hard hat against a low cross brace. "That's why," I answered, after I knew she was okay. Ever since then Liz is always the first to put on her safety gear in the field.

It has been fun over the years watching Roger and Liz learn about and adapt to the challenges and benefits of our dimensional form of experiential and immersive storytelling and grow to become masters of the art of Imagineering, just like Walt's first generation of animators did. Following that grand tradition, talented folks from the world of animation still find their places among the best of the best Imagineers. Liz, Roger, and their Pixar theme park team were wonderful partners in the design and development of both Nemo-themed attractions, and they continue to work their magic at Imagineering today. As a matter of fact, Roger, who lives in the Oakland, California, area, flies down to Imagineering so often he jokes his best friend is the car rental guy at the Burbank airport. But I don't feel sorry for him. Roger can commute to Glendale from Oakland faster than I can commute through LA traffic to Glendale from neighboring Orange County!

While writing on the scripts for both Nemo attractions, I worked closely with Roger to make sure I was staying true to the Pixar characters and the world in which they live. I also did my usual extensive research. In fact, I became a submarine expert because the script for Finding Nemo Submarine Voyage had to begin and end with official submarine-ish banter between the captain and his crew member. Their exchange had to sound and be legit. In addition to books, such as *Standard Submarine Phraseology*, I watched every submarine movie ever released, including my favorites, *Run Silent, Run Deep, The Hunt*

Roger Gould and I started a fun tradition fifteen years ago that we have to use a paper plate as part of our birthday greeting to one another. Here's a monstrous example!

for *Red October, Operation Petticoat,* and, of course, *20,000 Leagues Under the Sea.* (Fun fact: Jimmy Macdonald once told me in the part of the movie where the *Nautilus* surfaces and Kirk Douglas comes halfway out of the hatch and starts humming "A Whale of a Tale," that that humming is not Kirk's. They didn't record sound for that shot, so Jimmy performed the humming himself and added it in postproduction. Another fun fact: comedian Don Rickles was in the cast with Clark Gable and Burt Lancaster in the 1958 film *Run Silent, Run Deep* in a dramatic role. While watching this film, I never would have dreamed I'd be directing him a couple of years later in the role of a potato.)

While watching these movies, which, by the way, each had a subplot, I wrote down all of the submarine-sounding phrases and commands like, "Flood the main ballast tanks," and "Right full rudder, steady on course two-two-zero." In the final attraction script, I wrote this official-sounding line the captain says just after the bubbly "dive" under the lagoon waterfall: "Set course to six-zero degrees true." Two weeks after we opened Finding Nemo Submarine Voyage, I received a call from Bob Iger's office. It seems Bob had invited the admiral of the United States Navy's submarine fleet to be his guest on the attraction. Afterwards the admiral mentioned to Bob the captain's command was off by one degree. Boy, did I miss the boat on that one! I mean, come on, what are the odds the head of the U.S. submarine fleet would sail on one of our subs with the head of The Walt Disney Company and after all that thorough research I would miss the command by one lousy degree and then get the third degree? I was totally torpedoed. That just goes to show everything you hear in submarine movies you should take with a grain of salt water. We immediately called the Australian actor that played the captain to come back in and rerecord that one line. Crikey.

Redesigning the attraction proved to be quite a challenge in many ways, from the conversion of the diesel engines to electric motors to rethinking new ways of designing and fabricating an environmentally and maintenance friendly, more vibrantly colored coral in the lagoon. Designer Susan Dain cleverly figured that one out. Reasoning that since sea glass, pieces of broken bottles, tableware, and shipwrecks are rolled and tumbled for years until their edges are smooth, yet never lose their color, Susan proposed coating the coral understructures with real crushed glass. Problem beautifully solved.

Still, one of the biggest challenges we faced was figuring out the tricky show timing. In the original Submarine Voyage, the only words spoken were those by the captain and his crew; and they were naturally heard on board. Our new voyage required us to create the illusion the dialogue from the cast of *Finding Nemo* was coming from off board. The subs were essentially "moving theaters" transporting audiences through stationary scenes so the timing of the brief bits of dialogue, important to the storytelling, needed to be heard by all. Because the length of the submarines far exceeded the length of most of the show scenes, it meant guests riding in the front were already through a scene or two or three before guests in the back even arrived in those same scenes. We had to design the script and the audio portion of the show to tell the story to each guest positioned in front of a porthole no matter where in the sub they were seated.

To understand the action, staging, and timing of each scene relative to each "sweet spot" porthole position, Imagineer Mark Mine invented a way to virtually simulate the entire ride experience, as it would play, from both a visual and audio perspective, to each and every porthole in the sub. Using sheets of foam core board, we built a full-scale curved section of the sub complete with porthole and a "line array" of speakers that flanked either side. Using a scratch audio track of the show synchronized to rough virtual imagery of the characters and show sets, our team was able to experience how the show would look and sound from any seat on the sub. Using the array of speakers, we were able to simulate the "traveling" show audio as if the sub were actually moving through the scenes. This was a fantastic design and timing tool, especially for our show director, Rick Rothschild, whose job it was to ultimately put all of the pieces together into one seamless entertaining ride-through experience. Everything we learned, and as a result built into the show using our sub simulator, was later taken to the Disneyland lagoon to be permanently programmed on board. One of the things I learned in doing so was never to drink an entire pot of coffee just

All hams on deck!

before setting sail on a slow-moving sub to work offshore far from a restroom while completely surrounded by liquid. To heck with finding Nemo—I needed to find a speedboat.

Mark's virtual porthole tool evolved into our highly sophisticated on-site "Disney Immersive Showroom" (DISH) technology. The view inside the room-sized wraparound DISH extends outside of the peripheral vision, which allows us to virtually ride through any attraction scene, or entire land we create, as if it were the real deal. The DISH allows us to look up, down, and travel all around inside or outside anything we design. Before construction was complete and the show sets and figures were fabricated and installed for Radiator Springs Racers in Cars Land, I was able to "ride" through the entire attraction, from start to finish, using the DISH to flag and correct design and staging issues, and make important adjustments and changes to the show elements and timing where necessary. And in fact, the DISH allowed us to move through and fly over the entire land. Moving, changing, or deleting something in an early virtual representation of an attraction or land is faster, better, and a heck of a lot less expensive than doing so in a real one. We continue to use this cutting-edge design tool today.

Truly it was a dream to join Tony Baxter and the team to help bring the fleet of yellow submarines back into operation at Disneyland, and we have an adorable little orange clown fish to thank for it. It was such a joy to see the subs once again gliding gracefully across the even more colorful lagoon; and adding even more kinetics to the iconic setting are the three seagulls perched on a

I love this photo taken at the opening day press event for Finding Nemo Submarine Voyage. Back row (left to right): Brian Elliot, Eric Jacobson, Rick Rothschild, John Drager, Tom Fitzgerald, John Lasseter, Tony Baxter. Center: Kathy Mangum and me. Front row, Alfredo Ayala and George Scribner.

Submariners Tony Baxter, John Gizienski, me, and Skip Lange on opening day.

buoy crying, "Mine! Mine! Mine!" My favorite moment in the project came as we were wrapping things up a few days before the grand opening. I was sitting in the sub next to Marty, who was there to experience his first voyage through the newly completed show. Sitting between Tony and me, he was as happy as I've ever seen him. As the sub began to move forward and the new captain said, "Stand by to dive," I pulled my face out of the porthole to turn to look at Marty at the same time he turned to look at me. He didn't have to say a word because that famous Marty smile said it all. I was suddenly so choked up I pushed my face back into the porthole so he wouldn't notice.

Another wonderful thing that happened as a result of working on Finding Nemo Submarine Voyage is I really got to know Matt Ouimet, then president of the Disneyland Resort. I liked Matt a lot. I can't remember the exact date, but I was literally moonlighting one night with a small crew of Imagineering projection experts to find out what it would look like to project film and special effects imagery onto Sleeping Beauty Castle. It had never been done. At around 2:30 a.m., a thick fog started rolling in. Out of the corner of my eye I noticed the silhouette of a man, dramatically backlit by the lights on Main Street, walking out of the fog towards us. The man was Matt Ouimet. I was so impressed that he was out and about in his park in the middle of the night checking things out. Of course he was interested in what we were doing and he stayed with us for quite a while, until the fog got so thick it forced us to pack up and leave.

In 2005, Matt, who also spent a lot of time at Imagineering, spotted Rob't Coltrin and me having one of our crazy highly charged conversations in the hallway that is known today as The Monorail Hallway. "You two," Matt called out as he approached us, "are just the two I'm looking for." He took us by surprise when, from out of the blue, he told us he really liked the interactive-game aspect of Buzz Lightyear Astro Blasters and was hoping we could come up with another family-friendly attraction like it but that we'd have to "up the game." Rob't and I looked at each other knowingly, because if there's one thing we've learned over the years it's ideas have a better chance of being approved, designed, and built when it satisfies a need or a want from a park operator. And here Matt was personally asking us for a new game attraction. Game on!

"TIME FOR RECON!" That is Rob't speak for, "Let's take a trip to Anaheim and try to figure out what this new attraction is and where it's going." Matt Ouimet didn't tell us *where* he wanted it. He only told us *that* he wanted it. What it would be was up to us. We already knew, prior to our recon mission, this attraction concept would be a welcome addition to Disney California Adventure because the park was in need of more welcome additions. The first ride experiences to be added after the park opened in February 2001 were not designed for the general family audience. Flik's Fun Fair, which opened in 2002, was created to provide experiences for younger children, something the park lacked. (As a member of the Flik's Fun Fair design team, I created the attraction name and wrote the script for Heimlich's Chew Chew Train. In the recording session, I asked Pixar's Joe Ranft, who cocreated the story for *a bug's life* and performed the voice of its caterpillar character, to deliver the Spanish version of the safety spiel as the German-accented Heimlich. The result was hysterical! This is the first time a character would provide the Spanish spiel on an attraction).

The Twilight Zone Tower of Terror, which opened in 2004, offered an additional ride opportunity—but for thrill seekers. The time was ripe for the park to get an attraction that would entertain guests of all ages. Besides, Disneyland already had a game-based attraction with Buzz Lightyear Astro Blasters, so we set our sights solely on Disney California Adventure.

We arrived at the park hoping for a spark. Our plan was to simply walk and talk, keeping our eyes open for any possibility. As we strolled along Paradise Pier, we stopped in front of the boardwalk games and started talking crazy talk about how much fun it would be if we could play those games with unlimited objects to toss, not three only, and always come out feeling like a winner. This led to the "what if" question Imagineers always ask when brainstorming new ideas: "What if we could *ride through* these games and always walk away feeling like a winner?" KA-BAM! There was the spark we were hoping for. Actually, it was more like a lightning bolt. The ride could be built right here, somewhere on the pier, because thematically it was the perfect fit. While riding through, guests could somehow toss as many objects at targets as they possibly could in the time allowed.

We loved the idea, but it came with more questions than we had answers. What's the story that ties the experience all together? How do rider-players actually toss objects and what are they? How, in one ride, could players throw darts in one game and baseballs in another? How do we create a game attraction that is as fun and challenging for gamers as it is for non-gamers? How could the playability be intuitive and fun even if you've never played a midway game? Would Grandma have as much fun and be as successful as her grandkids?

234

On the job with some friends at Disney California Adventure

Neither Rob't nor I was a game aficionado, so the first thing we did when we returned to Imagineering with the big idea was bring Sue Bryan on board. She had just poured her heart and soul into the creation of Mission: SPACE at Epcot—plus had a slew of other interactive and gaming experiences on her impressive résumé—so we knew we could not pull this off without her. Sue is still today the best interactivity and game guru we've got.

As Sue was starting to wrap her head around this crazy game idea and ways to play it, Rob't and I started to explore story possibilities. But our story development effort didn't get the full-time attention it deserved because we were also wrapping up our work on Monsters, Inc. Mike & Sulley to the Rescue!

In addition to that, I was working on both Nemo attractions and a Car-*azy* concept I started on my own called Carland. (I would eventually call Rob't in for help on that one, too!) Rob't and Sue took a recon trip to the L.A. County Fair and returned with a whole zoo's-worth of stuffed animals that they had won at the games on the midway. Based on their experience that day, we made a list of their favorite games, including throwing darts at balloons, tossing rings, tossing coins, and tossing baseballs.

Suffice it to say there was a whole lot of tossing going on. These traditional games would be instantly recognized and intuitive to play for our guests. When we landed on our top choices for tossing games, our first thought was to invent some kind of mechanical device that would automatically gather up all of the objects players tossed and keep the ride vehicle constantly refilled. It

While researching games for Toy Story Midway Mania!, Sue Bryan and Rob't Coltrin prove they have a "plush" life!

didn't take long to determine all of that physical picking up would require some sort of complicated and noisy vacuum system—and that would suck. And even if it didn't, would such a device be able to gather up all of the objects from the ground before they got run over by the vehicles, the very notion of which would cause our ride guys to put the kibosh on the whole thing before we even got started? Three-dimensional imagery was the answer. It could give us the darts, baseballs, and rings we wanted as well as the perception of trajectory when tossed. Usually 3-D is chosen because it's the best way to deliver gratuitous in-your-face gags. But more important to us than 3-D gags, was making the booths and the games inside of them believable. They had to look as if they had real depth and dimension. We determined there had to be some sort of tangible tossing device that would never run out of "ammo" mounted to the ride vehicles and positioned directly in front of each player. We were starting to solve one practical game challenge at a time, but in the meantime, we had not yet hit the bull's-eye on the story.

The first place we went story-wise was the notion of having Mickey Mouse and his pals work the game booths. We even came up with a name to go along with it: Mickey's Midway Mania! But that didn't last long because it was difficult to land on an easy-to-get story hook that would work for Mickey and do him justice. It just didn't feel right having the most classic of our classic characters operating midway games. (For some reason, creating a story around Mickey for an attraction has always been a tough nut to crack for Imagineers, and this was no exception. I personally believe this is because Mickey is "every man" and goes everywhere, and does everything. He doesn't come with a distinct role or job, as does Wreck-It Ralph or Kim Possible, and he doesn't come from an instantly recognizable place like Radiator Springs or Arendelle. If Mickey had always lived and worked at a carnival or state fair, Mickey's Midway Mania! would have been a no-brainer. All that said, I'm so happy and proud that a decade later Rob't and I would finally crack that Mickey ride story nut by creating the original story for Mickey & Minnie's Runaway Railway, Imagineering's first-ever Mickey-themed ride-through attraction. Woo-hoo!)

And now, back to our story. Tossing Mickey out of the midway (with all due respect!), we started toying around with the connection between toys and games, which naturally took us to *Toy Story*. What if Woody, Buzz, and the gang were to set up Andy's "midway game play set" to play while he was away? And what if we could shrink to the size of a toy and play these games ourselves? Bull's-eye!

Taking into consideration the cast of *Toy Story,* we let each character's job and/or personality inform the types of game they might host. In doing so, the game and story sequence practically wrote itself! Hamm was a natural for an egg toss on the farm. Bo Peep was perfect for the dart-tossing balloon-pop game in which her sheep could be balloon animals. The Green Army Men could command the boot camp–themed, plate-breaking baseball toss. Buzz Lightyear could launch the ring toss around rockets in outer space. Barbie could bring on the beach ball toss (into floating swimming-pool rings), and Woody would wrangle the Old West–themed, suction cup–darts six-shooter game. Within a month of the original spark of the idea, we had the above-game sequence and attraction name Toy Story Midway Mania! pinned to our concept board. We thought these names for the games were right on target:

Hamm & Eggs
Bo Peep's Baaa-loon Pop
Green Army Men Shoot Camp
Buzz Lightyear's Flying Tossers
Barbie's Backyard Beach Ball Bash
Woody's Rootin' Tootin' Shootin' Gallery

One of our first game ideas that didn't make the cut was a ball toss in which you would try to knock Mr. Potato Head off the shelf. But that seemed rather mean to do, even for Mr. Potato Head! So, we moved our spud bud out to the front and cast him in the role of boardwalk barker to shill the attraction and invite all passersby to "step right up" and play Toy Story Midway Mania! Barbie's Backyard Beach Ball Bash didn't make the final cut either for various (ahem! legal) reasons. This broke my heart because I think Barbie is a real doll.

To complete our concept package, we sketched a proposed ride vehicle, which was actually inspired by Rob't's original design for the Monsters, Inc. Ride & Go Seek! vehicle in use today at Tokyo Disneyland. (Rob't and I came up with the idea for that attraction as well in between all of the other stuff we had going on!) The Monsters vehicle design was a single chassis upon which was mounted a row of three two-passenger canopied "pods" capable of turning quickly to the left or right. Each pod has a tethered flashlight positioned in front of each passenger to be used for our original "flashlight tag"-through-Monstropolis concept. In the case of Midway Mania, however, we invented a toylike spring-action shooter, sort of a string-pulling electronic popgun for each passenger. Once artist and designer Ray Cadd had our storyboard art completed, we were ready for our dog and pony show. We literally took our show on the road because instead of presenting the attraction concept to our corporate leaders at Imagineering, Marty Sklar was so excited about the concept he arranged to have Rob't and I pitch the idea as soon as possible in the executive offices at the Disney Studio. We tossed our concept and storyboards into the back of my pickup truck and schlepped everything over to the Team Disney Building in Burbank.

At that time, as mentioned, I was in the middle of working on the two different Nemo-themed attractions in California and Florida, and Rob't and I were busy on both Monsters, Inc.-themed attractions. Despite the heavy workload, I was selfishly and excitedly hoping to get going on this new idea, whatever it may be, because it was intended for Anaheim only, as was my concept for Carland. What this potentially meant is once the Nemo attractions were completed—and if another team could tackle Monsters for Tokyo—I could land designing an attraction close to home.

When Rob't and I pitched Toy Story Midway Mania! to our top three corporate leaders (Bob Iger, Jay Rasulo, and Tom Staggs) in their executive suite, I had sweet dreams they'd love it. So, with Mania and potentially Carland as my next projects, I could peace out in Anaheim. Well, they loved it all right. So much so they ordered two: one for Anaheim and one for Orlando! And they wanted them completed at the same time! Holy spring-action shooter! Take it from me, fellow dreamers, be careful what you wish for! (Today there is a third Mania in Tokyo Disneyland.)

"Well," I said to Rob't, "the good news is they loved it. The bad news is . . . they loved it!" It was bad news only because we had no idea how we were actually going to do this thing. The vision depicted on the concept board and storyboards we were pushing on a wheeled cart back to my truck meant we had done the hard part. But now came the *harder* part—figuring out how to make it real. I mean, I point-blank pitched to Bob Iger that the Audio-Animatronics Mr. Potato Head would actually pull off a part of his body while at the same time in my own head I was thinking I must be bonkers to even suggest such an impossible figure function. (Speaking of body parts, you should have seen all the jaws drop when I pitched this crazy notion of a motion to our animation team that would have to pull it off!)

It was now up to Rob't to site the attraction at Paradise Pier as promised and then, after determining the facility size and configuration we could get away with given the limited real estate available, design the ride layout to fit.

The day after we got the green light we took another trip to Paradise Pier to scout out an exact location for the new attraction. "I don't see how a ride can possibly fit here," I sadly said to Rob't, surprised at and disappointed by my nay-saying self because I never say "never" and always believe we can do anything anywhere, anytime. But this time, as we stood in front of the long, straight span of coaster track of California Screamin' that towers above and directly behind the game booths, and visually measured the distance from the edge of its track to the edge of the water behind us, it was clear there was not enough room to build another ride here. Another churro cart here may fit, maybe. Rob't saw how disappointed I was. "Here's what we do, Kev," he assured me. "We blow right through the coaster." Surely, he was joking. "You mean," I questioned, "blow right through the coaster as in blow right through . . . *the coaster?*" Rob't nodded affirmatively even though I believed we had our backs to the wall. My mind flashed to the scene in *Butch Cassidy and the Sundance Kid* when the pair is trapped on a precarious mountainside ledge high above the dangerous rock-filled water below. The terrified Kid sees no way out, but Butch has a plan. "We jump," he says. Sundance responds, "Like hell we will!" "No," said Rob't, "it'll be okay. We'll cut a hole through the coaster structure and enter the ride from this side and we'll put the ride building on the other side." Yikes! If this were even possible it would surely mean shutting down California Screamin', one of the park's most popular attractions, during our construction. As I continued to stare at him with my frozen expression of disbelief he reminded me of the promise we made to our execs by adding emphatically, "We have to." It was exactly like when Butch Cassidy said, "Would you make a jump like that if you didn't have to?" Like Sundance, I answered, "I have to and I'm not gonna. I'm not gonna suggest that to upper management, either." Rob't laughed, "I will," he said, "and do you know why?" I was afraid to ask. "Because we're gonna leave Screamin' open while we build under and through it."

Now I'd heard everything. If there's one thing about Rob't, it's he doesn't let anything throw him off track, not even the giant quagmire of cross-braced structural steel of an established and unmovable—and by all accounts, untouchable—roller coaster. We went backstage behind the gauntlet coaster to see what we could see, and we saw a big electrical substation smack-dab in the way of the only section it looked like we could possibly blow through. "We'll work around it," my crazy partner in creative crime confidently assured me. After a moment of thoughtful silence, he added, "Otherwise we're dead." The Sundance Kid finally admitted, "I can't swim." To that Butch laughed and said, "Are you crazy? The fall will probably kill ya!" I let out a yell and joined Rob't in the jump.

Working his magic at his drawing table, Rob't brilliantly sited and positioned the ride building right through the roller coaster structure and knocked out a track layout inside the building, proving against all odds this crazy thing could work. In order to get as many guests as possible through the ride, he cleverly created two identical show sets on either side of the single-track path, similar to the way Finding Nemo Submarine Voyage has mirrored scenes visible from either side of the sub. To make it work, he changed his *Monsters*-inspired, ride–vehicle design to place four guests in each swiveling pod back-to-back, with a shared seat back high enough to block the view to the opposite side of the track. Each peanut-shaped vehicle chassis or carriage, hidden under the floor, would carry two of these back-to-back four-passenger pods. Doubling the vehicles and show sets doubled our guest capacity! It was inspired and oh, so Rob't. We wanted the ride itself to be as fun as the playing of the games, so we worked in a little razzle-dazzle vehicle spin as they quickly transported guests between games. Protecting all of the show sight lines and designing the track layout, so as not to allow any character doppelgangers, also had to be figured out. After all, seeing two Buzz Lightyears or two Woodys at the same time would be as devastating as seeing two Santas!

While continuing to work on the version of the attraction for the Paradise Pier location, we were also working on how it could fit thematically into Disney's Hollywood Studios, where there was no boardwalk. By this time, we asked Lori Coltrin to come join us and Sue Bryan to help with the big thinking, keeping in mind the practical game and set production to come. As our production designer, Lori would ultimately be responsible for delivering the goods in both parks, each opening only one month apart. As our game designer, Sue was responsible for producing the games, and Roger Gould, Liz Gazzano, and their Pixar team were responsible for delivering the character animation.

Call her crazy, but Chrissie Allen took on the daring and daunting responsibility of being our cat-herding producer for both attractions throughout their simultaneous design, development, production, and completion. Hey, we didn't call it Mania for nothin'! But Chrissie, with her wicked smarts and even wickeder pluck, was definitely the right producer for this job. (One day Chrissie and I loaded up a bunch of stuff we needed to haul to Anaheim in one of those giant rental trucks. Before I could do it, she climbed into the cab and sat her undersized self behind the oversized steering wheel. "Gimme the keys," she said. When we pulled off the Santa Ana freeway near Disneyland and were waiting at a red light, she looked over at me and asked, "Hey, Kev, do you know what the difference is between me and Mangum?" I replied, "I dunno, what?" As the light turned green and she shoved the clutch to the floor and jammed it into first gear, she gave me the answer "Dirty Harry" style: "I drive the truck.")

The difference between the two versions of the attraction was the façade and queue. The ride and game experience would be identical. As the attraction was originally designed for Paradise Pier only, we had to rethink the entrance and queue area for its location inside a studio soundstage. Taking inspiration from our attraction's story (all the answers to any question or challenge that may arise during the design and development of any project can *always* be found by staying true to the story), we decided to design and deliver Andy's bedroom, the very place in which the toys have set up these games and at the scale the toys would view it.

While Rob't was circling in on fine-tuning the complicated attraction layout—and even more complicated ride timing—Sue was building game and vehicle mock-ups for play-testing. Our first vehicle "buck" was made of plywood, and the attached spring-action shooter mock-up was made from rope, over-the-counter steel, plastic pipe, and other random parts from a local hardware store. We set up a mock game booth in front of the buck, and Sue worked with Estefania Pickens and game designer Jesse Schell from Carnegie Mellon to develop some early games for play-testing.

There were a lot of learning curves along the way. When Jesse delivered his first-pass version of Hamm & Eggs, and we got the crude spring-action shooter to work in real time with it, every time an egg was tossed and knocked something over, a numerical score would pop out and float above the downed target (like you'd typically see in a video game). But we didn't want a video game! This was completely counter to the "reality" we were trying to achieve. We wanted the games and the booths to look like they were made out of flat "cutout" wood, painted and assembled. We didn't want any contemporary electronic game imagery or graphics you'd see anywhere else. Another lesson we quickly

With my creative partner in crime Rob't Coltrin at our first crude vehicle mock-up, made mostly of parts from the hardware store, for Toy Story Midway Mania!

learned was, using the dart toss as an example, we had to program the launched darts "stuck" in the back wall to eventually loosen on their own and drop "to the floor" out of sight. The reason for that is if you add up all of the games and all of the thousands of objects that all of the players are tossing/firing real time at the same time, the real-time computer required to simulate so much activity can be quickly brought to its knees. That's why the hundreds of objects you toss out every game quickly drop out of view to allow for the real-time regeneration of new objects being tossed. Making the games look simple—and the playing of them intuitive—was extremely complicated. We could not have done it without our mock-up and progressive play-testing. As our mock-up space was located directly across Flower Street from our main building in Glendale, we would often host John Lasseter and Bob Iger, who loved to stop by to play, much to the chagrin of their "handlers," whose job it was to keep them on schedule.

Over the course of our game development, Sue and Estefania hosted hundreds of play-testing sessions for invited gamers of all ages. These sessions proved invaluable in helping us to fine-tune the games and improve upon their playability. My favorite story was that younger gamers were reluctant to break plates (even though virtual) in the mock-up for the Green Army Men Shoot Camp. Sue discovered that, at that age, they were taught *not* to break things! That being the case, I brought the voice talent of "Sarge" from *Toy Story* into our studio to record this command that can be heard in the attraction today: "I am not your mother! You have my permission to break these plates!" Once we added that line, the kids broke free!

While the play-testing and target testing continued across the street, my aim was to write the overall attraction script and the separate "interactive" script for Mr. Potato Head. This, too, was complicated, in that I had to write any combination of real-time line possibilities he could say to any guest related to what they were wearing, saying, asking, and/or doing. "From expert to beginner, everyone's a winner!" he might say. "How about you, young man in the blue shirt?" I also happily wrote the lyrics to all of the songs he sings in his role of boardwalk barker to attract passersby and entertain those already waiting in line. Joyous was the time I spent working on all of the songs with Joey Miskulin, the accordion player (or the "Stomach Steinway" as he affectionately calls it) from the comedy Western singing group Riders in the Sky. Our connection with Joey, aka "Joey the Cow Polka King," is Riders in the Sky wrote and performed the song "Woody's Roundup" for *Toy Story 2*. Plus, they were also involved with other Pixar-related projects. Joey composed the music to go with my lyrics, which was like a dream come true for me because I was a huge fan of the group that does it "the cowboy way" long before they were involved with Disney and Pixar. Don Rickles, the voice of Mr. Potato Head, sang all of the songs with great gusto and glee. Here's the attraction's theme song's lyrics:

Midway Mania, you'll love this game it's so insane-ia
Everybody, I said everybody's playin', everybody's sayin'
You won't be the same once you play this game!
Midway Mania, how can I make it any plain-ia?
So, come on, pal, step right up and make some noise
It's time to play with all the toys!
You know, your life will never be mundane-ia
When you play Midway Mania!

How does a boardwalk barker, who also happens to be a potato, shill the attraction in song?

One potato, two potato, three potato, four
Five potato, six potato, play the game and score!
Seven potato, eight potato, nine potato, ten
Try your luck, ya hockey puck and play the game again!
Step right up and take a ride, my toy friends are all inside
There's no need to be afraid-O, trust me, I'm a hot potato!
Hurry! Hurry! Right this way everybody here can play
Feel what it's like, there's nothing greater
When you're a hot potater!
One potato, two potato, three potato, four
Five potato, six potato, you're gonna score
Seven potato, eight potato, nine potato, ten
Be a hot potato!

Two buds and
a spud!

One of the big breakthroughs on the Mr. Potato Head Audio-Animatronics figure is our animation team ended up pulling off his ability to pull off his ear. "You there, in the red shirt," he asks. "How would you like having a potato for a pet? We can do all kinds of tricks. Wanna see one? Okay, are you watching? Are you watching?" He takes off his ear. "Ta-da! Try getting a pony to do that!" He continues, "I like having interchangeable parts. Sometimes I wear my feet where my ears are supposed to go. Like that guy over there!"

Roger Gould and I spent thirty-three hours with Don Rickles in our recording studio at Imagineering. As you can imagine, it was an experience like no other! I had seen the showbiz icon on TV hundreds of times while growing up, and I must admit I was not a big fan of his insulting comedy shtick. In fact, the thought of working with the "Merchant of Venom" scared the heck out of me. Still, on Don's first recording day with us at Imagineering I thought it would be a nice gesture if I were standing out front of our main lobby to welcome him upon his arrival. I nervously watched as his long black limo turned in to our parking lot and stopped with its blacked-out back passenger side window within my arm's reach. The dark window went down to reveal the famous face of "Mr. Warmth" himself. "Get in," he ordered. I dashed around to the other side of the car, slid into the back seat next to the legend, and said, "Hi, Mr. Rickles, I'm Kevin. Welcome to Imagineering."

He scowled. "Now, you listen to me," he said, grabbing my shirt collar in his clenched fist and pulling my face right up to his, which wasn't anywhere near as pleasant as when Cindy Crawford did that to me, "'cause I'm gonna tell you something very important." He said that with the attitude of an angry parent who is about to warn, "If you ever do that again I'll ground you for a month!" I assumed Don was about to establish the rules of the road, the pecking order—the uncrossable boundaries between him and me. But what he actually wanted to do is tell me a funny story. And that story was followed by another and then another. The man was doing his act! I was at a Don Rickles show and the only one in the audience! I never said a word as I sat there in our parking lot in the back seat of his limo for a half hour listening to and laughing at his nonstop stories before he finally came in for a landing and let go of my shirt. "Now look what you did, Calvin," he scolded, "you made me late! You should be ashamed of yourself. If I was your father I'd ground you for a month!"

We had several recording sessions with Don, and he always came to our studio with the energy and enthusiasm of a man half his age. At eighty, he told me he had signed a five-year contract to extend his show in Las Vegas. Every recording session he had with us began with stories about his career and his relationship with Frank Sinatra and many of the biggest names in the business. But of all of Don's stories, my favorites were the ones I personally witnessed that happened at Imagineering. Jeff Webb, our vice president of project estimating, grabbed me in the hall and wanted to know if the rumor that I was working with his idol Don Rickles was true. "I'm so jealous," he said when I validated the rumor. Jeff told me he was a lifetime fan of the comedian and had been to many of his live shows. After one of our recording sessions a few days later, as I was walking Don through our main corridor back to his awaiting limo, I figured I knew him well enough to ask a favor. "Don," I said pointing to an office door we were approaching, "that office belongs to one of your biggest fans and a dear friend of mine. Would you mind just poking your head in and saying 'hi' to Jeff?" Not only did Don poke his head in, he marched his whole body in like he owned the joint and found our dutiful estimator crunching numbers at his desk.

I'll never forget the look on Jeff's face when he peeked over the top of his reading glasses and saw the man of whom he was a fan standing before him. "Look, at you, Jeff," exclaimed Don. "You're tired. You're overworked. You're underpaid. These Disney people are obviously taking advantage of you. Now, do you and me both a favor, huh? Get outta here. Take the rest of the day off. I mean it!" A few doors down the hall Don took me by surprise when he suddenly side stepped into video producer Ken Horii's office. "Hey, pally," he greeted Ken. "Yeah, I'm talkin' to you! What's a classy guy like you doing in a dump like this? Look at this place. I'm embarrassed for you. A big important guy like you should have better digs. Don't worry. I know people. I'll get it taken care of."

But my all-time favorite Don Rickles moment happened in the middle of one of our recording sessions. Roger Gould and I codirected Don's performances while sitting next to him in the studio. We worked him hard and he professionally knocked out everything we tossed his way.

Pixer's Roger Gould and I spent thirty-three hours in our Imagineering recording studio with Don Rickles (can you imagine?), where he brought my scripts and songs for Mr. Potato Head to life.

After one of his takes, which I thought was perfect, Roger asked him to perform the line once again with a different inflection on one of the words. "Roger," snapped Don, continuing in a rapid-fire pace, "why can't you be more like Kev? I like Kev. Kev's a good guy. Kev's a smart guy. I'm gonna take him on the road with me. But you! YOU! You're from around the San Francisco area, aren't ya? Look, do me a favor. Leave right now, fly back up north, hop in your car, drive to the Golden Gate Bridge, suck off all the red paint, then keep heading north and never come back again!" On the day when Don Rickles passed away I received this text message from Roger:

Don Rickles RIP. Pretty lucky we got to spend so much time with him. Makes me want to go suck paint off the Golden Gate Bridge.

I should have bought Don a Disney sweatshirt in Mickey's of Glendale to replace the one he was wearing!

Don became such a good friend that when he passed, people, including Marty Sklar, sent notes and cards of condolences to me. I should have known better than to be scared about working with Don. His insulting demeanor was all an act. What he did for a living was not who he really was. I was really blessed to be able to get to know the sweet, caring, and lovable guy who was the real Rickles. When our sessions were over, I sincerely thanked him for working so hard and for doing such a great job for us. He thanked me and said it was his pleasure because he does Mr. Potato Head for his grandchildren. Every line he performed, and there were hundreds, was for them.

Soon after Toy Story Midway Mania! had opened I received this letter:

June 9, 2008
Dear Roger and Kevin,
I figured I'd save stationery writing to you as a team!
Gentlemen, I can't thank you enough for my special Mr. Potato Head sweatshirt. I'll wear it proudly at the Donald Duck swim off contest at Disney! Meanwhile guys, take care of yourself and work on your personalities!
Love 'ya,
Don

DON RICKLES

June 9, 2008

Dear Roger and Kevin,

I figured I'd save stationary writing to you as a team!

Gentleman, I can't thank you enough for my special Mr. Potato Head sweat shirt. I'll wear it proudly at the Donald Duck swim off contest at Disney!

Meanwhile guys, take care of yourself and work on your personalities!

Love 'ya,

Don

Here are a couple of Midway Maniacs trying out their shiny new ride vehicle for the first time.

Every bit of designing and delivering Mania was *insane-ia*. But boy, was it fun! Not only was the attraction a toy and a game, it was also a puzzle. And in the end, all the pieces fit perfectly, including both versions of the attractions that were shoehorned into unorthodox spaces. On those occasions when you achieve your goal, the more impossible it seemed at the beginning, the sweeter and more gratifying it is when you get there. I worked on both Rock 'n' Roller Coaster and Twilight Zone Tower of Terror at Disney's Hollywood Studios, and prior to the addition of Mania, when the rope dropped on Hollywood Boulevard upon the park's opening, I was always so proud and happy whenever I saw guests turning to the right to head over to those attractions first. But once Mania opened—and I saw the wave of guests turning left—I jumped for joy. On the West Coast, adding this attraction to Disney California Adventure was a game-changer, because its popularity helped open the door for more expansion.

The ride and game experience was right on target, and the icing on the gingerbread cake—its highly detailed boardwalk-inspired architecture designed exquisitely by Oscar Cobos—in every way emanated a classic Disneyland vibe. And for Disney California Adventure, there was even more lovingly executed Disneyland-like detail to come on the road ahead!

THE ROAD TO CARS LAND

FOUR YEARS AFTER the opening of Disney California Adventure, Barry Braverman, then creative executive for the park, spotted me working alone in a conference room. "Kev," he said, drawing a deep breath. "I have a big favor to ask." The serious tone of his voice when he emphasized "big favor" sounded as if he were about to ask me to climb to the top of Mount Everest in the dead of winter in my underwear. I thought perhaps it was because he had not asked me to do anything since I had made all those excuses eight-ish years before, during the early-concept development phase of Disney California Adventure, about why I could not work on the new park project. Truth be told, it's not that I *could* not, it's that I *would* not. I'm a traditional build-a-berm-and-fill-the-inside-with-highly-detailed-immersive-stories-and-experiences-that-take-you-to-another-place-in-another-time kind of guy.

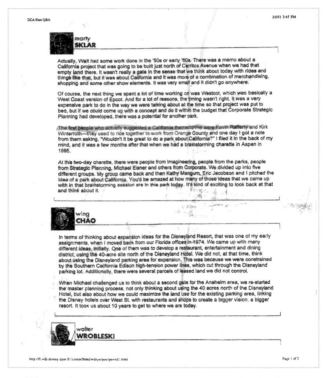

When the company was starting to think about adding a second gate park at Disneyland, Imagineer Kirk Winterroth and I suggested to Marty it have a California theme.

And I wasn't the least bit drawn to this new berm-less "build it and they will come" approach for a park, especially one that would reside next door to the mother of them all. I would do anything for Barry, including climbing Mount Everest in my tighty-whities in zero degrees, but I had zero desire to work on this new park. "Since you didn't work on the park," he continued, "I need your fresh eyes." I always felt guilty about bailing on Barry, so this time I promised to be there for him. "Great," he responded, "because I want to ask you to come up with something big, something that'll bring more Disneyland DNA to DCA." This was a huge ask for a daunting, terrifying, monumental task, but boy, oh, boy I loved the sound of it! "I get what you're asking," I said, "but what are you looking for specifically. A new ride?" "Yes, a new ride," he responded, but then it got even better. "Or even a whole new land."

When I was a kid, working at Disneyland, the southeast section of its parking lot—the very spot where I used to hang out with my fellow dishwashers after our night shift and dream about the fun new rides we would create there if given the chance (yeah, right!)—was the very spot Barry offered me to dream up a new fun ride. Or more! How crazy is that? The location offered a rare opportunity to build something from the ground up. And given my history of theoretical dreaming and scheming there, this was hallowed ground. It was also one of the precious and few sections of usable land left. Whatever was going to be built there had to be nothing less than spectacularly amazing. The pressure was on.

As soon as Barry departed, I started thinking about what some of my colleagues had done with their similar from-the-ground-up opportunities; and I came to the conclusion that they all shared something in common: the themes of their best and most groundbreaking (literally) work were inspired by their personal interests. Joe Rohde is passionate about art, nature, and travel to exotic places, and he helped parlay those personal interests into Animal Kingdom. Tony Baxter is passionate about Disneyland and Europe, and he helped turn those personal interests into Disneyland Paris. Steve Kirk is passionate about science fiction, world history, and travel to adventurous destinations overseas; he helped transform those personal interests into Tokyo DisneySea. What if, even though it seemed selfish, I could help turn my personal interests—classic cars and oldies music—into a new ride or even a whole new land?

Rock 'n' roll oldies and classic cars go together like sunshine and Southern California. Yet, despite the fact that a first-generation red Corvette was featured in the center of the opening day park poster, Disney California Adventure missed the mark in delivering anything about our legendary car culture in the Golden State.

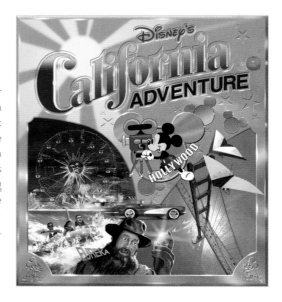

This opening day poster featured a first-generation Corvette, but the park didn't deliver on the popular car culture in California. This was actually one of my selling points when pitching the idea for a new cars-themed land.

Between all of the car clubs, car shows and gatherings, race courses, custom-build and paint shops, major automotive design studios, and manufacturing plants, car culture has always been in high gear in California. As long as I can remember, I was infatuated with cars and everything about them, inside and out, from top to bottom. While growing up, I built every model car I could get my hands on with my saved allowance; and I couldn't wait for every September issue of *Life* magazine because of its snazzy ads for the new car models, like the one for the "Wide-Track Pontiac," which was so wide, in fact, it always commanded a double-page spread.

I'll never forget watching the episode of *Bonanza*, sponsored by Chevrolet, that got me into more trouble with my pa than Little Joe Cartwright ever got into with his. The Sunday night show was on too late for a sixth grader, so my parents didn't allow me to stay up and watch. But I watched it anyway behind their backs—literally. My trick was to crouch behind the couch and

As long as I can remember, I was infatuated with cars and everything about them.

quietly watch it over their shoulders. I would have gotten away with it every week had it not been for the commercial introducing the 1967 Camaro. When the commercial cut to a close-up of the Camaro Rally Sport's hideaway head-lights opening like magic, I couldn't control my excitement. I gasped, choked, heaved, and spun around in a dizzying stupor until I, just this side of a faint, fell forward onto the back of the couch scaring the living crap out of Mom and causing Dad to pull me by the ear into my room. I remain a sucker for hideaway headlights to this day. Many new models were introduced in the 1950s and 1960s, and the evergreen models were always changing radically in their design every year. Advertising copy for them was terrific: CHEVY PUTS THE *PURR* IN PER-FORMANCE! and MOTHER WARNED ME THERE WOULD BE MEN LIKE YOU DRIVING CARS LIKE THIS. Compared to gems like those, car slogans today should be ashamed of themselves. GO FURTHER (that would also work for a laxative) and LET'S GO PLACES? (Like yours is the first car that can take us somewhere? That would also work for a laxative.) I can still tell you everything about every model from every manufacturer from that era, including all available engines, options, and colors. Show me a hubcap and I'll tell you the manufacturer, model, and year.

In 1962—one of my favorite years for perfect-line automotive design—I was playing in our front yard when I noticed a shiny new black Pontiac Bonne-ville, exactly like the one I drooled over in *Life* magazine the night before, glis-tening in the sun as it drove up the street towards our house. My eyes opened even wider when I recognized that the lucky stiff behind the wheel was my dad! We thought he was going to the hardware store. Well, he did, but on the way back he spotted "Bonnie" in the showroom window of the Anaheim Pontiac dealership and, bewitched by a beauty more ravishing than the bathing Bath-sheba, threw caution and money to the wind and traded our family station wagon for her!

Young Kev thoroughly enjoying Bonnie the Bonneville in 1962. "C'mon, dad, put the top down and let's cruise!"

I suspect all of this happened while Dad was in a euphoric hypnotic trance, like Snuffles the cartoon dog whenever he ate a dog biscuit. So, the entire affair was understandably out of his control. To surprise Mom, who was saving up for new living room furniture and knew nothing about this new car purchase, he pulled up alongside the curb, laid on the horn, and timed it so as she was opening the front door to step out, just as the automatic convertible top would be going down to reveal the beaming new owner inside. But when he lowered the top, she lowered the boom! The entire neighborhood came out to witness Mom's booming ballyhoo over Bonnie. As she stomped in a huff back towards the house—where the living room would now remain furniture free until the car was paid off someday—Dad called out to her one final time to try and bring her around. "And she has three deuces and a 389 under the hood! (Engine rev.) "HOT *cha-cha-cha-chaaaa!*" Mom slammed the front door so hard that two of the three glass panels in it cracked. Smiling, the old man raised his dark Ray-Ban glasses and winked at me. It was the greatest moment ever and the first time I realized that the power of a beautiful car is not found under the hood. The real power of a beautiful car is it can make you lose your mind. And your money.

Automotive design was in its heyday then, and I loved every line, headlight, taillight, and chrome trim. Today, when I want to go to a happy place, I climb behind the wheel of my classic car, "Sandra Dee," drop the top, turn up the oldies, and let her take me away—and that's without even leaving the garage!

My 1956 cascade green Corvette Sandra Dee at the First Annual "Car & Bike" Show held on the Green at Imagineering in March 2013. It took over eight years to restore her one piece at a time. She won Best in Show that day!

Here's the original land logo used for the first three years of concept development for what became Cars Land. After all, chrome wasn't built in a day!

Would it be possible to wrap an entire land around the single theme of the automobile? I was lucky to have spent my wonder years as the automobile became less of a means of basic transportation and more a form of personal expression, style, and freedom. That era would provide the perfect time period. The "where" should be small-town America. Would a 1950s, small-town main street in the spirit of Main Street, U.S.A., help bring some of that Disneyland DNA to DCA? It made sense that when Disneyland opened mid-century, its turn-of-the-century–inspired Main Street was compelling because it brought back to life, in a utopian way, a place from fifty years in the past. Yet, it was not so far back in time that older guests could not relate to its look and feel in a nostalgic and reassuring, "Hey, this reminds me of my hometown" kind of way. The same amount of time had passed from 1955 to 2004. If we created a *new* main street depicting mid-century America, it could work exactly the same way. "Cruise Street" was born. The name for the proposed new land came quickly, too, thanks to the challenge to bring more Disneyland to Disney California Adventure. Taking a cue from the names Fantasyland, Adventureland, Tomorrowland, and Frontierland, it seemed only natural to name this new land "Carland."

Although I knew a lot about cars, I began my usual research to help inspire ideas for possible shows, attractions, and restaurants for Carland. The first thing I did was make a list of all cars related to Disney, including Herbie the Love Bug and Professor Ned Brainard's famous flubber-fueled flying Model T from *The Absent-Minded Professor*. There were a couple of car-themed cartoon shorts starring Goofy called *Motor Mania* and *Freewayphobia*, and a few other Disney car connections here and there, but nothing with enough tread on its tire to become a full-fledged attraction. I even discovered, to my great surprise, an automotive event Disneyland hosted on September 5, 1959, called the First Annual Car Club Day and Autocade. Unfortunately, it was the first and only

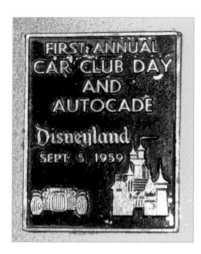

Few knew about the first (and last) annual car show at Disneyland. I discovered this event, which I had never been aware of while doing research for the original Carland concept.

such event—and the reason why was explained to me by someone who was there. According to his eyewitness account, "Things got a little out of hand because of all the hot rod hooligans with their slicked-back hair and cigarette packs rolled up in their T-shirt sleeves cruising down Main Street like they owned the place in cars that were almost as loud as they were." After the Autocade Parade, when the cruisers assembled and hung out on a dirt lot backstage, they raised even more of a ruckus. Still, for driving on down to Disneyland that day, each car owner, despite their undesirable behavior, received a desirable bronze dashboard plaque featuring the name and date of the event and side-by-side images of a hot rod and Sleeping Beauty Castle.

When I was a "little driver," my favorite ride at Disneyland was the Midget Autopia because the cars were my size; and that made them beyond special. The attraction opened in 1957 and closed in 1966 to make way for "it's a small world." But I didn't mind because by then I was just tall enough to segue over and drive a real car with a real gas pedal and steering wheel on Autopia. Short drives such as those on Autopia—or long drives, such as those on a "you can hold it until we get to the next gas station in a hundred miles" road trip—were my thing. My family took many cross-country trips in Bonnie the Bonneville. Our ex-station wagon would have been much more practical and spacious but certainly not as classy.

That's why, on one of our trips, I didn't mind traveling all the way home from Nebraska in our jam-packed back seat, filled mostly with my sister's stuff, riding on the back of a concrete donkey lawn ornament dad purchased at a roadside stand. And a few miles down the road that donkey ended up standing on top of a case of Grain Belt beer because dad couldn't get that Midwest brand in California. Beer on the bottom—donkey in the middle—me on the top. I was sitting so high up it was a good thing Bonnie had a soft top. That is until we hit the baseball-sized hailstorm in South Dakota. While we were getting bombarded with thousands of frozen pellets in the middle of nowhere, you should have seen Mom's "WHAT WERE YOU THINKING TRADING OUR STATION WAGON FOR A CONVERTIBLE?" glare at dad. That glare was even *glarier* when we had to stop in a long line of cars behind a summer road crew in Yellowstone National Park and a big old bear walked over to us on its hind legs and started clawing through Bonnie's vinyl top on Mom's side. "Take a movie!" dad excitedly suggested to her. But Mom just locked the door and screamed until she passed out. Holy convertible top! It was the greatest road trip moment ever! After we returned home, I remember lying on my back in all the spacious splendor of the sister-less, donkey-less, beer-less back seat and seeing blue sky through the shreds in the convertible top on our way to the furniture store.

Oftentimes on our family road trips, we'd stop to see the roadside attractions advertised on billboards along the highway: 100 MILES TO THE MYSTERY METEOR HOLE, EXPLORE THE MYSTERIOUS MYSTERIES OF THE CAVERNS OF MYSTERY, THIS MYSTERIOUS EXIT TO GRAIN BELT BEER, and HERE IT IS. The mystery there was we pulled off the highway at the HERE IT IS exit and couldn't find where *it* was. We were duped. Roadside attractions were the best! What if we combined a Midget Autopia ride system with the story of a road trip complete with roadside attractions? This question got me thinking about another Disneyland favorite back in the day: Nature's Wonderland in Frontierland, which was a train ride through the True-Life Adventures–inspired Living Desert with some now familiar-sounding sights along the way, such as Big Thunder Waterfall (which you got to ride behind) and Bear Country (featuring Marc Davis's classic gag of a bear scratching his back on a tree after a long day of clawing convertibles). The best part of the ride came after the natural arch bridge, comical cactus, wild pigs, bobcats, rattlesnakes, mountain lions, devil's paint pots, Old Unfaithful geyser, and even Balancing Rock Canyon, where the Stinky Pete-soundalike, onboard narrator warned, "Look out! They're startin' to tumble!" *Yessir*, the best part of Nature's Wonderland was its spectacular grand finale, Rainbow Caverns, which was filled with such wonders to behold as stalactites, stalagmites, color-ful waterfalls (cascading down on either side of the train), and even a choir of ethereal voices angelically accentuating the glory of it all. As a nod to Nature's Wonderland, the finale of the Midget Autopia road trip ride I named Scoot 66 (and later renamed Road Trip, USA) would feature a drive through the colorful and musical wonders of Rainbow Caverns.

And at the very end, just like my dad used to do (except for the trip after the "bear scare and tear"), guests would take a ride through the car wash

This proposed Carland attraction was inspired by favorite childhood memories from many cross-country road trips in Bonnie the Bonneville and by many rides on the Midget Autopia at Disneyland.

This storyboard art of Carsbad Caverns by Chris Turner shows the closing scene to the proposed Carland attraction, Road Trip, USA. It was inspired by the Rainbow Caverns in Nature's Wonderland, a Disneyland attraction that once existed where Big Thunder Mountain is today.

Prior to unload on Road Trip, USA, returning guests were sent through a car wash, where others on the Cruise Street side of the glass got to have some good clean fun!

This is the original "flavor" board I put together and used for pitching the crazy concept for a cars-theme land—and before I even knew Pixar was working on a movie about cars. This trifold board is what got the whole thing on the road!

located at the end of Cruise Street. Guests standing on the sidewalk side of the car wash could push buttons and pull levers to spray, bubble, brush, and blow-dry the road trippers returning to unload.

Pondering the E-Ticket thrill attraction, some kind of car or dragster race seemed like the way to go, but I didn't flesh it out as much as everything else in Carland. I figured I'd save the best (and hardest) for last. I continued working on the rest of the concepts on my own for a couple of months until I'd had enough research imagery and rough art to put together a high-level concept board that captured the flavor and feel of this proposed new land themed entirely around cars.

The portable trifolding board—the very first thing I used to pitch the idea for Carland—did the trick: Barry Braverman and other decision-making executives supported the concept and got it on the road to further development. To complement the concept art, the board featured the following copy:

Carland
Time Period: Late 1950s–early 1960s
Keywords: Drive-in, Drag Racers, Teenagers, Classic Cars,
Rock 'n' Roll

Carland puts California car culture on the map of Disney's California Adventure. The time is late '50s to early '60s[,] when songs like "Little Deuce Coupe," "409," and "Drag City" became the soundtrack of this classic era when the car became a symbol of personal freedom and expression.

Cruise Street, the land's "main drag," is home to Marty's Malt Shop, Ride 'n' Shine Car Wash (interactive water-play area), California Classics Showroom (displays and merchandise), Carland Dine-in Theater (restaurant) and Be-Bop Garage, a live show starring mechanics that discover the musical potential of car parts! Cruise Street also plays host to classic car shows and cruise nights. Major attractions include *Drag Racer*, a racing-themed roller coaster and Scoot 66, a Midget Autopia–type driving adventure along a meandering highway dotted with California Crazy icons.

Carland captures the "cool" and carefree attitude driven by the automobile!

Remember, this first concept board was put together in 2004. I had no idea Pixar had started work on a *movie* about cars while I was independently working on a *land* about cars. The baby moons (for non-car folks those are chrome wheel covers) were in alignment. This land was destined to happen! After I got approval to continue development, I added another major attraction to the land. It was Junkyard Jamboree, an idea for a show-controlled, indoor ride-through attraction in which you hopped into a junked jalopy body that transported you through a junkyard at the stroke of midnight when all of the car parts come to life and perform car-themed music.

In one scene, Johnny Revtone and the V8s—rock 'n' roll-playing car engines that popped up from under a car hood—performed "engine block rock." In another scene, long and low car bodies hopped, dropped, and danced to War's "Low Rider." Pickup trucks crooned a country tune. There was a hubcap-and-brake drum percussion band and the car-horn section had a brassy and sassy Tower of Power-type vibe. In the finale, all of the parts came together to literally rock the night away as the sun came up to return everything back to normal in the junkyard.

The Googie-style Cruise Street featured a build-your-own slot car shop, where you could also race them on giant tracks; a record store, where you could choose your favorite "car tunes" and make your own records; a real barbershop, where the talk was all about cars; a dealership showroom, where displays and tributes to a variety of classic car models would change out regularly; a 1950s "dime store" and automobile memorabilia shop; and, of course, a car wash in all its colorfully spired Googie glory.

At the end of Cruise Street was Marty's Malt Shop (where Flo's V8 Café is today), featuring a patio that overlooked the breathtaking view of the monumental rockwork, waterfalls, colorful geysers, and roadside attractions of Road Trip, USA. The malt shop's claim to roadside diner fame was its Car-B-Que, a custom barbecue that put the "hot" in hot rod. On the outskirts of town, the land's second restaurant, Carland Dine-In Theater, was the sister of Sci-Fi Dine-In at Disney's Hollywood Studios; but instead of showing trailers from

The junked jalopy body transported guests between musical scenes in Junkyard Jamboree. May it rust in pieces.

This concept sketch for the original Junkyard Jamboree illustrates Johnny Revtone and the V8s performing rock 'n' roll at the midnight hour, when all of the car parts come to life.

Early concept for the Car-B-Que, known to insiders as the "Sklar-B-Que," which Marty did not like! Strange, coming from a man who usually encouraged *engine*-uity!

science fiction movies it would show trailers from car movies like *Hot-Rod Girl* (CHICKEN-RACE . . . ROCK 'N' ROLL . . . YOUTH ON THE LOOSE!) and *Thunder Road* (THE HOTTEST HIGHWAY ON EARTH!).

I thought it would be fun if the "Dine-In Theater" part of the name on the marquee was fabricated from neon so the word "eat"—hiding out in the middle of the word "Th**eat**er"—would flicker as if it were shorting out to call attention to itself as an eatery. The music heard on Cruise Street would be every car-themed song you could think of this side of the 1970s. To further flesh out the rough concepts and their stories (and to help start thinking about how to make them doable and buildable), I asked my creative partner in crime, Rob't Coltrin, to join me on the road to Carland. And to create our concept art and story-boards, there was none better than my good luck charm (because his art has helped me to sell many projects over the years) and fellow car guy, designer/illustrator extraordinaire, Chris Turner.

Rob't and I went right to work trying to get that yet-to-be-defined E-Ticket racing ride off the starting line. Our intent was to make it the land's anchor attraction, so it had to be big, fun, fast, and repeatable. We kicked around a few concepts but didn't come up with anything that felt right or did the land justice. That's when we got wind of the timely, unbelievable rumor that Pixar was making a movie about cars! ARE YOU KIDDING? Who knew? I'm sure when Pixar found out Imagineering was working on a land about cars they said the same thing. It was, I must say, the strangest of coincidences. Or was it? The movie was about two and a half years out from theatrical release, so the film's director, John Lasseter, and his team were still very much in the devel-opment phase. Rob't and I flew up to meet with John as I had done in the past to brainstorm and consult on other attractions—only this time we were hoping *there might be something* in his new car-themed film *we might be able to use* in our land. Neither Rob't, nor I—or anyone else at Imagineering—knew anything about the movie.

John graciously and excitedly took Rob't and I through the concept art and story in the works for *Cars*. He showed us one of his favorite pieces of early-concept art, the first-ever bird's-eye view of the town of Radiator Springs, illustrated by longtime animator Bud Luckey. Afterwards, John took us into Pixar's main lobby theater to show us, on the big screen, some of the absolutely stunning test footage they had recently completed of rookie race car Lightning McQueen in a "Piston Cup" race and the scene in which Doc Hudson teaches the rookie how to steer on the dirt track around Willys Butte (for you keen-eyed editors out there, relax. "Willys" does not have an apostrophe because Willy is not possessive about his *butte*. The butte is named for the defunct car

Chris Turner's early-concept sketch of Cruise Street with a view to Marty's Malt Shop, the only weenie at the end of any Disney street where you could actually get a weenie!

company once known as Willys; S's with no apostrophe preceding them can be messy. I once knew someone whose first name was Roberts. So as not to keep confusing people, he shortened his name to Bobs).

When I saw the early clips from *Cars*, my incredulous head blew a gasket. I, like Mater, was hooked. All I could think was *Way to go, John*. Independently choosing cars as a theme for a movie while I chose it for a Disney Park land close to the same time made John Lasseter and me oil brothers, car-*noisseurs*, *afficion*-autos. While we were at Pixar, Rob't and I learned everything we possibly could about the movie, including, and especially, the lovable car characters and the town they lived in. Since I spent every summer vacation in the car, sometimes on Route 66, I loved that the "Mother Road" had such an important part in the story. But what Rob't and I loved the most about that Pixar trip is being introduced to race car Lightning McQueen at the very same time we were trying to come up with an idea for a race-inspired ride. That's all we excitedly talked about on the flight back to Burbank.

By the time we landed, fueled by Pixar's *Cars*, we not only had the big idea for our anchor racing ride, we also had it broken down into a three-act structure. Act 1 would be a relaxing drive through the mountains, like the one Lightning and Sally enjoyed together; Act 2 would be the show-controlled theatrical indoor experience with all of the Audio-Animatronics (or as I liked to call them, *AUTO*-Animatronics) characters; and Act 3 would be the thrilling race across Ornament Valley and around Willys Butte, where Doc taught Lightning how to turn right to go left. The whole thing felt right.

I loved our Act 1 road trip because it made the experience feel similar to major attractions at Disneyland that have a great opening act like the stretch room at the Haunted Mansion and the relaxing "firefly float by" alongside the Blue Bayou Restaurant at Pirates of the Caribbean. These Act 1 examples serve to decompress guests from all the other distractions and experiences of their day and get them settled in and ready to focus on the upcoming attraction story. Imagine if you had to hop into a Doom Buggy first thing after stepping through the front door of the Haunted Mansion or if the boats in Pirates of the Caribbean were dispatched directly into the first drop. Our relaxing mountain drive in the great outdoors would allow our guests to settle in and get ready for their *accelerating* surprise encounter with Mac, which gets the story started.

Radiator Springs Racers was the first attraction name I hand-printed on a three-by-five-inch card—and it never changed. Rob't and I never even suggested any other name options. More than two years before the movie *Cars* would be released, the two of us had the entire Racers ride sequence storyboarded in hand-printed words and thumbnail sketches. It took about six weeks for us to get to that point following our recon trip to Pixar. Then, after receiving some proprietary character model sheets from Pixar to help keep his depiction of the characters honest, Chris Turner started replacing our "placeholder" words and sketches with his sensational storyboard art.

I am so proud to say our completed first-pass story sequence as represented in our original attraction storyboards for Radiator Springs Racers, which we wrapped up in 2004 (about three months after we found out Pixar was making a movie about cars), represented beat-for-beat almost exactly the attraction you can experience in Cars Land today. The only differences between our original storyboards and the opening day attraction is our first-thought queue and load area took place at a Dinoco gas station at the entrance to Ornament Valley. Our first-thought postrace finale scene, featuring Mater, Lightning, and Sally, took place in a garage. But we quickly changed the uninspiring garage interior to the inspiring Carsbad Caverns, home to stalactites and stalagmites in the shape of spark plugs and other "natural" car part–like formations. When we went back to Pixar to pitch Radiator Springs Racers to John Lasseter, after we picked him off the floor because he was so revved up about the ride as you can imagine, his only suggestion was that we turn Carsbad Caverns into Taillight Caverns. After that, I started calling the stalactites "stalac-lights."

Since we ended up requiring a longer outdoor queue area with more shade and structural cover than the Dinoco gas station could provide, I created the story for Stanley's Oasis, which is the current queue and load area for Radiator Springs Racers. Pixar had already established a short Stanley story by featuring him as Lizzie's long-departed husband and the founder of Radiator Springs. The town honored their founder with a bronze statue of his likeness in front of the courthouse. In the bonus material on the *Cars* DVD, John Lasseter adds a bit more to that by explaining Radiator Springs was founded in 1909 by a character named Stanley who discovered the original spring, "Nature's Coolant," while crossing Ornament Valley in the summer heat. That's about as far as Pixar took Stanley's story. So, I picked it up from there to provide a backstory for the covered structures we needed to design and build for our meandering queue:

During the sweltering summers of the 1900s, automobiles traveling through Ornament Valley overheated with so much pressure, their radiator caps blew off. Losing a cap meant big trouble for those traveling alone. One such car, a radiator cap salescar named Stanley, started losing steam in the middle of nowhere. He carried extra caps but they were of no value to him without coolant in his radiator. Poor Stanley thought his miles were numbered—that is until he rolled down into a shady spot and happened upon lifesaving water bubbling up out of a rock. Nature's own coolant! As he filled his radiator to the brim in the comfortable surroundings of this hidden desert oasis, he decided to stay and direct overheated travelers to the spring and then sell them a new radiator cap.

Stanley put down stakes and went to work building the Cap 'n' Tap radiator cap shop. He then constructed a water tower with a pipe that carried coolant over to a long trough, so thirsty cars could park side-by-side and get their fill. The enterprising young car set eye-catching signs out on the road that read FILL UP & COOL DOWN and REFRESHINGEST RADIATOR REJUVENATOR ON ROUTE 66, and opened "Stanley's Oasis the 8 3/4th Wonder of the World" for business. Stanley had no idea the steady stream coming from his spring would attract such a steady stream of radiator cap customers!

Stanley added a filling station to his oasis where visitors to this restful and refreshing place could fill up with gas and get their oil changed. In those days, motor oil came in bottles, so Stanley saved up enough empties to build the Oil Bottle Garage, a popular roadside attraction. Many cross-country travelers pulled off Route 66 to rest and refresh in the shade of this special place, including a lovely little Model-T named Lizzie who instantly fell head-over-wheels in love with Stanley. Lizzie did not want to leave so she talked Stanley into letting her set up a souvenir stand in a corner of his radiator cap shop. Soon Stanley started to take a shine to his new business partner. To provide lodging for Lizzie and overnight visitors, Stanley established the Comfy Caverns Motor Court offering overnighters a free Lincoln Continental breakfast inside the "Naturally Cooled" Fender Cave.

Stanley's Oasis eventually expanded from the higher rocks to a flat stretch of nearby land where there was plenty of room to expand. Lizzie opened a larger curious shop and soon other businesses began to spring up establishing a new town. Stanley named the town after the natural wonder that saved his life and started it all: Radiator Springs. Thanks to the many travelers on Route 66[,] business was good and life was even better. When the courthouse was completed Stanley and Lizzie were the first to get hitched. And they lived happily ever after in the cutest little town in Carburetor County.

John liked the story of Stanley's Oasis so much Pixar turned it into an animated short called *Time Travel Mater*.

Written and laid out eight years before the opening of *Cars Land* on June 15, 2012, Radiator Springs Racers was the perfect anchor attraction for what was still known then as Carland. The six-acre attraction was to be located on the outskirts of town with its impressive Ornament Valley-inspired rockwork and waterfall serving as the "weenie"—the iconic draw—at the end of Cruise Street. The third-act outdoor racecourse layout of Racers intertwined and shared the expansive landscape with Road Trip, USA in the same way the Submarine Voyage, the Monorail, the PeopleMover, and Autopia intermingled to create the kinetic "world on the move" theme for the 1967 version of Tomorrowland. Junkyard Jamboree, a large-scale indoor attraction, was housed in a show building on the opposite side of town, and Cruise Street was complete with shops and smaller scale–themed experiences.

This pre–Cars Land concept rendering shows the entrance to Radiator Springs Racers added to the end of Cruise Street.

This photo was taken in 2006 before Carland became Cars Land. The only thing related to the movie *Cars* at that time was Radiator Springs Racers, the land's anchor attraction.

With my dear friend and longtime colleague, Cars Land executive show producer, Kathy Mangum. She "rocks," as you can see. Kathy and I started together at Imagineering as kids. Now we're just kids all grown up.

With all of the elements identified and sited, we created an illustrated bird's-eye view of Carland and went to work on a large-scale model. In 2006, Executive Producer Kathy Mangum and Executive Project Manager Jim Kearns joined our team, so we knew things were getting serious.

Carland was well on the road to becoming a reality. As is his style after he helps launch and grow new concepts until they are designed and ready for production, Rob't left the project to develop other new blue-sky ideas. Creative Director Tom Morris and Art Director Greg Wilzbach joined me to continue work on the land's further design and development, right up and into its production phase.

Tom and Greg would be instrumental in helping to refine the detailed ride layout, show sets, and a large-scale walk-through model of Radiator Springs Racers and the land. Everything was running on all cylinders and speeding along quite nicely until 2007, when our little Carland team would suddenly take an unexpected detour.

A year after the movie *Cars* was released in theaters, it would establish itself as a phenomenally strong and growing franchise. As a result, John Lasseter asked if we would consider turning Carland into *Cars* Land. I must admit, after all of the hard work we had done, I felt like the carpet was getting yanked out from under us, especially since we had already created so many original stories and experiences for the new land. Turning Carland into Cars Land would mean everything that was not related to the Cars franchise would be wiped off the map. But I respected his instincts, so I remained open-minded. In fact, the more I thought about his request, the more I realized, dadgum, he was right. (It's interesting to think that creating an entire twelve-acre land based on one movie, which had never been considered, much less done, would probably not have happened were it not for the slow and steady evolution of Carland to its eventual transformation into Cars Land.)

In our business, sometimes you have to toss out the stuff you love—always painful at first—to get to the place you'll love even more. It's all part of the process. Heck, we already had Radiator Springs Racers designed, which took up half of the land, so we were halfway there. Our go-ahead mission then was to swap out Cruise Street with the town of Radiator Springs at the same scale, replace Marty's Malt Shop with Flo's V8 Café (in the same location), and come up with two new *Cars*-themed attractions to replace Junkyard Jamboree and Road Trip, USA. Kathy called the troops together to immediately get to work turning Cruise Street into the cutest little town in Carburetor County. The fun part for me was realizing we were still going to be able to create new Imagineering stories because movie audiences never got to go inside

The "Three Car-balleros": me, Tom Morris, and Greg Wilzbach.

Flo's V8 Café, Lizzie's Curios Shop, and Sarge's Surplus Hut, as well as parts of Luigi's Casa Della Tires and Ramone's House of Body Art. We got to create almost everything that was inside of everything! So many new stories came out of the effort to re-create the town of Radiator Springs to make every nook and cranny of it accessible for guest exploration and enjoyment, including Doc's Museum and the Motorama Girls gold records display at Flo's. I had had a blast writing all of the songs and album titles (such as "Jeep Date," "Blue Suede Brake Shoes," and "Fuelin' Around"), plus the backstories for Mater's Junkyard Jamboree, Luigi's Flying Tires, Stanley's Oasis, and the story for the entire land: "It's Race Day in Radiator Springs."

But before we even got started on all that, John suggested we experience the same Route 66 road trip he and his animation team took when they began their research to learn as much as they possibly could about the legendary road. He arranged for us to have their same ride-along guide, the man who wrote the quintessential book on the subject (*Route 66: The Mother Road*) and who performed the voice of Sheriff for the movie, Michael Wallis. Seven Imagineers—including myself, Producer Kathy Mangum, Creative Director Tom Morris, Art Director Greg Wilzbach, architect Joe Kilanowski, interior designer Emily O'Brien, landscape architect John Sorenson—plus our Pixar pals (Director Roger Gould and Producer Liz Gazzano), got our kicks on Route 66 for ten days with our own personal guide and master storyteller, the Sheriff himself. Michael met us in Amarillo, Texas, where we piled into three SUVs and immediately took to the interstate, which he referred to as "The Super Slab." We also immediately took to Michael. He greeted us with a devilish grin on his lips, mischief in his eyes, and something up his sleeve. The first thing he said to us in his deep, dramatic voice was, "Are you frightened?" I wasn't until he said that. Michael was clearly the beloved son of the Mother Road and he couldn't wait for us to meet her.

We stopped for the night at the Big Texan Steak Ranch, home to the famous seventy-two-ounce steak and a fake cow that was so big you can probably see it from the moon. We met the manager, Becky, who invited us to step into her *Cars*-themed office. There we were, standing with the Sheriff himself, in a wall-to-wall shrine to the movie. But that was only a drop of water in the giant radiator of stuff *Cars*-collector and uber-fan Becky had acquired. She invited us to her house, arranging that we ride over in Cadillacs (really *Cattle*-acs) with steer horns on the hoods and car horns that sounded like moos. Every square inch of Becky's house was covered in *Cars* collectibles—truly the mother lode of the Mother Road. I couldn't help but ask what her favorite movie was, and she answered *Beauty and the Beast*. Becky's home and business reflected the irony of the many moms and pops that almost lost their shops because of the interstate bypassing their towns—as happened to the residents of Radiator Springs—but then, thanks to the movie *Cars*, experienced a strong resurgence of customers. Most of the small businesses we visited had some sort of a display dedicated to the movie because the owners felt it told their story and claimed it helped spark an interest in Route 66 tourism, which helped their bottom line.

We drove to our easternmost destination, Erick, Oklahoma, and then motored west stopping at almost every diner, curios shop, and interesting and/or historical spot along the way. Michael personally knew every small-business proprietor along the over one thousand miles we traveled, because they were his siblings, the daughters and sons of the Mother Road. These warm and welcoming people gave a face and heart to their particular dot on the map, and they helped us feel the friendly spirit we knew we needed to capture in Cars Land. My favorite of these folks was Angel Delgadillo, a long-retired barber in Seligman, Arizona. With a twinkle in his eye, Angel told me about the days when travelers stopped in for a long chat and a short haircut. Even though they we out-of-towners, every one of them remained his friend for life. "Having this place where my friends can stop and visit," he said, "makes me feel good." And then he put his arm around my neck, looked seriously into my eyes, and whispered, "If that new land you Disney people are making gives you that same feeling, it will be a success." More than anything, I wanted our new land to make our guests feel as welcome as the "Angel of Route 66" made me feel that day.

With Michael Wallis at *Cadillac Ranch* in Amarillo, Texas. I have to say, these cars really stuck out.

Our Cars Land team was welcomed with open arms to Erick, Oklahoma, from which we "motored west" for ten days.

Members of our Cars Land core team listening to one of Michael Wallis's many stories about the Mother Road. The voice of Sheriff, Michael wrote the quintessential book about Route 66. From left to right: Greg Wilzbach, me, Liz Gazzano, Tom Morris, Michael Wallis, and landscape architect John Sorenson.

Enjoying my model friend, Pixar's Roger Gould, at the Radiator Springs Racers model. Roger and I have worked on many Disney-Pixar attractions together and he has become one of my dearest friends.

Throughout the trip, we took hundreds of reference photos; filled our sketchbooks cover to cover; stood on a corner in Winslow, Arizona, and sang every word to the Eagles' "Take It Easy"; sampled every comfort food dish from every roadside restaurant; and listened to the song "Life Is a Highway" from the *Cars* soundtrack a million times. No, I'm kidding. It was more like *ten* million times. Roger Gould alone consumed 8,746 packages of beef jerky. (His salt level was so high that whenever we'd stop for gas and more beef jerky, cows would come over and lick him.)

At the Midpoint Café, in Adrian, Texas, we were treated to a dozen flavors of Ugly Crust Pie created from the owners' grandma's recipe. (Later in the project, we met with one of the chefs at the Disneyland Resort, a gentleman from France, to suggest adding Ugly Crust Pies to the menu at Flo's. "No, no, no, no, no!" he denied us emphatically. "I will serve nothing that is ugly. Everything must be beautiful!")

One afternoon, after driving up a switchback road on a mountainside in New Mexico, we stopped at the summit near an abandoned adobe church. The old church presented a breathtaking view of the entire valley framed by magnificent mesas. Disrupting the glorious view, however, was the straight dissecting line of Interstate 40. It suddenly occurred to me this was the very view Sally presented to Lightning when they reached the mountaintop at the Wheel Well Motel. I played that scene back in my head. "Look, they're driving right by," Lightning laments to Sally as he watches the cars cut straight across the landscape to make time. "They don't even know what they're missing." At that moment, I heard Michael Wallis, who was standing next to me whisper, "It's such an incredible sight, that road." I was taken aback by his comment, shocked that Michael—of all people—would be talking about the Super Slab with so much affection. But then I glanced over and noticed his eyes weren't on the interstate. He was staring straight down the cliff towards the cracked and broken weed-covered remains of what was once a portion of Route 66.

We returned to Imagineering inspired, invigorated, ten pounds heavier, and loaded with fresh memories of the people, places, sights, sounds, tastes, textures, and emotions we felt on the road. That "something" Michael Wallis had up his sleeve when we first met him was the very heart of Route 66, and that's what inspired the design of just about everything in Cars Land that was not already established in the movie, from the menu items to the interiors of the shops, Flo's V8 Café, and everything in between. Almost every square inch of Stanley's Oasis was inspired in its design, materials, color, and texture by our research photos and sketches. John Lasseter was right to suggest we go on that trip.

Cars Land most certainly would have looked and felt different in many places had we immediately zeroed in on the destination without first having experienced the journey, especially considering the land was much more than a "cookie-cutter" representation of Radiator Springs from the movie. We had a blast working on all of the things you never saw in Cars but were "always there." For example, if in the movie the camera were to travel down through the center of town and turn right at the courthouse, you'd see the entrance to Stanley's Oasis," now a historical point of interest. In stepping into Radiator Springs Curios, we wanted it to look and feel the same as when we stepped into any one of the many curio shops we visited. But we did absolutely adhere to the layout of Radiator Springs as designed for the movie when we started brainstorming ideas for our smaller scale Cars-themed attractions. The reason is if we were to change or move any of the buildings in our Radiator Springs from where they were located in the movie, that visual disruption would be a contradiction and the town would not feel real. Had it been an unbelievable fake-believe and not a believable make-believe, we would not have heard a young boy ask his mom on the opening day of Cars Land, "Was this where they filmed Cars?"

Among our secondary-ride ideas were Sarge's Boot Camp, a Midget Autopia-sized off-road Jeep adventure that started out behind Sarge's Surplus Hut. Luigi's Leaning Tower of Tires put you on top of a tall and precarious stack of tires that leaned to-and-fro in all directions. But then we changed that to Luigi's Flying Tires, inspired by the Flying Saucers that floated on air at Disneyland from 1961 to 1966. Mater's Junkyard Jamboree took its story cue from Mater deciding to host a tractor-pullin' square dance in honor of Race Day in Radiator Springs, much like Sally did by converting her Cozy Cone Motel rooms into cone-themed snack shacks for this special day. We decided the time period for the land was post-movie, soon after Lightning McQueen moved to town. After deciding upon the stories and ride layouts for Mater's and Luigi's—and upon

While on our Route 66 road trip, we took thousands of pictures like this one to help inform the colors and textures for our new land.

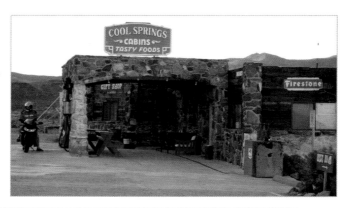

Art Director Greg Wilzbach brought his sketchbook instead of a camera.

Inspired by our photos from our Route 66 road trip, this early-concept sketch was created before I created the (queue line) story for Stanley's Oasis. Still, you can see some of the design influences that made it into the Oasis.

the completion of concept art and a scale model depicting the exciting new twelve-acre addition and everything in it—I pitched Cars Land to our corporate executives, Jay Rasulo, then chairman of Walt Disney Parks and Resorts; Tom Staggs, then chief financial officer; and fellow car guy (and oh, CEO) Bob Iger.

After my pitch, the first question came from Jay. "Can you explain," he inquired, "why there are people walking around in a place inhabited by cars?" I couldn't tell if he was being serious, facetious, or just playfully toying with me as he often did. I went with the latter. "Well, Jay," I responded, "for the same reason people are sitting in Dumbo's guts in Fantasyland." Before he had a chance to fire me I followed up by explaining that in Cars Land, people are honorary cars and would be treated as such. For example, a cast member taking an order at Flo's V8 Café might say, "How may I help you fill your tank today?" The next morning, I found a photo that had been mysteriously placed on my desk of guests riding Dumbo the Flying Elephant. The guests were saying—in Eric Jacobson's handwriting—"Mom! I'm sitting on something gushy! It's icky! Oh,

When Jay Rasulo asked me why humans are allowed in a place inhabited only by cars I asked him to explain why humans are sitting inside of Dumbo. Later I found this anonymous note—in Eric Jacobson's handwriting— on my desk.

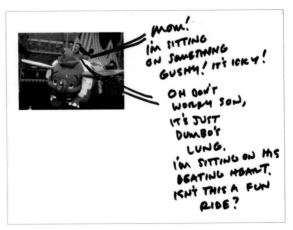

don't worry, son, it's just Dumbo's lung. I'm sitting on his beating heart. Isn't this a fun ride?"

I'm not a money guy (I can't be trusted with this stuff), but I knew Cars Land could not possibly pencil out from a return-on-investment perspective. But I credit Jay for doing the right thing and championing the project because, as he said himself, "It's the right thing to do."

So many crazy and remarkable things happened over the course of creating Cars Land, and among them are some of the most memorable moments of my career. Like when I was walking on the nearly completed site with John Lasseter and some of his family members and he asked me to sing for them the

Now this is what I call "creative license"!

theme song for Mater's Junkyard Jamboree, as would be sung by Mater himself. I started off with a bang:

> Here we go tractors whip and whirl
> Make them trailers twist and twirl
> Circle to the left and circle to the right
> 'Round the Junkyard Jamboree
> Boy, them tractors sure is dumb
> I just sing and here they come
> Look at 'em TOW-si-do, dadgum!
> At the Junkyard Jamboree . . .

That's about when I forgot my own lyrics and started filling in the blanks by singing, "somethin', somethin', somethin'—" John cracked up at that and asked me to tell Dan Whitney (aka Larry the Cable Guy, aka Mater) when I was with him in Omaha, Nebraska, the following week for the recording session to do a version of the song where he "forgets" the lyrics. He sure did, and now you can hear it every so often as it plays randomly on the attraction where those cute little tractors are pulling guest-hauling trailers all around the junkyard. Here's another unexpected bonus you might hear at Mater's: I suggested we put the first-ever "joke button" on an operator's console there so an operator could, on occasion, treat guests to Mater suddenly telling a joke like "What does the popemobile say when he backfires? Holy smokes!"

While directing all of the show and audio programming in Radiator Springs Racers, Joe Herrington told me one rainy night at 2:00 a.m. we were about to

With Dan Whitney, (aka Larry the Cable Guy), aka Mater, at the recording studio in Omaha, Nebraska, about to get 'er done!

go on our seven hundredth ride (it takes a lot of ride-throughs to get everything tweaked just right on a major attraction). I started counting from there, and before opening day we had traveled together through the show 879 times.

When Joe and I were mixing sound in the tire-changing scene in Luigi's, I could *hear* Guido at work beneath our car. But I could not *feel* him. So, Joe and I went out to the construction site, found a four-foot-long piece of steel rebar, and recorded the sound while whacking it against the side of our audio toolbox to get the desired effect. We then channeled that sound to the sub-woofer located under the vehicle seat. So, the next time you're on the ride in that scene and you feel Guido working under your car, that's why!

On another rainy day we were experiencing many technical difficulties in Racers. Everything was dark and gloomy—and that was inside the attraction. It also happened to be the day John Lasseter was going to stop by to see how everything was going. The timing for his visit could not have been worse. The site was still under construction so, thanks to the nonstop rain, there was nothing but mud to walk through on our walk-through. When the time came to

Media designer and sound effects wizard Joe Herrington and I have worked together on many attractions. Here we're installing the soundtrack we created for Radiator Springs Racers. Joe and I rode Racers together 879 times before opening day!

With the Cars Land crew making sure everything is "on track."

We built a track loop to test out our cars for Radiator Springs Racers. Man, was that fun! I'm sitting with Special Effects Designer Todd Wilder, and behind us, left to right, are Ride Engineer Eric Davis and Art Director Greg Wilzbach. Looking on in the background is Executive Producer Kathy Mangum.

After a rainy day on the construction site, the clouds parted and a rainbow appeared, stretching from one side of the land to the other. John Lasster proclaimed, "It's a sign!" I said, "Naw, it's just our lighting designer, Ken Lennon, playing around."

meet John at the entrance to the land, the rain suddenly and strangely stopped. At that moment, the clouds opened enough to allow the sun to paint a brilliant brushstroke of glowing gold across the Cadillac Range. Then suddenly, I'm not kidding, a rainbow appeared and stretched over the land from the Cadillac Range all the way over to Mater's Junkyard Jamboree. The rainbow appeared at the same time John did, and when he saw and reacted to the scene, we all started

For some strange reason, while working on Cars Land, I started seeing Mickey everywhere! I had this cactus for over thirty years before it grew ears! I spotted that "hidden Mickey" on the drain the day after the rainbow appeared.

shouting, "It's a sign! It's a sign!" I took a picture of John with my smartphone with the glowing Cadillac Range and the end of the rainbow over his shoulder.

The very next morning, as I was walking backstage behind Racers, I looked at the ground, and lo and behold, there were two perfectly round pools of water on either side of a round drain cover that together created a special not-so-hidden Mickey just for me. I knew everything was going to be all right going forward.

Cars Land and I had a very special relationship that way. A few years later, these "signs" continued. After completion of Luigi's Rollickin' Roadsters, I was back in my office in Glendale suffering separation anxiety from the land. I already went through a separation in June 2012 and it took months to get over it. I never imagined I'd be suffering through it again three years later after returning to deliver the new story for Luigi's. Driving home to Orange County that night, I was thinking about the special times I'd slip away to take a quick break and step out onto the street in Radiator Springs at 3:00 a.m. and have the whole place to myself. There I would enjoy the breathtaking view of the beautifully illuminated Radiator Cap Butte rising high above and behind the courthouse. While reminiscing about this very thing, I came to a stop in freeway traffic and happened to look into the sky to my left. There I saw a cloud in the shape—not in a *kind-of-like-it* shape—but in the exact shape of the Radiator Cap Butte. Coincidence?

Soon after Cars Land was completed, I was stuck in LA traffic reminiscing about those many late nights I had the view straight down the street of Radiator Springs to the magnificent Radiator Cap Butte all to myself. I looked out my car window and saw this amazing sight. Coincidence? This photo is not retouched or photoshopped. That cloud was a *butte*!

Getting Cars Land on the road and having the privilege to work on every bit of its evolution from the first day to opening day was not only the greatest honor of my career, it was also the *headlight*, er, I mean the highlight. Throughout the course of the project, I got to bring together all of my personal interests from childhood to adulthood and do all the things I love to do, from going on road trips to living and breathing all things cars, and from creating attraction ideas and stories to writing songs, scripts, and directing the talent for them. I even got to work on an animated short, too, when John invited me to come to Pixar to write puns for A Cars Tune short entitled *The Radiator Springs 500½*. My first pun of the short happens when some bad guy off-roaders come to town, and one of them asks Mater, "Who are you?" Mater answers, "Mater." The bad guy car asks, "What's a Mater?" Mater responds, "Nothin'. What's a *Mater* with you?" A forklift with a snare drum does a rim shot and then shows up again to do it again after every pun to follow.

After I finished the pun project, Pixar sent a beautifully framed *car*-icature of me entitled *All Hail the Punisher!* signed by everyone on the shorts team.

Ah, Cars Land, the gift that just keeps on giving! Working on the land, though, was the hardest and most work I've ever done on one project. But it was also the most fun I've ever had as an Imagineer. Of course, to create a land on

John Lasseter invited me to come to Pixar to work on a couple of "Cars Toons." Imagine my surprise when afterwards this beautifully framed piece was delivered to my office, signed by the Cars Toons team. I always wondered what I would look like as a car!

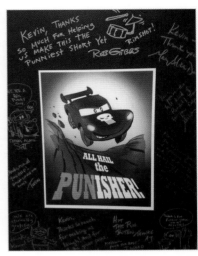

the scale of Cars Land, it takes hundreds of talented and dedicated Imagineers representing all Imagineering disciplines to, as Mater says, "*git* 'er done!" But establishing the up-front vision for the Mother Road of all lands—the one that brought Disneyland DNA to DCA on an epic scale—will forever be in my most grateful heart. I never ever could have imaged when I was a dishwasher dreaming big dreams in the very parking lot spot where Cars Land stands today that someday my dreams really would come true.

Now, as the sun starts to set on my day as an Imagineer, I find myself thinking more often about that rare Cars Land experience and all of the other Imagineering project experiences I've had that have terrified, gratified, challenged, and changed me. When all is said and done, two magical memories rise to the top of the millions I have, and both happened in Cars Land. As soon as the land opened, I invited my in-laws to see for themselves what I had been working on, but couldn't tell them about, for so many years. As I helped my eighty-four-year-old father-in-law step into the front seat of our car at Radiator Springs Racers, my mind flashed back to the time I asked for his daughter's hand in marriage. He had little faith in me then because I was an art major and he was certain my career opportunities would be, in his own words, "Marginal at best." His advice to me was to take a more "practical" road. A child of the Depression era who climbed out of poverty to earn a master's degree in engineering, which led to a long, solid, and successful career, I sensed he didn't think I would amount to much.

Patty and I sat in the seat behind her parents, and I watched Dad the entire ride, all the while thinking had I heeded his advice, not followed my heart, and taken a more *practical* road, he would not be on *this road* now.

Before: the southeast corner of the Disneyland parking lot, where I used to hang out after work with my girlfriend Patty or my fellow DMOs and dream of things to come.

After: as a Disneyland cast member, I used to park my car around the area where the courthouse stands today in Cars Land.

Project Manager Jim Kearns and I were thrilled to accept the Themed Entertainment Association's "Award for Outstanding Achievement: Attraction" for Radiator Springs Racers.

My then eighty-four-year-old father-in-law riding Radiator Springs Racers. Thirty-five years prior he gave me some career advice: "You should consider taking a different road." As I was taking this photo, I thought about that moment. Had I taken his advice, he would not be on this road right now!

When he stepped out of the car at unload, he smiled and silently but firmly shook my hand for a long time. He didn't say a single word. He didn't have to.

My other favorite memory happened in the very same place. It was a moment that reminded me that making make-believe believable is the most important thing an Imagineer can do. On the opening day of Cars Land, quite frankly, my engine was running on fumes. But all of the aggravations tied to the impossible days and late nights melted away like an ice cube in Ornament Valley in the heat of summer when I stood on the unload platform to watch and listen to returning "racers" as they happily stepped out of their cars after experiencing the attraction for the first time. Jumping out of his car with his family, a seven-year-old boy was so excited and overwhelmed by the experience, he could not formulate what he was trying to communicate. All he could do was excitedly jump up and down while repeating, "That was . . . that was . . . that was . . . that was . . . that was . . . that . . ." Finally, he stopped and stood still, knowing exactly what he wanted to shout out loud enough for the whole world to hear: "I NEVER WANT TO LEAVE THIS PLACE!"

TO THE NEXT-GENERATION IMAGINEERS

I WRITE THIS having just returned home from X Atencio's funeral mass. I've been to a lot of masses in my day, but this was the only one in which the recessional song was "Yo Ho (A Pirate's Life for Me)," the lyrics, of course, written by X himself. It was the perfect ending to the well-lived ninety-eight-year life of this beloved Disney Legend. I idolized this warmhearted and talented Imagineer because he started out as a Disney artist and ended up a Disney writer. He showed me such things are possible. Among the last of the first Imagineers, X was the perfect example of someone who didn't know what else he was capable of doing until he started doing it. That is so Imagineering! Never having written a song lyric in his life, X's first attempt turned out to be the popular theme song for Pirates of the Caribbean. Not bad for a visual artist who had no idea he was also a writer until Imagineering handed him the pirate map that led to the buried treasure of his hidden talent. Talk about bringing literal meaning to the idiom "X marks the spot"!

In 1965, Walt Disney asked X to transfer over from the studio to WED to design the Primeval diorama for the Disneyland Railroad. After that Walt asked him to write the script for Pirates of the Caribbean and that's when he teamed up with composer George Bruns to pen the song that has been heard millions of times by millions of fans for more than fifty years. As both a fan and a dedicated student of X's work, I can tell you the true treasure of this gifted storyteller is he took his clever and humorous approach to show writing quite seriously. When I was a young Imaginer, I discovered a shelf in the back of our Information Research Library upon which were dozens of dusty books on the subject of pirates. "I wonder . . . ," I whispered to myself as I peeked inside the cover of the first book I randomly pulled from the shelf. Sure enough, my curiosity was more than satisfied when inside I saw the name X ATENCIO hand-printed on the library card above two other names: Claude Coats and Marc Davis.

X did his homework before thinking long and hard about the story he wanted to tell through lyrics, narration, and dialogue. While carefully crafting each line, he strung an unusual collection of words together like perfect pearls to say what he wanted to say in a most uncommon way. Case in point: at the moment when the Haunted Mansion stretch room is stretching, for example, any other writer may have provided the Ghost Host with this line (and it would have worked fine): "I can tell by the pale expressions on your faces you are frightened because this room is changing." But X didn't go for normal. He went for paranormal. Staying absolutely true to the story and place, this talented showman *stretched* his imagination until he was able to dig up this killer line: "Your cadaverous pallor betrays an aura of foreboding, almost as if you sense a disquieting metamorphosis." What a difference, huh? That's the difference between something that works and something that works far *beyond*.

Although the above example is specific to the art of writing, if you are an Imagineer, the notion of stretching your imagination until your work, whatever it may be, arrives at a level beyond all expectations—even your own—should always be your goal. But to achieve this kind of rare excellence, the kind that only comes when you take the extra time and effort to build a full-on 747 jumbo jet out of toothpicks instead of making a paper airplane like everyone else, takes more work than the average person is willing to do. Thankfully, Imagineers are not average people. And because of that, they end up doing more and being more than they ever expected.

In 1955, a young college grad who wanted to be a sportswriter started his career as the editor of *The Disneyland News* but ended up becoming the chief creative editor and longtime leader of Walt Disney Imagineering. Marty Sklar never became a sportswriter, but he did become the head coach of an unbeatable team. When you add up the number of individual projects and whole new parks created on Marty's watch, the sheer volume and every-time excellence of all that work seems absolutely impossible for one man to oversee. Yet, he was the creative funnel through which all of our projects flowed from beginning to end. There are few times in history when the right leader comes along at the right time to make everything right. Marty was that leader. But he never expected to be. It happened thanks to his creative instincts, strong and tireless work ethic, personal experience in delivering many projects from start to finish, love for and knowledge of all things Disney, built-in story and design chops, and respect and passion for people, whether they were his Imagineers or his beloved Disney park guests.

In true Imagineering fashion, Marty started off as a new kid on the block but grew to become a giant in our industry. He was a world-class leader, a powerhouse of energy and creativity, a courageous pioneer, a difference-maker, a game-changer—a life-changer. We worked for and with Marty not because we had to but because we wanted to. He was all about unbridled optimism, the team dynamic, and the belief that many brains working together can figure out how to do anything, including the impossible. "Don't tell me you can't *because* . . . ," he loved to say. "Tell me you can *if* . . ."

Every day Marty helped his dreamers and doers see the value and importance of generating that "One Little Spark" that brightens our sometimes dark and crazy world and helps to make it a better and more reassuring place. When I heard the news of his passing, it hit me as hard as when I lost my own dad. Marty was family. One of the most difficult things I've ever done was to speak at his memorial service at the request of Leah, his wife (of more than sixty years), and daughter, Leslie. What an incredible honor it was to stand before Marty's friends and family and speak from the heart about this one-in-a-million magical man. He took a chance on me and many others from my generation of Imagineers in the same way Walt Disney took a chance on him. Marty's first generation of Imagineers kept the torch lit and burning brightly after Walt was gone. My second generation carried that torch and used it to illuminate our way to several more Disney theme parks and many other unique Disney experiences all over the world. Now the time has come for you, dear third generation and beyond, to fan your spark into a flame and keep that torch lit and burning brightly.

With great respect and admiration for you up-and-comers who inspire me every day with your fresh enthusiasm, passion, and dedication, I'd like to offer you some helpful hints rooted in lessons learned and wisdom earned from my long career. The fact that you're an Imagineer says you're not the average Joe or Josephine. That means you should never limit yourself to only what you think you're capable of doing, because you can do more and be more. That's the Imagineering Way. X was not a trained or experienced writer when Walt challenged him to make words flow out of the end of his pen instead of drawn Disney characters. And look what happened. In my humble opinion, Francis Xavier Atencio was the greatest show writer WED ever had. Will you grow to become the greatest at what you do?

Whatever you do, you're an Imagineer for a reason. You may not know the reason now, but the first time you see a guest enjoying something that has your fingerprints all over it, you will know. Be and make your work as original and one-of-a-kind as your own fingerprints. Create, don't replicate. If you're working on something new and someone asks you to describe it and you start by saying, "It's *like* . . ." slam on the brakes and ask yourself, "Why am I working on something that is like something else?" How can you invent the future when you're digging up the past? Learn from the past, of course, but make the future your own. Johnny Cash tried to break into the music business by performing covers of other singers' songs for record-company executives. The only door that opened for him was the one back onto the street. But man, as soon as he found his own sound, he found fame. Find your own sound. Then bring it to the orchestra that is your Imagineering team.

Consider that every day thousands of résumés get delivered to 1401 Flower Street in Glendale, California, from good and talented people all over the world whose dream is to become an Imagineer like you. The résumés and inquiries are many, but the positions are few. These talented folks would give anything to be able to do what you do. I know because I'm constantly contacted by young people who, in their noble quest, want to meet with me to hear my story and perhaps gain some insight as to how the same thing can happen for them. Well, it has already happened for you, so count your blessings as you count yourself among those fortunate few who get to live the dream by making dreams come true. That itself is a dream come true. Be mindful and thankful every day of this privilege and responsibility entrusted to you. Realize the importance and value of your contributions in helping to design and deliver new ventures and adventures as only Disney (that's you) can do. The Disney parks and cruise ships and other dimensional and live-entertainment experiences will never be completed as long as there are Imagineers in the world. Since Imagineering is at the heart of their creation, that's where your professional heart needs to be.

Our Disney park fans, TRULY THE GREATEST, NICEST, AND MOST-APPRECIATIVE PEOPLE ON THE PLANET, are counting on you. What you do can help give them the best day of their life. The. Best. Day. Of. Their. Life. That, my friend, is not just a job (if you think of it that way then amscray! I mean it).

Walt Disney Imagineering has always been—and still is today—the themed entertainment industry leader. It can only stay on top if you stay on top of your game. That means you must *imagineer* with the excellence and perfection of Baryshnikov dancing, Whitney Houston singing, and Michael Jordan getting nothing but net. Don't look now, but you're performing at the Carnegie Hall of our industry. That doesn't mean when you do well you're here for good and can kick back and sip your latte-*da* drink on our Big D patio. You are only as good as your last performance, so you must keep going and growing. There's always more magic to make! So, make sure you stay sharp, relevant, and productive, not just every once in a while, or when you feel like it, but every day in every way. Work today to be better than you were yesterday. Never stop learning everything there is to know about everything. Always do your research. Ask questions. Seek advice. There is no Imagineering major in college, so the best school on the subject is right here on this busy campus. Study and learn from the failures and successes of those that came before you. Find out what worked and didn't work—and why!

If you have not yet been there and done that, listen to those who have. Welcome and grow from constructive and caring criticism that comes from those who have many successes under their belts and tribal knowledge in their brains. Be disruptive in a productive, contributing way. Shake things up. Shake things down. Stay alert and in the know. Take action. Take responsibility for your action. Believe in the power of your dreams, because dreams have the power to change everything, including you. Never fear, Imagineer, because every single time you step out of your comfort zone to betray that aura of average, you will sense a disquieting metamorphosis that will keep you stretching until you can reach the stars.

Okay, I'm going to stop now before my cantankerous perspicacity prompts an aura of *snore*-boding. But I do want to leave you with one more thing: when Walt Disney Imagineering celebrated its fiftieth anniversary in 2002, I was asked by Marty to write some words about what Imagineers dream and do for our in-house publication called the *WDEye*. I'd like to reprint that piece for you here as something to ponder as you set sail into the future.

Don't Miss the Boat

This month I'm supposed to write about how, in addition to theme parks, Imagineers create resorts, cruise ships and other incredible stuff. But right now, I feel like expounding about butter.

My dad told me a terrific story about an unforgettable moment that happened at a business dinner he attended. It seems the guest of honor, a famous coach, was growing increasingly impatient with the overworked waitress. He was in dire need of butter, apparently, a matter of life and death. The waitress had twice as many tables to cover that evening because the other waitress called in sick. While doing her best to accommodate everyone's requests in the order received, she politely assured the coach that she would bring him some butter as soon as she possibly could. He grabbed her by her arm as she raced past him trying to deliver a tray full of salads. "Do you know who I am, young lady?" he barked. "Yes," she calmly responded, "But do you know who *I* am?" The shocked coach shook his head. She continued, "I'm the one with the butter!"

Imagineers are the bread and butter of Disney's dimensional design and development. For fifty years, we've been churning out our product like nobody's business because we've always been driven by art—not business. If we are going to make our next fifty years as fruitful as our last, we need to let the *art* and *showmanship* of what we do continue to navigate our incredible journey. As the winds of change fill our sails, we must ensure that *creativity* and *vision* remain at the helm. To continue to sail successfully into the future, we must first remember where we've been. Fifty years ago, the Imagineers who charted our original course were moviemakers. Now, more than ever, it would serve us well to keep thinking like moviemakers. Our business is not "business." It's *show* business. Our job is to keep setting the scene to the best of our ability so we can continue to immerse our guests, as if they are the camera, into our stories. THAT is what Imagineering is all about.

We are the Herbie Rymans, the Claude Coats, the Mary Blairs, the Marc Davis's and the X Atencios of today. Sure, they may have worried a little less about budget in their time, but I wonder how these highly imaginative and talented people would rise to the occasion if they were still imagineering today? If Marc had to give up a character or prop in one of his comical scenes, do you think his ideas and sketches would turn out to be any less clever, hilarious[,] or charming? I think not. The IDEA is the thing.

Some argue that we would not and could not build Pirates of the Caribbean or Haunted Mansion today. Well, I'd love to see the above-mentioned group (and their colleagues) take up that challenge today. I'd be willing to bet that these attractions would still turn out to be beloved Disney "classics." The IDEA is the thing!

Let's take on the next fifty years, not only as developers and technical wizards and people who pencil it out, but first and foremost as a group of uniquely talented dimensional moviemakers. Let's be driven by the *idea* and the *story* because if we allow ourselves to be driven by anything else, our products will reflect compromise and our guests will respond accordingly. What will some future Imagineer write about *us* on the one-hundredth anniversary?

Oh, boy, and while I'm all fired up, what's all this nonsense about focus groups? Pah! Can you imagine the following scenario?

IMAGINEER: "Say, Walt, about this new Matterhorn idea . . .
WALT DISNEY: "Yeah, what about it?"
IMAGINEER: "Well, I'm worried people will think it's crazy to put a big snowcapped mountain smack-dab in the middle of Disneyland. Don't you think we should see what people think about it first?
WALT DISNEY: (You fill in the blank.)

Don't worry about opinions and trends and what other people think. Worry about what *you* think. You're the Imagineer! Make the future your own, not simply some reinterpretation of something someone thinks it ought to be. This company survives on the strength of brilliant, original ideas and stories, not on second-guessing. And while I'm at it, don't waste precious time fretting about the state of the company or its stock price or any other bogus buzz about the biz. Stop thinking "bottom-line" and start thinking queue line. Don't wait for a job number. If you have to wait around for a job number, then it's only a job. Get busy! Don't wait for someone to tell you to do something. Do it! Take the initiative. Take the chance. Make something happen. Nothing will happen if you do nothing!

Think about how much has been accomplished in the past fifty years by Imagineers who let their CREATIVE VISION steer their course. For crying out loud, Walt Disney World is the number one vacation and honeymoon destination IN THE WORLD. The top five theme parks in the entire universe are OUR PARKS. Where did it all start? Right here. How will it keep going? You guessed it.

Dreams from Joe Lanzisero

Don't look now, but we are setting sail for our next fifty years. Leave your baggage behind, jump on board[,] and create theme parks and resorts and cruise ships and other incredible stuff no matter who or what grabs you by the arm and tries to stop you. Remember who you are. You're the one with the butter.

BY THE TIME this book is published, my final major attraction project, Mickey & Minnie's Runaway Railway, should be pretty darned close to being completed for Disney's Hollywood Studios at Walt Disney World. Creating, writing, and directing the first ride ever to star Mickey, the mouse that started it all, is truly the perfect ending to my Imagineering fairy tale. It's the best cherry I can think of to put on top of the sweetest forty-year career I never expected. Sharing the vision and leading this incredible attraction project with me from start to finish are two extraordinary colleagues who have supported me and inspired me every step of the way: Laura Alletag, who by trade is a mechanical engineer but is now our razor-sharp and fearless project manager, and Charita Carter, who started with the company in finance but is currently our talented-theater-and-art-savvy creative producer. That is so Imagineering!

When I started working on Luigi's Rollickin' Roadsters, my project manager, a young and brilliant up-and-comer named Nick Ross, quickly demonstrated he had the wisdom and management chops of someone twice his age. While minding the store for schedule and budget, he always put creative and story above all else because he knew that was the *real* value of an Imagineering project. Not yet thirty, Nick could conduct a meeting with twenty people his senior, and with all due respect to them, flat out own the room. Luigi's was his first attraction flying solo, yet Nick was the best manager that project could have had. After the attraction was completed, I walked away feeling sorry for myself because I didn't think I'd ever find another Nick Ross. Enter Laura Alletag, who turned out every bit as talented, every bit as wise, every bit an owner of the room, and every bit a keeper and protector of creative and story. And they say lightning doesn't strike twice in the same place! What are the odds I'd hit the jackpot with the best project managers and the best project teams ever assembled on my last two attractions out of the box? Rock solid young superstars like Nick and Laura (and others like them) on my current project team give me great hope for the future. Thanks to them I will be able to sleep at night after I retire (not retire as in sleep, retire as in retire) knowing the place will be in excellent hands.

I bring up Nick, Laura, and Charita not only because I adore and admire them but because I know when they started at Imagineering they never dreamed they would be in their current roles knocking it out of the park (or should I say knocking it *into* the park?) while representing the very best our company has to offer.

But that is the gift of Imagineering, the gift that stretches and shapes and polishes you until you fit perfectly into the setting like a precious jewel. Look, everybody, here's the deal. Even if you think you're small change, like I did on my first day at WED, if you truly believe in the power of your dreams, if you truly believe the only place you're going to find success before work is in the dictionary, and if you can get up every day—and slay that fiery dragon of your fears, no matter what anyone tells you to the contrary including yourself—you can make a career out of doing what you love to do. Oh, it won't happen overnight. But if you keep doing what you're good at until you discover what you're even better at, it will happen.

When I look back at my young pre-Imagineering days and think about all of the things I could have been, I feel so blessed I was drawn to the thing I should have been. I'm glad I didn't become an animator, artist, movie director, TV writer, screenwriter, advertising copywriter, car designer, or songwriter, because when I became an Imagineer, I got to be every one of those things all wrapped up into one. I gave my focus, passion, and dedication to Walt Disney Imagineering, and in return, it gave me the gift of turning all of my interests and hidden talents into a rare and special career—and one with great and important purpose. There has not been a single day when I have not felt honored and thankful for the privilege of getting to do what I've been able to do all these years. Not a single day! For those of you who aspire to become an Imagineer, it is indeed a noble and worthy aspiration. But be warned the hours can be long, the pressure can be intense, the travel can be far, the work is hard, the challenges are impossible, and you will love every minute of it. I would not change a minute of it.

Thanks to Imagineering, my imagination has taken me to more places and allowed me to do more things than I could possibly imagine. I'm not a trained writer, and I never went to school with the aspiration to become one. But I've written everything from the drink menu at Trader Sam's Enchanted Tiki Bar to poems, plaque copy, songs, names for more stuff than I can list, scripts for TV shows, park shows, comedy shows, small and major attractions, CEO speeches, and holy blank sheet of paper—now this book. Thanks to Imagineering, I have traveled to more destinations around the world than anyone could have ever dreamed they'd go. I've had a Singapore sling in Singapore and cheese fondue and peppermint schnapps on a hundred-year-old ferryboat in the middle of the Rhine River under a full moon. I've lectured many times at the four universities I wanted to attend as a student but couldn't afford: USC, UCLA, Chapman University, and the California Institute of the Arts. I've raced a Corvette, stayed awake all night in three haunted hotels, befriended a dolphin, piloted and landed a 747 (in a flight simulator in England), given a speech to an audience of seven thousand, gotten my kicks on Route 66, taken off (just barely) on a bumpy country road in a small sputtering charter plane with a farmer who wasn't really a pilot (but pretended to be because the real pilot called in sick), walked the entire length of track at Space Mountain in the middle of the night with the lights on, played the theme song to Mater's Junkyard Jamboree on my banjo to an audience of three hundred educators, sang and danced in a tux with dazzling showgirls in front of the Disney family and my surprised and shocked Disney leaders, learned about writing from Ray Bradbury, learned about color from John Hench, come up with ideas for attractions that were actually built in Disney parks, not gotten fired every time I should have been, watched a space shuttle launch, and hung out with astronauts, scientists, composers, celebrities, singers, and musicians and rock 'n' rollers, many of whom I adored as a kid. And get a load of this—I've even held in my trembling hands George Washington's personal diary, written in his hand during the Revolutionary War, and done so much more. Who does this stuff? It all seems so impossible. It all seems like a dream. If it is a dream, for crying out loud, don't wake me up!

Well, the white-gloved hands on my Mickey watch are telling me it's almost time to hang up my Imagine-Ears. These past four decades have gone by in the blink of a WDI. It seems like only yesterday I stepped into the 1401 Flower Street lobby on my first terrifying day at WED and noticed the black-and-white picture at the top of the stairs of Walt Disney at Disneyland, the magical place where washing pots and pans led me to Imagineering plots and plans. Maybe it's my age—or that I'm getting close to enjoying my happily ever after—but these days I find myself reminiscing quite a bit about the many moments of my uncommon career, almost as if my entire Imagineering life is flashing before my eyes. I've been remembering and thinking about the "firsts" I experienced, like the first time I was put on hold on the phone and the hold music was a song I wrote. Or when I was in Japan for the first time and my colleague, Jim Elliott, asked a drink-stand owner for a can of Calpis, but when he said it, the L sounded like a W and I said to myself, "Holy cow! What am I getting myself into over here?" Or the first time Patty saw me on TV and exclaimed, "Hey, that's YOU!"

I've been thinking especially about how strange it is that the Disney park I didn't want to work on at first is now the one that contains the highest concentration of things I've worked on, including it's tough to be a bug!, Flik's Flyers, Heimlich's Chew Chew Train, Francis's Ladybug Boogie, Tuck and Roll's Drive 'Em Buggies, Monsters Inc. Mike & Sulley to the Rescue!, Twilight Zone Tower of Terror (before it was transformed into Guardians of the Galaxy—Mission:

BREAKOUT!), Toy Story Midway Mania!, Cars Land (including Mater's Junk-yard Jamboree, Luigi's Rollickin' Roadsters, and Radiators Springs Racers), and how they are all on the same piece of land I used to park "Old Unreliable," my leaky convertible, when I was a dishwasher with big dreams. All of my dreams have come true. If this isn't the stuff of fairy tales, I don't know what is.

With special affection, I've been retracing the steps I used to take when I'd run around through the confusing maze of hallways exploring and learning everything I could before my break time was over during the early design days of Epcot. I'll never forget when I first set foot into the magical mother ship of Imagineering and marveled at the attraction posters hanging on the walls in the very place where the attractions themselves were dreamed up and designed. I never could have imagined then—seriously, not in a bazillion years—that many more posters would be added to those walls for attractions I would eventually help to dream up and design.

This morning, in my ongoing reverie, I went to the 1401 Flower Street lobby to stand at the bottom of the stairs and look at the picture of Walt Disney stepping through Sleeping Beauty Castle. "Thanks, Walt," I whispered. "What a ride!" I stared at that picture for the longest time with heartfelt thanks to Walt for this magic journey and heartfelt thanks to God for Walt. If it weren't for Walt Disney, there would be no Imagineers. Without the Imagineers, there would be no Disneyland. If there was no Disneyland, I would not have the loving wife I met there, my two beloved sons, my long and rewarding career as an Imagineer, or my dear friends and colleagues, my Imagineering family, past and present.

Last but not least, there would be no little guy jumping up and down at the exit to Radiator Springs Racers so excited about his experi-ence that all he could say was "That was . . . that was . . . that was . . . that was . . . that was . . . I never want to leave this place!" I know how you feel, kid. I know how you feel.

How lucky I am to have something that
makes saying good-bye so hard.
Winnie the Pooh